THROUGH

—THE—

GLASS

DARKLY

SELECTED COLUMNS

THROUGH
—— THE ——
GLASS
DARKLY
SELECTED COLUMNS

BY
BILL McCLELLAN
ST. LOUIS POST-DISPATCH COLUMNIST

ST. LOUIS POST-DISPATCH

THROUGH THE GLASS DARKLY:
SELECTED COLUMNS BY BILL McCLELLAN

Editor: Tracy Rouch
Illustrations: Dan Martin
Designer: Vicky Frankel

Copyright (©) 2006 by The St. Louis Post-Dispatch
900 N. Tucker Blvd.
St. Louis, Missouri 63101

First edition, first printing
ISBN 13: 978-0-9661397-6-1

Printed by Walsworth Publishing Co., Marceline, Mo.

To order additional copies on-line, go to www.stltoday.com
and click on "Post-Dispatch Store Front."

Bill McClellan

*To all the people who have
shared their stories with me,
and especially to those who
have not subsequently taken
legal action.*

TABLE OF CONTENTS

Chapter One

Chapter Two

TABLE OF CONTENTS

Chapter Three

TABLE OF CONTENTS

Chapter Four

Chapter Five

Bill McClellan

INTRODUCTION

I write messages, put them in bottles and throw those bottles into the sea.

That is how I make my living. I write four messages a week. "This is really about the times in which we live," I sometimes shout when I throw the bottle into the waves.

Very seldom do I actually see anybody reading one of my messages. Now and then, I might be at a coffee shop, or a doctor's office, or a fast-food restaurant, and I will see somebody pick up a newspaper, and I'll look closely and see that the person is holding the section of the newspaper in which my message appears, and if I look even more closely — and I always do — I can sometimes see that the person is reading my message. My heart races, even after years of doing this.

This is, in some ways, an odd job. It's great for the ego. I get my picture in the newspaper and I can spout off about anything. On the other hand, this can be a difficult job for someone who is basically insecure. Which most of us are. The exceptions are attractive women and cool guys.

They're welcome anywhere and they seem to know it. But being cool is like having good form. Captain Hook was obsessed with good form, and he was tormented with the thought that Schmee had it without thinking about it, which was, of course, the only way to have it. So it is with cool.

In your heart, you know you are only as cool as you were in high school, and I was in the B crowd. That's probably not true. I went to a large public high school in Chicago and the A crowd was easily defined — the athletes and the cheerleaders and the dancing girls from the half-time show. The B crowd was more nebulous. My friends and I claimed the title, but I suspect an impartial observer would have selected a different group. One comes to mind. The boys were smart, and the girls

INTRODUCTION

were pretty. Most importantly, it was a co-ed group. My crowd was just a group of guys. We were minor athletes. I was a swimmer, but because I wasn't fast, I swam longer distances. My specialty was the 400-yard free-style. That was 16 lengths of the pool, and often I was lapped. Even today, the smell of chlorine reminds me of humiliation.

So I come to this job with a deep-seated sense of insecurity.

But, oh, how I love it. I meet so many interesting people. I argue with some of them, and when I later think of what I should have said, I say it in the newspaper.

I was, of course, thrilled when the newspaper decided to publish another collection of columns. Instead of a stack of yellowing newspapers in the basement, I will have another book. Pick out about 100 of your favorites from the last six years, the bosses told me.

That was not easy. I went through hundreds of columns. In certain moods, I liked almost everything. In other moods, I liked nothing. And what if the earlier columns were decidedly better than the more recent ones? How would I explain this decline? Perhaps the safest thing would be to pick some of the worst columns from the earlier years, and the better columns from the more recent years. "He's not very good, but at least he seems to be improving." I could live with that kind of criticism.

Also, there was this — certain columns have a prominent place in my personal history, but maybe they aren't so interesting to everybody else. I remember when I wrote about two lawyers from Belleville who specialize in class-action lawsuits. I wrote that the two lawyers reminded me of bank robbers, and then I corrected myself and said that such a comparison was not fair to bank robbers, who are too honest to pretend to rob the banks on our behalf. They just rob them. That caused the lawyers to sue me for slander, and in the next column, I explained that because the lawyers were from Illinois, they didn't understand that in Missouri, we like bank robbers. Jesse James is a state hero. If you own

INTRODUCTION

a cave in Missouri, you advertise that Jesse James once stayed there. The lawyers made that second column "Exhibit Two" in the lawsuit and our feud raged on.

How could I leave those columns out? Or the columns in which I have been visited by a strange and ambitious woman from my past?

I also considered columns that dealt with politics. I was opposed to the war in Iraq, not because of any understanding of geo-political issues, but simply because I believe that it is almost always honorable to oppose a war. There is never a shortage of people ready to pound the drums and wave the flags.

But really, what I most often do and what I most enjoy doing is writing stories about people, not politics. I like love stories, and crime stories, and stories about unexpected kindnesses. For the most part, then, these were the columns I selected. In the end, I just grabbed a bunch of them, hurriedly stuffed them into bottles and threw them into the waves. If this book washes ashore near you, I hope you enjoy at least some of them.

Bill McClellan

Bill McClellan

CHAPTER ONE

IT'S YOUR LIFE

ENJOY THE BUMPY RIDE, GRADS, AND BE KIND TO FELLOW PASSENGERS

May 18, 2003

Editor's note: After taking St. Louis University to task for inviting former American Airlines CEO Donald Carty to give its commencement address, Bill McClellan found himself as Carty's replacement. Below are excerpts from the remarks he prepared for Saturday's graduation ceremony.

When St. Louis University announced that I would be giving a talk this morning, Kevin O'Rourke sent me a note. He's a Dominican, an ethicist. He founded the Ethics Center here at the university. His note said: "You got into this ceremony the same way Pontius Pilate got into the Creed. By accident." He was referring, of course, to the fact that I was not the original choice to give this address. That would be Donald Carty, who was, at the time the invitation was extended, the CEO of American Airlines. But he ran into some trouble, and he lost his job, and the opportunity to give this address. So I was invited.

It was a strange choice, and I sympathize with the graduates who say,

"Last year, the speaker was a former provost, who now heads a university. The year before, the speaker was an official with the Council for Opportunity in Education. The year before that, August Busch. These are all people of accomplishment. And we get a newspaper guy?"

But don't be too upset with the university. This was a last minute deal, and all Father Lawrence Biondi could offer was an honorary degree. The people on the A-list already have degrees. I don't. Because this will be the first degree I have ever received, this is my commencement, too. So I wish we had a more distinguished speaker.

So I stand up here today not even trying to be an example. I'm more like an object lesson. In that sense, my timing is good.

You are graduating into an uncertain economy. Actually, there's nothing uncertain about it. It's a lousy economy. Some of you are not going to get that perfect job. You're going to have to temporarily "settle for" something. You may feel frustrated about that. You may feel that some of your peers – the ones who did get that "perfect job" – are running well ahead of you in the big race.

Don't worry. That's my message. When you look back on things years from now, early setbacks mean nothing. Triumph and disaster morph together. Consider my resume. "Started college at the University of Illinois. Dropped out and entered the Marine Corps."

That doesn't sound successful, but it sounds acceptable, maybe even patriotic. But when it was happening, it was awful. I dropped out of school right before I would have flunked out. Flunking out seemed so disgraceful. Dropping out had a certain panache. Not that I was fooling anybody. You come home a couple of weeks before the semester ends, people figure it out.

I left school during Vietnam, so I was drafted. This was in the beginning of 1969. Richard Nixon had just taken office. During the campaign, he had talked about a secret plan to end the war. So I was rooting for him. I was actually apolitical in those days. I believed in beer. But when you're about to lose your student deferment, you start paying attention and you pull for the guy with any kind of a plan to end the war.

So Nixon took office, and I was drafted. I didn't even know the Marine Corps could draft people. I remember being at Camp Pendleton, a helmet jostling around on my head -- it took me forever to figure out how those straps worked -- when suddenly the realization hit me: I was Richard Nixon's secret plan.

I wanted to write him: Mr. President, With all due respect, sir, you have misjudged me badly. I'm incompetent. Ask anybody who knows me. Ask my dad.

My dad had little faith in me, and justifiably so. When I left school, he asked what my plans were. "Beats me, Dad," I said. Then I got drafted, and he wondered how somebody with no self-discipline would survive in the military. "Beats me," I said. I remember him telling my mom, Mildred: "It's not that he's a bad kid. You just can't go around saying, 'Beats me,' all the time."

I wish he were alive now. I'm on a local PBS discussion show, and the moderator will ask me about some issue, and I say, "Beats me, Martin." And people say, "Gee, he's thoughtful."

So everything comes around.

Things did not go smoothly for me as a young man, but I'm glad it all happened the way it did. You'll find that, too. I can almost guarantee you that if you end up with some job you didn't want to take, years later, you'll be happy you did it. So enjoy it while it's happening. Don't worry so much.

I kid around about being a reporter, but it's really wonderful work. I get to meet people and hear their stories and sometimes those stories can really make you think.

For instance, I've written about a fellow named William Stradford. He sold pretzels on Cherokee Street. California and Cherokee. That was his corner. He once worked in a warehouse. Actually took inventory. A pretty good job. Mostly, though, he was a father. A wonderful storyteller. He did different voices for each of the characters in the story. His kids say he was better than television.

Then something went wrong with his mind. He went into the hospital. This was years ago, and we knew even less then about the mind than we know now. Mr. Stradford was heavily medicated, and when he came out, he was different. That first night at home, his son ran up to him, and said, "Tell me a story, Dad," and the greatest storyteller in the world got a pained look on his face and said, "I don't know any stories."

Then he became a pretzel seller. He'd get on the bus at the end of a day selling pretzels, and he'd sometimes have trouble figuring out the fare. He'd stare at the coins in his palm, trying to add things up. Finally, he'd come down the aisle. He'd been out all day in the weather, and he looked it.

Often, it was a crowded bus. Not every seat was taken, but there might not be any empty rows, and people would put their bags on the empty chair next to them, or they'd be sitting on the aisle, and they'd turn in, with their body language letting Mr. Stradford know that they didn't want him sitting next to them. Almost nobody wanted this strange man as a traveling companion.

But now and then, somebody would notice this little drama, and say, "Sir, here's a seat."

Be that person.

To be successful, in the sense that Mr. Carty was successful, requires a lot of luck. The right people have to notice you, and like you. A vacancy has to come open just when you're ready for it. Not everybody has that kind of luck. Some of you will never be president of a big company.

But to be the person on the bus who calls out to Mr. Stradford, that requires nothing external. That's all you. And if you are that kind of person, then you'll be a credit to your parents, and a credit to St. Louis University.

Let me read you a brief quote. Commencement speakers have to quote somebody. It's like a rule. And newspaper readers, when they learned I was going to be here this morning, sent me dozens of quotes. Kind people. I've selected one from Ogden Nash.

"Speaker, oh speaker. You labor under a delusion.

"The words the audience longs to hear are, in conclusion."

And so, in conclusion, don't worry so much, be kind and remember, if at first you don't succeed, you've got something in common with your commencement speaker.

Congratulations and good luck.

———

Bill McClellan

WHEN ILL WINDS BLOW, YOU DO WHAT YOU HAVE TO DO

DECEMBER 19, 2004

The Christmas Lights on the modest brick house in Overland speak to the holiday spirit, but the wooden ramp that leads to the front door suggests something less joyful. The truth is ever sadder. The ramp is not really needed anymore. Beverly Aitken no longer leaves the house. When I visited this past week, she was in the living room, lying in a reclining lift-chair. One of the family's three cats was resting on her stomach.

Beverly was born about 50 years ago and spent most of her childhood in south St. Louis County near the Jefferson Barracks National Cemetery. She was close enough that she could hear the haunting sound of taps from the funerals. Day after day she heard those notes. A strange sound to associate with childhood, perhaps, but things are what they are. When Beverly was 10, her mother fell ill and the family took a trip to the Grand Canyon. It was, in effect, her mother's farewell. She went to some kind of a sanitarium in Colorado. She died when Beverly was 11. Later, Beverly would learn that she had died from ALS.

But you get on with life, and Beverly did. She graduated from Mc-Cluer High School and went to work for the phone company. She was a mail clerk, and then a service order writer. The salesmen who called in the service orders were mostly just that - men. So she met a bunch of fellows, but they were voices without faces. On Christmas Eve 1977, she spent almost two hours talking to one of these faceless voices. It was a very slow night. So they talked and they talked.

They talked again in March and she mentioned that she was a bowler and that she'd be bowling that night, and he showed up. His name was Dave. He had been raised in St. Ann. He graduated from Ritenour High School and went to UMSL for a year before getting on at the phone company. His first job was as an operator. The company was just starting to put men in women's jobs, and vice versa. Dave was only the second male operator. The first fellow couldn't handle it, but Dave was so easygoing and so unimpressed with himself that he had no problems. He eventually transferred into service and sales.

After Beverly finished bowling that evening in March, she and Dave went to Rich and Charlie's on Delmar for pasta. And that was it, really. Neither of them ever dated anybody else. They were married in April

1980. They bought their home in Overland the following year.

In 1982, the first of their four children was born, and Beverly quit work. It was something they had talked about. How important was that second income? For Dave and Beverly, the answer was, "not so important." Beverly quit work and never went back.

About five years ago, Beverly's equilibrium began to fail her. She and Dave went to school one night for some kind of event, and she fell in the parking lot. No reason. No warning. Stairs were suddenly a problem. She did not mention it to Dave, but when she went into the basement to do the laundry, she would sit down on the top step and then slide down to the next step and so forth. She'd come up the same way. She knew, of course, that her mother had been afflicted with ALS. Could it be happening to her?

On Mother's Day of 2001, she told Dave she had to find out what was wrong. By the way, a month earlier, she had bowled a 200 game. This thing, whatever it was, came and went. She went to a doctor and then a specialist and she got her diagnosis. Familial ALS. Very rare. You have a better chance of winning the lottery.

Her condition deteriorated. Dave took early retirement in 2002 to be with her. He kept his health insurance, and that has been a godsend. Since his retirement, they have been living on their savings, but that is gone now, and Dave figures they will dip into his IRA now. You do what you have to do.

By the way, remember the story that appeared in this paper last week about the high school student who was working at Schnucks and found the bag with $21,500 in cash in the parking lot? He took that bag home and talked to his folks and then turned it in to the police station?

That was Jeff Aitken, the third child of Dave and Beverly.

—

MODERN LIFE HAS NO ROOM FOR SALOON WITH STORIES LIKE KELLY'S

APRIL 1, 2005

One of the last great downtown saloonkeepers leaned against the bar Wednesday – his last day as a saloonkeeper – and talked about the ways in which the world has changed since he served his first drink so many years ago.

"The do-gooders are coming after you with both guns blazing," he said. "You shouldn't drink. You shouldn't smoke." He nodded toward the portable oxygen machine on the bar in front of him. "I know smoking's no good, but it's a choice, right?"

The phone rang and he picked it up. "Kelly's," he barked.

Actually, Kelly's Korner, which has existed in three different downtown locations, has never been on a corner nor has it ever been owned by a Kelly.

"The sign was in the window when I bought it," said John McMahon, who bought the saloon in 1970. At the time, the saloon was in the 700 block of Market Street. Twelve years after buying it, McMahon moved to the 800 block of Chestnut Street. Four years later, he moved to South Broadway.

"I've always stayed one block ahead of the Gateway Mall," he said with a laugh.

It's fitting that urban renewal has chased Kelly's Korner from one location to another. Modern life has been chasing it, too. When McMahon served his first drink, the world was a different place. Jogging had not yet been invented. Bottled water? No way. People drank at lunch and again after work. Oh, did they drink after work! They'd crowd into downtown bars – yes, there were downtown bars – and they'd drink hard for an hour or so before going home. And those were the moderate ones.

Not that a lot of moderate ones hung out at Kelly's Korner. McMahon's place attracted a more Runyonesque bunch. Cops and lawyers and sheriff's deputies and bail bondsmen. The courthouse crowd.

Shortly before a long ago Christmas, one of the sheriff's deputies stopped in for a quick pop or three before delivering the various legal papers he had been assigned.

"Let's see those things," said McMahon. The deputy slid one over and McMahon studied it. "Why, this is an eviction notice," he said with total disdain. "It's almost Christmas and you're going to evict a poor family."

"Not me," said the deputy, and with a dramatic flourish, he tore up the notice.

"Let's see the rest of them," said McMahon, and sure enough, they were all part of the same sad song. There were a number of garnishments – "This man won't be able to buy his children anything," lamented McMahon – and more eviction notices and warnings about this or that. Fueled with the Christmas spirit and cheered on by his comrades, the deputy took the entire stack out to Market and, as the snow gently swirled to the ground, he threw the notices into the air. He stood there, arms extended, snowflakes falling around him, and there wasn't a dry eye in the crowd. It was like being in "It's a Wonderful Life," watching Jimmy Stewart do something grand.

At least, that's how the story is told. I wasn't there. Nor was I there the day McMahon served a 7-year-old.

"That was the world record," McMahon told me Wednesday afternoon, as his last day edged toward his last night. "I was standing there behind the bar. Of course, I'd had a couple myself. I looked up and there was this little kid, kneeling on a bar stool, staring at me. I said, 'What do you want?' and he said, 'A beer.' I said, 'How old are you?' and he said, 'Seven.' So I thought, 'This'll be a record,' and I served him a beer.

"Then I started worrying, and I asked him where he lived. He said he lived on Shenandoah, and I asked him how he got down here. He said he had a Big Wheel. I didn't want him riding that bike home after the beer, so I gave him a couple of bucks and told him to take a bus. I said, 'Don't forget your bike.' He looked at me and said, 'It's a blanking Big Wheel.'"

None of this is right, of course. Nobody should tear up legal papers, and nobody should serve a child, and the world is a better place now that people don't drink after work. Still, some people are really going to miss Kelly's Korner and John McMahon. So they tell me, anyway.

———

Bill McClellan

CHILDREN SAY FATHER WAS MORE WONDERFUL THAN ADVERTISED

FEBRUARY 24, 2002

Don Bopp was born in 1923, and he grew up in Kirkwood. His up-bringing was middle class. He was 19 when the Japanese bombed Pearl Harbor. He and his best friend, Lou Greenwell, joined the Marine Corps together.

They fought in the Pacific. They were together at Tinian, Saipan and Tarawa. Lou came out of the war unscathed. Don was wounded at Tarawa. His wound, by the way, was in the rear end. He made a lot of jokes about that. He had tried to run, but he wasn't as fast as he thought he was. Stuff like that. He didn't need much to make a joke. He went to St. Louis University on the GI Bill. He studied journalism. He also worked as a bartender at the Ten Mile House Tavern in Affton. He graduated in January of 1950, and a couple of weeks before he graduated, he ran an ad in the Post-Dispatch.

"Young man, 26 years old, ex-GI, forced to seek employment because of graduation from college. Bachelor's degree with journalism major; available after February 1 unless G.I. insurance refund check arrives; has studied marriage laws of primitive tribes, adolescence in Samoa, ancient history under ancient professors, geology, psychology and women; took enough courses to get a degree; has had experience as a parking lot attendant, stable hand, soda jerk, caddy, material expediter, office clerk, pro at a miniature golf course, drug clerk, in own business, in the Marines and with women. At present is working nights as a bartender, present employer is satisfied or seems to be, can mix a good martini or whisky sour; is a fair dancer but has a lousy voice, can listen sympa-thetically to tales of woe; is honest but has never been tempted with a million dollars. Can drive a car or tank, but doesn't own either; will-ing to buy a car but not a tank; believes in God, nickel beer and the St. Louis Browns. Is against communism, women in the White House and belted-back suits. Will consider any type of employment, but, of course, would prefer an executive position."

Somebody in the city's personnel office must have liked the ad because somebody tore it out of the newspaper. It ended up in a file cabinet, and 52 years later, when Kathy Sullivan was cleaning the file cabinet in preparation for moving the office to the old federal building, she found the ad. She enjoyed it, and she gave it to me. I wrote about it. I wondered in print what had happened to the job-seeker who could drive a tank or a car, but owned neither.

Pete Greenwell contacted me. He's Lou's brother. I remember that ad, he said. Don Bopp wrote it.

The late Don Bopp, sadly enough.

The clever ad did not lead to a great job. Don got a job driving a fuel oil truck. He lived at home with his mom, and he spent most of his evenings hanging out with his friend, Lou.

Then Lou's older sister, Dorothy, moved back to town from Arkansas. She was newly divorced and had four children, the oldest of whom was 14. Dorothy was five years older than Don. She was also a remarkably independent woman for that time. She worked downtown as a manager of a beauty salon and supported her kids. She and Don fell in love, and they were married in a civil ceremony in February of 1956.

The oldest of Dorothy's children, Terry, still lives in town. She was 18 when her mom married Don. I asked her what she called Don.

"Dad," she said. "Maybe that sounds strange, but I guess you had to know him. He was the kindest person you could ever meet, and he had such a sense of humor. Such a storyteller. He'd tell you a story, and you'd be listening intently, and then he'd start laughing and say, 'Nah, that never happened.'"

The younger kids fell in love with him, too. Ray, who was 12 when Don became his stepfather, remembers that his siblings took to Don at once while Ray tried to resist.

"I was the lone holdout," Ray told me. "Everybody else called him 'Dad,' but I called him 'Pop.' I didn't want to be disloyal to my father. I even tried to dislike him, but that was impossible.

"I found him to be a better person than my father, and that troubled me. He was so generous with his time, and he didn't have a bad thing to say about anybody. You couldn't ask for a better father. He was incredible."

Ray, who now lives in California, also remembers Don as the world's best storyteller.

"He could tell you the same story you'd heard 15 times before, and you'd still laugh!"

Don had seen combat in the Marine Corps, but to his new children, he did not come on like a toughie. Just the opposite.

He was afraid of bugs, he told them. He was especially afraid of spiders. So the kids or Dorothy would catch bugs or spiders and scare him. He claimed to be frightened of lightning and thunder, as well.

He and Dorothy had one child of their own, Libby. She now lives in Alaska. Like her siblings, she remembers her father's sense of humor. She remembers how they'd pull up to another car at a stoplight, and Don would pull a tire gauge from his pocket, and pretend to talk into it. "They think I'm a secret agent," he'd say to the delight of his children.

As he said in his ad, he had a lousy voice, but as the kids recall, it was a strong voice.

"He would sing very loud in church - off key, of course - just to annoy Mom and raise giggles from others sitting around us," Libby said.

One day when Libby was about nine, she and her father were walking to a neighbor's potluck dinner. Don dropped the meatloaf he was carrying. He picked it up, brushed it off and took it to the dinner. Neither he nor Libby ate meatloaf that night, but other people did, and one neighbor asked admiringly what the crunchy stuff in it was. Gravel, said Don, and everybody laughed, but nobody laughed harder than Libby.

Twenty-five years after Don married Dorothy in the civil ceremony, they renewed their vows in a Catholic ceremony, and on their 35th anniversary, they were married again in Hawaii. Don told Pete and Lou that marrying their sister was his favorite thing to do.

In 1993, Dorothy died of cancer. Don died two years later. A broken heart, is what everybody said. Don and his bride, which is what he always called her, are buried at Jefferson Barracks.

I know I haven't mentioned his career. He had one. He ended up as a salesman, and although he never became wealthy, he did fine. He also wrote a book that was never published. But it's an odd thing about this story. When I first read the ad and decided to see what had become of the man who wrote it, it was work I was thinking about. What did he end up doing? What kind of a career did he have?

Then I started to learn about Don Bopp, and I realized that work and career aren't really the mark of a man. Pam, who was five when Don married her mother, sent me an e-mail that concluded: "My dad was the warmest, gentlest, most considerate, most honest and tolerant and understanding and caring person I have ever known and he truly loved all of us children equally and he adored my mother." And I realized, without a doubt, that the man who wrote that ad in 1950 did, indeed, turn out to be a very big success.

—

TWENTY-YEAR-OLD TWINS HAD BEEN INSEPARABLE. THEN AN INTRUDER RUINED THEIR LIVES.

APRIL 25, 1999

Bosco Boulia never had much going for him.

That's not quite true. He had his twin sister April. The two of them were inseparable. They'd been that way since their father died 14 years ago. They were 6 at the time. They turned 20 on the fourth of this month. Their mom never really recovered from her husband's death, and a lot of people would tell you that April was as much mother as sister to Bosco. But however you'd want to classify the relationship, April was certainly the leader. She'd consult with her brother – she was not bossy – but she made the decisions.

They were born in St. Louis, but raised in Jefferson County. They dropped out of high school together during their freshman year.

Life is not easy with no education. The twins have been living in St. Louis for the last couple of years, working whatever jobs they could find. A lot of it was fast-food stuff. A couple of weeks ago, Bosco got a job with a company that installs pools. That job paid $9 an hour. It seemed like a fortune.

It wasn't what he really wanted to do. His dream was to become an artist. He'd always had a knack for drawing. If he couldn't be an artist, then maybe he'd be a preacher. He was very much into the Lord.

In fact, he had started attending the River of Life Revivals Inc. on

Jefferson Avenue. The Rev. Charles B. Thompson remembers him.

"He started coming this winter. He would talk about how he loved the Lord, and how he wanted everybody to be saved. He was hungry. He wanted to know more and more. He was very interested in the book of Revelations," the reverend told me Friday.

But if installing pools wasn't a dream job, it paid so darned well that it had the potential to be a life-changer. For a long time, the twins had struggled just to pay the rent. They had an apartment on Pennsylvania that cost $275 a month. They shared a 1986 Buick. For a long time, they didn't have a refrigerator.

Suddenly, they could begin to think about buying things. Maybe even think about a vacation. Neither had ever been out of Missouri. Bosco always wanted to see an ocean.

On the other hand, even with the promise of more money, life had gotten a little more complicated. April had a boyfriend. His name was Tony Albert, and he had moved into the twins' apartment.

If Bosco felt at all jealous, he didn't let on. In fact, he and Tony seemed to get along fine.

Bosco had never had a girlfriend. He wasn't bad-looking, and at 5 feet 6 inches and 130 pounds, he was trim. But he never seemed to click with girls.

Tony started acting very strange on Wednesday. He was twitching his neck, and moving his head, and not replying when either of the twins asked what was going on. But what could they do?

Sometime in the middle of the night, Tony got up and went into the kitchen. April followed him. He took a butcher knife out of a drawer and began to sharpen it.

"What are you doing?" she asked.

"I'm not going to hurt you," he said.

Then he rushed into the bedroom where Bosco was sleeping and began stabbing him. Bosco woke up and began to fight him. April came in and tried to drag Tony off. Bosco told her to run, and he finally pushed his assailant away and ran out of the apartment.

He collapsed outside the apartment. April cradled him in her arms and laid him gently on the concrete. Then she knocked on a door to get help. She called the police. Tony drove away in the twins' car.

Shortly after the cops arrived, Tony came back. He denied he had stabbed Bosco. "Billy did it," he said. The cops asked him if he knew where Billy was. "Yes, he's over there in the corner," he said.

The cops soon discovered that Tony had a history of mental problems. He had been admitted to the Metropolitan St. Louis Psychiatric Center on several occasions. At various times, he had been diagnosed with a number of maladies, including psychotic delusions and schizophrenia. In addition, he'd been arrested previously for assault. The character "Billy" seemed to have popped up in other reports.

Bosco died.

April went to the police station to be interviewed. She saw Tony. He was in handcuffs. He denied having stabbed her brother.

The cops got warrants charging Tony with murder, and then a judge remanded him to Fulton for a psychiatric evaluation. He was taken there Thursday afternoon.

April didn't know what to do. Her aunt, Darlene Chambers, took over. Darlene is more accustomed to difficult situations. Her husband, Jim Chambers, is on death row.

In fact, he had a brief bit of notoriety during the U.S. Senate contest last year. When Attorney General Jay Nixon ran an ad alleging that when Senator Kit Bond was governor, the state had commuted sentences and at least one of these men who was released early then committed a murder, the man who was featured was Jim Chambers.

At any rate, Darlene took over and arranged the wake and the funeral. But even with the least expensive casket and no limousine and a donated suit, the bill was too much for April or her relatives to afford. The Kutis Funeral Home on Gravois agreed to provide the services and bill the family later.

Darlene also went to St. Pius Catholic Church, and the church agreed to donate a burial plot.

"My father was active in the St. Vincent De Paul Society at our church in Old Mines," Darlene said.

She also established a trust fund at NationsBank.

"April needs all the help she can get," Darlene told me. "You know how guilty she feels. The man she brought into their lives killed her brother."

Indeed. And there's one more thing. April is pregnant with Tony's baby.

—

GED CLASS STUDENT REMAINS FOCUSED DESPITE ADVERSITIES
MAY 15, 2005

Maury Buckman is friendly and chatty, but his mind operates on a slightly different level than do the minds of most folks. That's because of a head injury he suffered almost 50 years ago when another child hit him in the head with a shovel.

"Do you want to know how long I spent in the hospital?" Maury asked me. I nodded. "Six months, 19 days, five hours and 10 minutes."

Despite the long hospitalization, Maury did not have a complete recovery. Fortunately, his folks were affluent. His father was a psychologist. His mom had a teaching degree. They were able to provide him with much love and plenty of therapy, but still, love and therapy can only go so far. Maury did not get through high school. He never moved out of his parents' home. He never got a job. He remained, in many ways, a youngster.

Eight years ago, as he approached his 50th birthday, Maury decided to get a GED. He enrolled in a GED program. An instructor recalls that he was barely able to read and unable to do more than very simple math, but he was a determined student. He began to make progress. All things considered, it was remarkable progress.

Four years ago, the government announced that the GED exam was going to be revised and made more difficult. Maury decided to take the old test before the changes were made. He missed a passing grade by two points.

That was disappointing, but then again, there is a theory that the journey is more important than the destination, and so Maury continued his journey. The GED class is at the Missouri Career Center on Lindbergh Boulevard just north of Midland. The students are a varied lot – youngsters with court referrals, older folks who've seen longtime jobs go overseas, and a good number of people just trying to better themselves. They tend to come and go, but Maury was a constant. Five days a week, five hours a day.

He continued to come to class even as his life began to fall apart. His mother died. His father became ill. Then Maury was diagnosed with cancer.

"I had melanoma on both sides of my lung and one here," he told me, patting his side. I had stopped by the Career Center on Wednesday to talk. "They took out part of my lymph nodes, but not enough, I think. They say I'm terminal."

He got that diagnosis in November. His father died the day after Christmas. "I broke down," said Maury. Fortunately, there is a trust fund and a younger sister to make sure that things go the way the parents intended, which is that Maury stay in the family home. He has a health care worker to care for him.

Through it all, Maury continued to come to class. He said he wanted to get his GED before he died.

The instructors were dubious. Maury had made progress, yes, but the new test is tougher than the test he failed and all the upheaval in his life had to have taken a toll. It will take a miracle, was the consensus.

One of the instructors wrote the state director of the GED program and asked if Maury could be given an honorary GED. This is a federal program, said the state director. The instructor wrote to the secretary of education. We can do nothing, responded an assistant. The instructor wrote the director of GED testing in Washington. There was no response.

Last month, the instructor contacted Sen. Jim Talent. We will get on this, responded an aide.

Bill McClellan

The senator's staff was able to get certain accommodations for Maury because of his disability. For one thing, he was able to take the test without a time limit. More importantly, I suspect, because of tremors and seizures, Maury was allowed to dictate his answers to an assistant, who then wrote them down. There are actually five tests -- math, science, literature, social studies and writing skills. Each has a total of 800 points, and to pass, a person must average 450 and score no lower than 410 on any of the five tests.

Maury's scores ranged from 660 to 450. To those who know Maury best, it did indeed seem like a miracle.

Maury will give the speech at the GED graduation this week.

—

WITNESS WHO WASN'T TAKES HIS CHANCES WITH IRE OF STATE
MARCH 3, 2002

Bruce Cummings celebrated his 21st birthday on Tuesday, and on Friday, he came to court to be sentenced for robbery. He was wearing his brown jumpsuit from jail.

"Nervous?" I asked from my seat in the front row. There were no other spectators. "Yeah," he said, and he smiled and shook his head. I had expected something gruffer. His personal history seems to be that of a dead-end kid for whom all roads lead to prison. He was kicked out of high school for fighting. He's got an arrest record for drugs and weapons. Perhaps more to the point, he was born shortly after his father went to prison for murder.

"That 10 years probably sounds good about now," I said. He smiled again, and nodded.

He could have gotten a deal for a 10-year sentence, which is the minimum for first-degree robbery, which happens to fall under the truth-in-sentencing statute. A person has to do 85 percent of the time. So 10 years isn't a great deal, but it's a lot better than 20 years, which is the sentence the state was seeking on Friday. The state was very unhappy with Cummings.

This unhappiness had nothing to do with the robbery. It had to do with the murder of Melvin Norman in May 2000. Norman was 19 when he was killed in one of the seemingly senseless shootings that has long plagued the neighborhoods around Fairground Park. In this particular instance, a group of fellows from one gang came cruising in a truck into enemy territory, where they encountered a group of fellows from a different gang. The encounter ended with Norman shot four times and lying in an alley. He was alive, but barely, when the cops arrived. He would not talk to them, and then he died.

The cops later learned that Norman had been one of the fellows in the truck. He apparently left the truck hoping to ambush one of his rivals, but he was discovered and shot as he tried to run. A crowd gathered around him. "Shoot him in the head," urged Base-Head Betty, a crack addict, but the shooter hesitated. Then came the sirens, and everybody ran.

Who was the shooter? The cops found two people who were willing to talk, but only on the condition that they would not be publicly identified. That meant, of course, that they were not willing to testify, but still, any kind of help was appreciated. Rodney was the shooter, the cops were told.

Six days after the shooting, Rodney was arrested. He had the murder weapon, but so what? Without anybody willing to testify, the weapon didn't mean much. Rodney was not charged.

Nor was he forgotten. In December 1998, he had been arrested for a different murder. This one involved a drive-by shooting and an unintended victim. In this case, the shooter missed his target and killed a 14-year-old boy who was playing basketball on a nearby playground. Rodney had been acquitted in that case.

In April last year, 11 months after Norman's murder, Cummings was arrested for the robbery of the Grand Currency Exchange. The clerk identified him. The cops recovered some of the money. Cummings confessed. The state had an airtight case.

Bill McClellan

Cummings had one thing on his side. He had been among the crowd in the alley the night Norman was shot. A deal was struck. The state would agree to the minimum sentence of 10 years on the robbery if Cummings would testify about the murder. He testified to the grand jury, which then returned a true bill against Rodney.

A month ago, Cummings pleaded blind, which meant he pleaded without any kind of a deal. The judge said that when it came time for sentencing, he would take into account Cummings' testimony in the murder trial.

That trial was supposed to start last Monday, but it didn't. Cummings backed out.

"I don't put my nose where it doesn't belong," is the way Cummings explained it to me.

Judge Robert Dierker sentenced Cummings to 16 years. Meanwhile, the murder case remains unsolved. At least, officially.

—

WOMEN'S FRIENDSHIP ENDURES, EVEN IF THE DETAILS ARE SHAKY

OCT. 1, 2000

Several months ago, Susan sent me an e-mail about Norma. She wrote that Norma had been in a mental institution. She got out and was doing quite well. According to Susan, Norma was a very kind woman.

Too kind, it turned out. "Often, she would offer the couch to those who needed a place to crash for the night," wrote Susan. "And in the morning, she would send them off with a loaf of bread, fruit and soda."

One day, a niece came over. As Susan told the story, the niece was shiftless, almost a street person. As Norma busied herself at the stove, making breakfast, the niece looked through a pile of unopened mail. She found an envelope containing a telephone calling card. She stuck it in her purse.

The next month, Norma got a bill for more than $500. Her niece had shared the card with her friends, and they had made dozens of calls – to friends, to psychic hot lines, all sorts of calls. Norma called the telephone company and said she didn't know anything about the bill, but she wasn't able to work things out, and the next month, she got a bill for another $500. This would be hard on anybody, Susan explained, but it was a huge hurdle for Norma. An absolute disaster. First, there was the frustration of trying to work things out with a big company, and then there was the matter of paying the two bills.

After the second bill, the phone company canceled the calling card, but Norma still had to pay the bill. Susan explained that Norma tried to cut her expenses. To save electricity, she wouldn't turn on the lights. To save water, she bathed only twice a week. Finally, realizing that she would never pay the bill with only her disability check, Norma got a part-time job at a second-hand store run by a charitable organization.

"Now she looks forward to getting out every day," Susan wrote. "She is wearing make-up. She curls her hair. And she has almost paid that bill in full. Such a proud and determined lady. Her life is good. I have heard that God works in mysterious ways. What do you think?"

I didn't know what to think. Interesting story, I wrote back.

A month later, Susan e-mailed me again.

"Now the newest development of this twisted blessing. Norma smokes. Like many people with a mental illness, smoking is very important to her. But when she is working, she is not allowed to smoke. After smoking her entire life, she decided to quit. It has been seven days now since she smoked!"

I like stories in which God works in mysterious ways. I wondered if Susan worked in – maybe managed – the second-hand store. I wrote and asked her.

She wrote back with some biographical information. She is a housewife who lives in the suburbs. She is the mother of some very successful children. She is also a person with another life, a more spiritual life.

"I write letters to prisoners. People say my poetry is good. I do what God directs me to do. I am a volunteer. My best friends are a group of mentally disabled adults. Most of them have Down syndrome. We study prayer and religion together."

I meant to visit Norma, but weeks went by, and then months. Last week, though, I wrote a story about a man who has spent 15 years in the state hospital on Arsenal Street after being found not guilty by reason of insanity for a minor, nonviolent crime. He wants to get out. He has been diagnosed as a schizophrenic. Norma shares that diagnosis. If she has been successful, perhaps that means that he could be. I searched through my old notes and found Norma's phone number. I called her and then went to see her.

She lives in an apartment in Wood River. She was sitting at the kitchen table when I arrived. A pack of cigarettes and an ashtray were in front of her. The room was smoky. Her hair was not curled, and she was not wearing make-up. Still, she was out, and on her own.

She said she had been raised in a small Illinois town not far from Mount Vernon. She'd gone to work after high school in a factory and she had gotten married at the age of 20. She had two kids – they're both doing great, she said – and then things went terribly wrong. One day things just starting spinning around. She was diagnosed with schizophrenia. She was in and out of mental hospitals for years but has been living independently for about the past four years, she said.

"You seem to be doing great," I said. I asked if she felt like a success story. She hesitated before she answered.

"I think so," she said. "Sometimes I get nervous."

She showed me the bills from the phone card. One was for $542 and the other was for $532. She said she gets a monthly disability check of around $900. Her bills eat up most of that. She said she pays about $200 a month for her prescription medicines. I asked about her job at the second-hand store.

"What job?" she asked.

She said she had not worked at the second-hand store. She earned a little extra money cleaning houses with Susan, she said, but that stopped when Susan went back into the hospital. That's how she met Susan, she said. You probably know that, she said. We were in the hospital together.

I thought back to the dream-like quality of some of Susan's notes. "I write letters to prisoners. People say my poetry is good."

Susan is out of the hospital again, Norma said. She seems to be doing fine.

On my way out of town, I stopped at the second-hand store. I wondered if Norma had worked there and forgotten about it. Or maybe Susan had been mistaken. Then I figured it didn't really matter. This is not a story about who worked where. It's a story about friends and hardships, and happily enough, it is, at the moment, a story about success.

—

A FATHER LEAVES RIGHT TOOLS TO CONNECT THROUGH THE GENERATIONS
JULY 16, 2006

This is my father's birthday. My daughter was 2 years old when he died. So he knew Lorna only as a toddler and it is impossible to get a good reading on a toddler. I am not as observant as a newspaper reporter ought to be, but I bet my father watched her closely, and I can imagine his eyes darting from her to me and then back to her. He would have been trying to take her measure. Was she going to be like me?

I was incompetent. Anything even vaguely mechanical left me befuddled. I was able to tie my shoes, and that was about it. I couldn't use tools. Oddly enough, it was a congenital condition, and I say "oddly enough" because I came from a long line of skilled craftsmen. My father was an electrician. An uncle was a carpenter. But no amount of instruction was enough. I remember taking a shop class in high school. My project was to make a doorjamb. I might as well have been trying to build a rocketship.

My father repaired televisions in his workshop in the basement, and when I was little, I was his helper. I handed him tools. I never progressed beyond that point. I was also his helper when he would work on the car. Sometimes, he would try to explain things. He might as well have been speaking a foreign language.

He did not act disappointed as much as he acted puzzled. But he accept ed things. One day, shortly before his death, he said, "If you ever need any electrical work done, you won't try to do it yourself, will you?" I said that of course I would not. That seemed to satisfy him.

When he died, his will was simple. Half of everything was to go to my late sister's children, and half was to go to me. An even split except for one thing. "My son gets my personal tools," he wrote. Was this meant as a joke? It could have been. He had a lively sense of humor. Or maybe he figured that incompetence did not run in the family and so the tools might prove useful to my children. Who knows?

Although Lorna has never used any of his tools, she did turn out to be competent. She is very much the granddaughter of an electrician. She is also the granddaughter of a nuclear physicist, and the daughter of a dentist. Competence runs in her blood.

She graduated from the University of Illinois in May with a degree in biology. Biology? I tried to stay away from science classes, and I still flunked out of college. And the college? The University of Illinois.

During her senior year, she decided to join Teach for America. What a nice program that is. Graduates teach in under-performing school districts. Lorna volunteered for California, and was assigned to the Richmond School District. That's near Oakland. She will teach high school biology.

She and I drove to California a couple of weeks ago. Only a father can understand what a privilege it is to drive across the country with a child who is about to start a new life. We took a scenic route and visited Mount Rushmore, the Little Bighorn Battlefield and Yellowstone National Park. We listened to music, and we talked. She did all the driving, and I did a lot of daydreaming.

One of the nice things about getting older is the way the past changes. What was good seems terrific. What was awful seems pretty good. I am especially blessed in that regard. Reality has little to do with my memories. I now think I was a pretty good athlete when I was a kid. Self-confident in high school, too. Very sure of myself. Boot camp was kind of fun. And have I always been totally incompetent? No. I might not be the most talented guy around, but I seem to remember something about a doorjamb. Plus, my dad did leave me his tools. That must mean something.

With this kind of mind-set, I sometimes snapped out of my reveries long enough to give Lorna various bits of advice. Oh, I forget exactly what the advice was, but it was the sort of valuable stuff that a competent father would want to pass on to his daughter. And Lorna, bless her, would listen attentively.

Toward the end of our trip, we stopped in a cheap motel in California. We had been north, and we had been in the mountains, and this was our first time in real heat. I went into my room and tried to figure out the air conditioner. It was very complicated. Well, fine. I've slept in heat before. I stretched out on the bed. There was a knock on the door. It was Lorna. Her room was down the hall.

"Dad, did you figure out the air conditioner?" she asked. I started to say I had not really looked at it, but she was already walking across the room. She reached the air conditioner and opened something, and then she pushed something, and in a moment, the unit began to purr.

"Good night, Dad," she said, and she left. She really is her grandfather's granddaughter.

—

ON ST. PATRICK'S DAY, DRINK A TOAST TO ALL FRIENDSHIPS GOOD AND GREAT
MARCH 14, 1999

Nobody, not even an Irish kid, grows up thinking that he'd like to become a leprechaun. It's something that just happens.

For Hap McAlevey, it began to happen 17 years ago. Wait a minute. This is an Irish story, and no real Irish story would admit to starting as recently as 17 years ago. So let's back up to sometime in the middle of the last century.

That's when Timothy Clancy came to these shores from County Clare. He came here so many years ago that nobody now living knows when or why. Or even where he settled. What people do know is that his son, Frank, came to St. Louis.

And this first Frank had a son named Frank, who also had a son named Frank. This third Frank Clancy was born in 1927 and was to become great and good friends with the aforementioned Hap McAlevey, and was to become instrumental in his friend's transition from man to leprechaun.

Let's stick with Frank for a moment.

He went to Visitation grade school, and there he met his future wife, Elizabeth Ann. They were fourth-grade sweethearts, and the romance never soured. In 1944, Frank turned 17 and joined the Navy and went off to the war. When the war ended, he came home, married Elizabeth and settled into life as a butcher, which had been the traditional job of Clancy men since at least the days of Timothy.

Shortly after the war, Frank and Elizabeth Ann moved to the far reaches of West County. Frank opened a butcher shop on Manchester in Ballwin.

Not long after moving to West County, Frank met Hap at the Holy Infant Church.

The two men had a lot in common. A couple of years older than Frank, Hap had grown up in Maplewood and gone off to the war. He came home, became a plumber, got married and moved to West County. You could get more house for your dollar if you moved to the sticks. That's the way he felt.

The years went by.

Frank and Elizabeth Ann had 12 children. Six became butchers. One of the six, Patrick, was killed in 1977 when he sliced his artery with a saw while cutting meat. Other than that terrible tragedy, though, life was good for the Clancy clan.

Frank had moved his butcher shop from Ballwin to Ellisville. He had a place just off Old State Road, just south of its intersection with Manchester. Just up the hill from the shop was an old house that Frank's dad had built as a summer place back in 1933.

In 1982, Frank took that old house, did a little bit of remodeling and turned it into Clancy's Irish Pub and Grill.

By this time, Ellisville was the heart of suburbia, and Manchester Road was becoming a string of strip malls. It was an unlikely spot for an Irish pub.

Of course, the very best customer was Frank's old friend, Hap McAlevey. Proof of this came when the city of Ellisville named the road leading into the pub McAlevey Lane. It helped that then-Mayor Ed O'Reilly came in a bit.

Life had been good for Hap, too. His wife, Helen, was a seamstress. They had three kids. As Hap aged, he became less the wiry working man, and more and more began to look like a leprechaun.

People had begun to notice even before the pub opened. When your name is Hap McAlevey, and you stand 4 inches over 5 feet, and you've got the eyebrows, well, people begin to notice. But when the pub opened, there was suddenly a reason to look like a leprechaun. You could give your friend's place a certain style on St. Patrick's Day.

And so the tradition began. On the first of October, Hap would begin growing his beard. His costume was the best, too. How many would-be leprechauns are fortunate enough to be married to a seamstress?

It was for only one day a year – Hap would shave on the morning after – but what a day! Hap was the perfect leprechaun.

On St. Patrick's Day in 1993, a pub in Manchester had a leprechaun contest, with the winner earning a trip for two to Ireland. There were plenty of would-be leprechauns shooting for that trip, but when Hap came sauntering in just minutes before the judging was to end, you could hear an audible sigh from the other contestants. It was as if a real leprechaun had showed up.

Hap and Helen went to Ireland.

Other than that, though, the whole show was at Clancy's. Hap was their leprechaun. Year after year. The two friends, Frank Clancy and Hap McAlevey, led the St. Patrick's Day celebration at the decidedly unfancy Irish pub in the unlikely West County location.

Hap was diagnosed with cancer five years ago. Still, he was the leprechaun at Clancy's. Each year the thought was, One more year.

Frank died a couple of weeks ago.

Cancer it was, and it went quickly. Seven weeks from diagnosis to death.

The family gathered for his service, but it's a tribute to Frank and Elizabeth Ann that the family always gathers. One of the girls, Bridgette, moved to Texas a couple of years ago, but the 10 other kids all live within a four-mile radius of their dad's butcher shop. There are now 37 grandchildren.

The butcher shop and the pub are both still in Clancy hands, too.

Matt, the ninth of the 12 kids, runs the pub with his wife, Angie. They are, of course, gearing up for a big St. Patrick's Day affair.

But it will be different this year. No Frank. No Hap.

"I'm dying," Hap told me when I visited him at his home on Friday. "I'm not going to be able to get to the pub this year. I think I'll spend the day at my daughter's house."

He's 75 now. The cancer has cut his weight to 120 pounds, 30 under his prime leprechaun weight. Still, he grew the beard this year, and the smile has not left his Irish eyes.

If you make it to Clancy's pub this Wednesday, or even if you don't, you might want to raise a glass to friendship. Have a drink to a patriarch and a leprechaun. Good and great friends they were.

—

REVENGE PROVES TOUGH TO COME BY WHEN A SON IS LOST

JUNE 29, 2003

Last November, Walt Volkenannt died of a heroin overdose. He was 30 years old. I remember sitting in the kitchen of his parents' suburban home in St. Peters a couple of weeks after he died. His parents, Walter and Donna, said they did not want to shade the truth. They wanted to talk about the fact that heroin can reach into the upper middle class. Walter, in particular, seemed driven. He said he knew who had sold his son that last, deadly dose of heroin, and he wanted that man charged with murder.

The man's name was Michael McCoy, and the case against him was circumstantial, but fairly solid. Walt had called McCoy from his cell phone not long before he died, and he died about half a block from McCoy's house on the south side of St. Louis. It seemed likely that Walt had bought the heroin, gone back to his car, shot up and died. Plus, there was a young woman who supposedly could testify that Walt had bought the heroin from McCoy. Walter relayed this information to the St. Louis Police Department. He also talked to the circuit attorney. He was a man on a mission. He wanted justice for his son, and he thought a murder conviction was the answer.

The detectives assigned to the case thought murder was a bit of a stretch. Cops on the street understand that the drug trade is driven by demand more than supply. Addicts don't buy heroin because somebody has it. Somebody has it because addicts will buy it. Furthermore, there is the matter of intent. The last thing a heroin dealer wants is to kill his customers.

Walt was not the only young man who died from an overdose in early November. Two days earlier, another young man had died. There was a chance – later disproved – that he had gotten the fatal heroin from McCoy. So the cops got a search warrant for McCoy's house – actually, his mother's house – and busted him. He had about eight grams of crack cocaine and less than three grams of heroin. An ounce is 28 grams. He also had a gun, and approximately $1,000. He seemed like a small-time dealer. He was 52 years old, and while he had been arrested a few times, his only felony conviction was almost 30 years in the past. He had been convicted of robbery, and put on probation.

The notion of a murder charge didn't last long. Toxicology tests could not tie McCoy's heroin to the heroin that had killed the young men. Also, the young woman who was supposed to help had disappeared, and when she resurfaced, she was in jail in St. Charles County. I'll help now, she said, but the cops said that train had left the station.

Because McCoy had a gun, the case went federal. He was charged with possession with intent to distribute crack cocaine, possession with intent to distribute heroin, felon in possession of a firearm and possession of a firearm in furtherance of drug trafficking.

He went to court last week, and pleaded guilty to the crack cocaine charge. In return, the government dropped the other three charges. He will be sentenced in November. He faces somewhere between five and eight years.

He is a small man, and he seemed older than his 52 years. He was soft-spoken and polite when he spoke to the judge.

Bill McClellan

I called Walt's father Friday morning to see what he thought of the plea agreement. He said he thought it sounded fair. He said he no longer hated McCoy, and he understood that the responsibility for Walt's death belonged primarily to Walt. He said the family had a farm in Osage County, a peaceful place where Walt is buried. The father said he wanted to turn it into a place where recovering addicts can go for rehab. These two-week detox programs don't work when the guys have to go back from where they ca me, he said. He added that he had learned that from his son's experience. He said he had a lot of work yet to do, but he was excited because this was something that could help people.

As a memorial to Walt, that sure beats a murder conviction.

—

COUPLE EMBRACED THE WORLD AFTER FINDING EACH OTHER
JANUARY 10, 1999

In 1925, a fire caused heavy damage at St. Joseph's Catholic Church in Clayton. Adolph Gutman, a Jewish businessman who owned a nearby department store, delivered a large check to the priest. I think Clayton needs a Catholic church, Gutman said.

If the church can ever do anything for you, said Father Victor Stepka. The businessman game him a quizzical look.

If your kids want to get married at the church, there is always a place for them, said the priest. Both men laughed.

That is the story that has been handed down. Handed down and nearly forgotten until this summer, when David Gutman, Adolph's grandson, married Susie Ziervogel at St. Joseph's

David was 56. Susie was 40. It was the first marriage for each.

Before Susie met David, she was doing OK. She worked at a fast-food restaurant for eight years, and then she got a job at a grocery store as a bagger. A very nice job.

Plus, she was living alone.

So, she had reason to feel good about herself. She had been a Special School District student in the days before mainstreaming came into vogue. As a developmentally disabled kid, she had gone to school with other developmentally disabled kids. When she was 17, she went to Columbia, Mo., to live in a group home for developmentally disabled people. When she returned to St. Louis three years later, she enrolled in a Life Skills program. As its name suggests, its goal is to teach people how to live independently.

Which is exactly what Susie was doing. Working and living alone.

She was blessed with a strong support system. A mother, a stepfather, a father, siblings, an extended family. But still, she was making it alone. That meant a lot to her.

David was out in the world, too. He lived with his stepmother, but he worked at the St. Louis County Election Board. He started working there in 1966. He hardly ever missed a day. As of last week, he had accumulated 1,897.9 hours of sick time. It is, people say, an unofficial record.

He was a cheerful sort, even before he met Susie. He'd show up every morning with a bag of pretzels, or a box of bagels. Cheerful and happy, but sheltered. Didn't get out much. Absolutely unstylish. Went from home to work, and work to home. His only diversion was bowling.

Susie's mother, Susan Davenport, had heard about David. Neighbors of hers were related to him, and she had heard that he was a very nice man, and she found herself wishing that Susie and he could meet. Actually, David and his stepmother lived quite close to Susan and her husband, Jack.

But Susan didn't do anything until April 1997, when she heard from her friends that David's stepmother had died. Susan stopped by to offer her condolences.

He was nice, and soon they were talking, and he mentioned that he liked to bowl, and Susan asked him when and where he bowled, and she said, maybe my daughter and I will come out to watch you, and he said that would be fine.

So that's how Susie and David met. At a bowling alley.

I talked to Susie this week, and I asked how long it took her to realize that David was Mr. Right. She laughed.

"Second frame," she said. "Right away."

David was just as smitten. David and Susie became inseparable.

Susie was like a teen-ager, so much in love. David was changed, too. For one thing, he was going out. Work was still important, but now there were other things, as well. He was going to restaurants. He was planning trips. He even became a little conscious of his clothes. Most noticeably, he started wearing dark socks.

David and Susie were married this past July. July 10, to be exact. Father Jerry Kleba of St. Joseph's and Rabbi Joseph Rosenbloom of Temple Emanuel co-officiated.

"These were two people who had thought they would never find some-one," Father Kleba said. "And then to find each other. They were just aglow. We are all broken and fragile people, but these two people came together to make a perfect whole."

Rabbi Rosenbloom said, "If you were writing a novel, you couldn't do better than this."

In fact, the emotions were so high that the wedding party had a difficult time getting through the rehearsal. When it came time for David to acknowledge his love, he was crying.

Father Kleba was prepared for the actual service. As the ceremony approached the point when the bride and groom would have to speak, the priest said, "In the 157-year history of this church, we have had a number of double-ring ceremonies. This is our first double-hankie ceremony."

Then he pulled out two handkerchiefs, and handed one to Susie and one to David.

The couple honeymooned at Disney World.

They were soon taking other trips. Kansas City, Chicago, even Quebec. So many places to see now that they each had somebody with whom to see these places.

Last Saturday, they went to a movie. The weather was bad, and they came out into the cold, and maybe the cold triggered David's asthma attack, but he suddenly fell to his knees in the snow.

"Are you all right?" asked his wife.
He looked up at her, and said, "I love you, Susie, and I always will," and then he fell headfirst into the snow.

"I love you, too, David," said Susie.

As Rabbi Rosenbloom prepared the eulogy, he decided he would be directing his remarks to Susie. He took his pen and scratched out some thoughts.

"Your loss is tragic," he wrote. "A good man, a wonderful relation-ship, cut off all too soon, too suddenly - but your love, your memories, will live on."

Yes, that was the tone he wanted.

His eulogy went over well, and Susie understood exactly what the rabbi meant. A love story is never judged by its length.

—

BIG PINE ANCHORS MANY MCCLELLAN FAMILY MEMORIES

SEPT. 8, 2004

The Pine Tree was there when we bought the house 21 years ago. It was a big pine –75 feet or so – and decidedly unfancy. It wasn't a spruce, blue or otherwise. It was just a pine. A scrub pine, I would have called it, but I later learned it was an Austrian pine. It stood in the middle of the front yard.

Over the years, the squirrels used it as a means to get on the roof and from there into the attic. We'd hear them scurrying around somewhere above us. I was always of a live-and-let-live mode, but my wife was more practical. "They'll chew through the wires," she'd say, and we'd hire somebody to chase the squirrels out of the attic and nail some mesh over wherever it was they had used as an entrance. That's something I should mention about the pine. The squirrels used it as a highway, and perhaps as a home, but birds seemed never to nest in it. I watch for that sort of thing. In a month or so, when the leaves fall off the trees, I'll notice which trees have a nest or two, and which are empty. My heart always breaks a little for those that are empty.

Still, the big pine was not a tree that elicited much sympathy. It had its squirrels, after all, and more than a few birds rested on its branches. We could view them from the living room window. Also, there were regular visits from a woodpecker. To somebody like me, raised in a city, a woodpecker is almost a mythical creature, something from cartoons or fairy tales. I'd stand at the window and stare. It was like watching a unicorn.

But the pine's real purpose was this: It was first base. When the kids were young, we'd play whiffle ball in the yard. We played so much the base paths were visible in the grass. The grass? OK, the weeds. Our lawn has always been the kind that if you applied weedkiller to it, all that is green would die. But who cares? You could follow the base paths from the corner of the sidewalk to the pine to a magnolia to a small sycamore next to the street and then back to the corner of the sidewalk. Anything hit into the air toward right field ended up in the pine. What should have been a blast – maybe all the way to the alley! – would instead hit the pine and, more often than not, drift gently down toward the pitcher. Just a loud out, I'd say.

Several years ago, some of the needles began to turn brown. Not all of them, though, and it was easy enough to pay attention to the ones that were still green. You could even see new growth on the tree, little bud-type things at the ends of some branches. But soon enough, there was more brown than green. This year it was all brown.

"I think we need to get rid of the pine," my wife said.

You're in charge of it, I said. I'm the one who cried when we took our daughter to college a couple of years ago. No way could I handle getting rid of the pine. Of course, by "handling" I mean hiring someone to do it. Even if I were not a sentimental wreck, I am incompetent with tools.

My next-door neighbor, on the other hand, installed his own air-conditioning system. For all I know, he designed it. Not long ago, he decided to take down a big tree in front of his house. He made elaborate preparations with pulleys and ropes. All the neighbors gathered around as he made ready to bring the tree down. "It should land over here," he said, pointing toward the sidewalk that runs in front of our houses. We all nodded, but exchanged glances of disbelief. A sense of expectant disaster was in the air. I was reminded of a time, many years ago, when I went to a racetrack to watch Evel Knievel jump over 16 buses. But the tree came down just where it was supposed to come down. For that matter, Evel Knievel made his jump.

My wife called a tree service. They came while I was at the newspaper, and when I came home, the tree was down. I thought about the woodpecker, and I looked at the grass to see if I could see any trace of the base path that was once so obvious. Maybe I was seeing with my heart, but I thought I could see it, ever so faintly.

—

MAN WAITING FOR TRIAL CONTEMPLATES FREEDOM VERSUS MEDICAL CARE

JUNE 9, 2002

Freedom's just another word for nothing left to lose.

"What would you do if you were free?" A look of puzzlement came over Tyrone Dickerson's face. I got the feeling this was a question he had not yet considered.

"Would you stay here?" I asked. Dickerson is currently at the Normandy Nursing Center. All things considered, it's an excellent place for him to be – a clean room, meals, medication, transportation to a dialysis center and people making sure he's all right.

"No, I don't think so," he said.

He said he might look into living with his sister in East St. Louis. Well, sure. That would be nice. Then again, if living with relatives were a realistic option, Dickerson probably would not have spent so much of his life on the street, and he wouldn't be facing the legal problems he's facing.

Regular readers might remember Dickerson. He was arrested in May last year, and accused of using a coat hanger to fish dollar bills out of a pay box at a downtown parking lot. It was the 11th time he'd been busted for the same offense. All the previous times, he'd spent a little time at the station – at most, a night in jail – and then he'd be released. Minor penance for a minor sin.

For some reason, though, the 11th time was the charm. The system took a hard look at Dickerson. In 1993, he had been arrested for rape. He pleaded guilty and got five years. He did every day of his five years, and was released in June 1998. Somewhere along the line, he became HIV-positive. So the prosecutors saw a convicted sexual offender who was HIV-positive. A third misdemeanor stealing conviction can be upgraded to a felony, so the circuit attorney's office upgraded the charge against Dickerson. He went to jail to await his trial. He was looking at a possible seven years in prison.

His kidneys began to shut down. End-stage kidney disease, said the doctors. He needed dialysis. Then he developed pneumonia. He also had mental problems. He was diagnosed as suffering from schizophrenia. He was transferred from the jail to a hospital. Because he was in custody, he was ineligible for Medicaid.

I wrote a column about the situation. Shortly thereafter, Judge Robert Dierker ordered Dickerson released from custody. Dierker cited the fact that the "continued incarceration was costing the city treasury very large sums." Dickerson was moved to Normandy Nursing Center. His application for Medicaid is pending. So is his trial. It's scheduled for September.

He is represented by public defender Amy Fearncombe. This has been a str ange case, and some city officials have accused Fearncombe of representing Dickerson too zealously because she didn't try to get him out of jail. She shrugs at the criticism. He was getting medical care while he was in jail.

I visited him at the nursing home this week. He's 34 years old. He is slightly built, and he seemed frail. He told me his biological mother put him in foster care when he was 4 months old. He considers that foster family to be his real family. He quit school in the 10th grade, and began living on the street.

He went through job-training programs twice, but nothing came of either. He said he once had a job cleaning a bar in East St. Louis, and for his work, he was allowed to sleep in the bar.

Before he got arrested last year, he was sleeping in cars, he said. And doing what for money? Fishing for dollars, he said, but on his lawyer's advice, he did not want to talk about the circumstances of his pending case. He had nothing but nice things to say about Normandy Nursing Center. He's getting dialysis three times a week, and he's getting medication for his mental problems. Did he get medication while he was on the street? Oh, no, he said.

But still, if he were acquitted, or found guilty and sentenced to time served, if he were free, he'd want to leave the nursing home and head off on his own. He said he thinks he might make it this time.

—

EXCOMMUNICATE AT CHRISTMAS? IF ARCHBISHOP HAD A WIFE . . .

DECEMBER 26, 2005

Every boss needs someone who will occasionally say, "Whoa! Let's think about this, Chief." But few bosses want to hear that, and consequently, the sort of people who tend to rise in the corporate world are the sort who say, "That's a great idea, Boss!" even when they know it isn't. Underlings concerned with advancement tend to keep their doubts to themselves.

That's why wives are so important. They don't keep their doubts to themselves.

In that sense, it's really a shame that Roman Catholic priests cannot marry, because if anybody needs a wife, it's Archbishop Raymond Burke. Shortly before Christmas, he announced that the six lay members of the board of directors of St. Stanislaus Kostka Church and a priest they had hired to be their pastor had been excommunicated. He made the announcement in a column he writes for the archdiocesan newspaper.

That column would never have appeared if the archbishop had a wife.

"Let's see what you've written for the paper, Raymond."

"Here it is, Martha."

She starts reading it, shakes her head and looks at her husband.

"You can't be serious. You're excommunicating them at Christmas?"

"In a technical sense, they have excommunicated themselves. I am simply declaring it. I am just an instrument. That is the point I'm trying to make in this column, Martha."

"Nobody is going to understand that, Raymond. All that comes across is that you are excommunicating these people right before Christmas, and you're doing it because they want to celebrate Christmas Mass at the church they love."

"Martha, you have to understand that . . ."

"No, Raymond. You have to understand. This fight was never about religion. It's not like they're worshipping Satan over there. This has been a fight about property rights. Property! Past archbishops let it slide. I know you well enough to know you're not doing this for the money, Raymond. You're just a little over the top about order and everything being in its rightful place. But the bottom line is, you took away their priest and now you're excommunicating them because they've hired a new one."

"He's been suspended, Martha."

"Suspended? So what? Haven't you ever read any Graham Greene novels? Think about the priest in 'The Power and the Glory.' He was a drunk, Raymond. He fathered a child. But he loved God, and he was willing to lose everything to bring the sacraments to the people. There is something heroic about a flawed priest who loves God, Raymond."

The archibishop stands there, taking in his wife's words. She continues.

"If you do this, the focus of the entire holiday is going to be on St. Stanislaus. They'll probably draw 1,500 for the Christmas Eve Mass. Maybe 2,000. It's magical – a flawed priest bringing the sacraments to the people. Also, did you see what that priest did at his news conference when he arrived in town? He went around and introduced himself to every single reporter and photographer there. He shook their hands. He welcomed them. When was the last time you spoke with anybody from the press?"

"You know I don't talk to the press, Martha."

"I know you don't, Raymond. And I'll admit, they are a rather common lot. And liberals, too, most of them. They did give you the business during the election. But still, you need to learn to mingle with all kinds, Raymond. You really do. But that's a lesson for another day. Right now, I want you to throw out this column. Write something about love and faith and joy. Leave the canon law and the property fights for another day. I mean, Raymond, this is Christmas. "

—

BARRIERS OF CULTURE, LANGUAGE EMERGE AT MURDER TRIAL

MARCH 25, 2001

On the first day of 2000, a St. Louis police officer pulled a car over for running a stop sign at Michigan and Potomac. Four men and a woman were in the car. Three of the men were Bosnian, and spoke very little English. The fourth man was Vietnamese. He had been stabbed in the chest and was badly hurt. The woman was also Vietnamese. She spoke English, but in a limited way.

It was a very confusing situation. The woman said they had just come from her house on Michigan. An officer went there and found a Vietnamese man still holding a bloody knife. He had lacerations on his face and head. He spoke no English.

It was still a confusing situation.

The man in the car died at the hospital. His name was David Stark. Before long, the who and the what of the crime were put together. Phat Nguyen, the man who had been holding the bloody knife, had stabbed Stark. But the why was a complete mystery. The woman in the car – her name was Victoria Tran – was Nguyen's wife. What was she doing in the car with Stark? And how did the Bosnians fit into the whole thing?

Through an interpreter, Nguyen told homicide detectives that he and

Stark had had an argument earlier in the day. He said that Stark had come to his house with the Bosnians, and they had pushed their way into the house and attacked him with sticks. He had stabbed Stark in self-defense, he said. The police had already impounded the car that had been stopped earlier. After interviewing Nguyen, detectives searched the car, and found a bamboo stick and a pipe – both about 5 feet long – in the trunk.

Meanwhile, the Bosnians, also interviewed through an interpreter, said that Stark, an immigrant himself, occasionally helped other immigrants with paperwork. Consequently, one of the three Bosnians, Hariz Osmanovic, knew him. On this particular day, Stark and the Bosnians were going to go get something to eat. Stark wanted to stop at a house on Michigan to deliver a stuffed animal to a child. He went up to the house with the toy while the Bosnians waited by the car smoking cigarettes. The next thing they knew, Stark came running out of the house holding his chest. That was the story the Bosnians told.

Where did the woman come from? She just showed up, the Bosnians said.

She, too, was interviewed through an interpreter. She said she had gone to the market to get some food. As she approached the back door of the house, her husband came running out. He told her he had been attacked by Stark and some Bosnians. She then ran around to the front of the house and saw Stark lying on the ground. She went with the Bosnians to direct them to the hospital. That was her story.

What was her relationship with Stark? Friends, she said.

There is, however, a dispute about the exact translation of that first interview. She says she said she liked Stark. The police say the interpreter said Tran said she loved Stark.

It was the city's first homicide of the new millennium, but police and prosecutors decided it had an old-fashioned motive. This is about jealousy, they said. Nguyen was charged with first-degree murder.

He went on trial last week.

Defense attorney Nick Zotos decided to waive a jury trial and have the case heard by a judge. Legally, it's a simple case of self-defense, Zotos told me, and the danger is a jury could get distracted by all the interpreters and cultural issues.

The first cultural issue came during Tran's testimony. Prosecutor Dwight Warren asked about her car. Wasn't it true that Stark had bought it for her? Wasn't it true that her husband had not even known that she had a car?

As the interpreter, Ly Lac, repeated the questions in Vietnamese, Tran's eyes flashed with anger.

Stark had not paid for the car, she said. He had told her about the car, and she had given him the money to buy it. As for her husband not knowing she was buying a car, that is the way it is.

Whatever the woman wants, she can get. She doesn't have to tell her husband.

Weren't you having an affair? Warren asked.

I am Vietnamese, she said. We are not like Americans.

By the way, Tran's father was an American GI, and that ancestry is evident in her features. She is an attractive woman – cute rather than beautiful – but her European features were a detriment in her home country. She was 9 years old when the Communists took over in 1975, and life became very difficult for her mother and her. She told me she has known her husband since they were children, and I imagined a wonderful love story. Ostracized by most, but loved by one.

That was a fascinating thing about the trial. With refugees from Vietnam and Bosnia, there were plenty of stories. For instance, Lac, the Vietnamese interpreter, escaped from Vietnam in 1982. He was 14 years old. His family had owned a furniture company in Kien Giang, south of Saigon. Although the company and the family home were confiscated by the Communists, Lac's mother hid enough money to finance his escape. He got away on a boat, but once at sea, the escapees ran out of water. It looked like the end, but then the boat was raided by pirates from Thailand. The pirates took all the jewelry and money the boat people had, but gave them water. That's how they survived. Saved by pirates.

Tran was allowed to come to this country in 1989 because of her American bloodlines. In addition to her husband and daughter, she brought her mother. They were located in St. Louis. Tran got a job in a beauty shop. Her husband worked in a restaurant, and then got a factory job. They had another daughter. Both kids go to parochial schools. I spoke with the girls and realized that the American dream does not always work for the parents, but almost always it works for the kids.

Speaking of kids, Stark's children were at the trial. They seemed very nice, and while their father was Vietnamese, they were born in this country, and are, of course, completely American. They politely declined to talk to me.

According to Stark's brother, Leo, who also attended the trial, Stark came to this country in 1972 when he was adopted at the age of 14. He became a successful businessman in Union, and moved to St. Louis a couple of years ago after a divorce.

Tran's testimony was certainly helpful to her husband. She said that when she got home and saw her husband at the back door, she ran to the front of the house and saw two Bosnians coming out the front door.

The Bosnians testified later and told a completely different story. They didn't go inside the house. They didn't hit anybody. By the way, only two of them testified. The third, Osmanovic, has gone back to Bosnia.

Their interpreter deserves a mention. Her name is Lilly Svrakic, and when Judge Philip Heagney was asking about her qualifications as an interpreter, she responded to one question with, "Yes, your majesty," and to another, with "Yes, your honesty."

Needless to say, the judge decided she was very qualified. Apparently, she was. So said Shirley Rukcic, a local attorney who is fluent in Serbo-Croatian and sat in on the trial when the Bosnians testified.

The defense had only one witness, Nguyen. He said that one of his daughters showed him a stuffed animal, and told him that Stark had given it to her. Nguyen said he didn't like the fact that someone he hardly knew would give his child a gift, and so he took it back. A couple of hours later, he said, there was a knock on the door and as he began to open it, Stark pushed his way in. He had the "Soviets" with him, Nguyen said. They began beating him with sticks, he said, and he managed to get into the kitchen where he grabbed a knife to defend himself.

It was, I thought, a pretty good story, but defense attorney Zotos had something even better. He had photographs showing that Nguyen had lacerations on his head and face. Somebody hit him with something, and the bamboo rod in the car was much like the bamboo stick Nguyen had mentioned to the police.

Cultural issues and age-old motives aside, the photos and the stick seemed to make a strong argument for self-defense.

Judge Heagney is expected to announce his verdict Monday.

—

WHEN MAGIC BLENDS WITH REALITY, LIFE IS A BIT SWEETER

APRIL 11, 2005

One of the loveliest streets in the St. Louis region is Wydown Boulevard, which runs from Skinker to Hanley, and I am blessed to walk that route every Saturday morning as I march to the U.S. Bank branch at Hanley and Forsyth.

I maintain an account there for sentimental reasons. It was to this very location that the late Thomas Jacobsen, the former top dog of Mercantile Bank, retreated after negotiating the sale of Mercantile. Like all the fellows who sold our local banks to out-of-towners, Jacobsen made sure the deal was good for him. In fact, he pocketed $13.5 million worth of cash and stock. And by hurriedly moving from his opulent downtown office to decidedly less posh digs at Hanley and Forsyth, he avoided paying city earnings tax on his loot. Before stiffing the city like that, Jacobsen had served as president and chairman of Civic Progress.

So the branch serves as something of a monument to me.

At any rate, I was walking along Wydown on Saturday and the weather was great and everything was blooming and for some reason, I thought of a young woman named Manuela. My wife and I met her when we were in Argentina for our 25th wedding anniversary a couple of months ago. We met her in a place called Bariloche. I promised my son to Manuela. As regular readers know, I believe in arranged marriages. Especially for sons. You cannot trust a young man's judgment on something as important as a wife. When I was at that stage of life – Flawed Man Seeks Perfect Woman – my future wife happened to move into the apartment next to mine. That sort of lightning does not strike every young man.

Bill McClellan

"You should marry my son," I told Manuela.

"Maybe he will be prince of my dreams," she said.

Actually, I bet I know why Manuela came to my mind on Saturday. Everything was blooming. Manuela had told us a story about a plant, cana colihue. It looked like a regular bamboo plant to me, but Manuela said that cana colihue blooms every 50 years. It has an orange flower, she said, and that flower emits a strong odor of cheese. This odor attracts mice who gorge themselves on the starchy flower. The starch makes them thirsty and they go down to the lake to drink. The starch expands inside the stomachs of the mice and they explode. Every 50 years, this natural disaster befalls the mice of Bariloche.

She said her mother had told her the story and her mother would not lie.

I would not want to get off on the wrong foot with my son's future mother-in-law, but I am not convinced. Still, I like the magical quality of the story. It is the very quality you find in books of the Latino genre. "One Hundred Years of Solitude." "Like Water for Chocolate." Always magic blends with reality. That is the way life should be. We need magic.

I turned north on Hanley and headed toward Forsyth. There is a car wash along Hanley. I enjoy watching the fellows as I march past. They're usually laughing and chatting. Doing something productive, something that can be quantified. Taking something that is dirty and making it clean.

But yikes. The car wash was closed. What will happen to the workers? Upon closer inspection, there was a sign on the door. Temporarily closed. Let's hope so, I thought.

I reached the bank. While the branch is a monument to the greed of bosses, the workers are generally friendly and helpful. I stood in line to deposit my check. "Next, please," said a teller. Her name was Faye. I gave her my check and my deposit slip. I glanced around while she entered my deposit and pulled out my cash, which she counted out as she handed it to me. Then she gave me my receipt for the deposit. I started to put the receipt away when I noticed something. A stamped "Thank You" on the slip.

"Is this new?" I asked her.

"Oh, I did that," she said, and she pointed to pens of various colors. So it wasn't a stamp. It was something Faye was doing, and for no particular reason except to do it. Just thanking the customers, and if they noticed it, fine, and if not, that's fine, too.

Maybe the story about the mice is true.

—

COUPLE BELIEVE GOOD FUTURE IS NEAR AFTER LIVING TOUGH PASTS

NOVEMBER 22, 2000

Sherry works the morning shift at a fast-food restaurant in St. Louis. She works at the grill, frying this and frying that.

She's 41 years old, so she's a bit older than most of her colleagues. That's fine with Sherry. She's like most people. You have work, and then you have the parallel universe of life. In Sherry's parallel universe, she has a fiance. I met him once. It was a very brief meeting, and he seemed shy. Sherry told me he suffers from a social phobia. She defined it as a fear of being around people. Whatever the medical definition is, it's enough to get him a small disability check. He gets $429 a month.

Perhaps Sherry could get a disability check. She says she has a bipolar condition and suffers from depression and attention deficit disorder. On the other hand, she is able to function in society. She has a GED. She even enrolled at a local community college once. She dropped all of her classes except for English composition. She got an A in that class. Plus, of course, she is capable of holding a job.

Not that life is easy. She went to jail once. It was, she said, sort of a misunderstanding. She said she found a bag at the airport. The bag was filled with camera equipment. She needed some money, so she took some of the equipment to a pawn shop. A short time later, the police showed up at her apartment. She was charged with felony theft, but she said she didn't really steal anything. The bag was just sitting there. She found it. She didn't steal it. Wouldn't she have tried to fence it on the street if she thought she had stolen it? Instead, she went to a pawn shop and used her own name. Still, she pleaded guilty and got probation.

Sometime later, she got messed up with drugs and was arrested for selling crack cocaine. She wasn't really selling it, she said. This guy asked if she could get him $20 worth of crack, and she said, sure, and she got it for him. That's a sale? There was no profit. But that was enough to get her probation revoked on the earlier theft conviction. She did a total of about seven months.

She was sent to a drug and alcohol treatment center in Farmington. She met a guy there and, when she finished treatment, went to live with him and his mother near there. The three of them lived in a trailer, and things were pretty good. She got a factory job. She was a seamstress. About the time the romance had run its course with the fellow from the treatment center, she met another guy and moved into his trailer. She said they got engaged but it didn't work out because he was violent and still in love with his ex-wife.

At any rate, she ended up back here. She met her fiance about nine months ago. At the time, she wasn't working, and his disability check wasn't enough to make a deposit on an apartment or pay first and last month's rent, so they lived on the streets.

Sherry and her fiance are happy – grateful, actually – to accept meals from the churches and missions that provide them, but they try not to spend any nights in the various shelters. They prefer the streets.

Not too long ago, they found a nice place. Pretty nice, anyway. It's the shell of a place that burned down. At night, they take a roll of toilet paper, soak it in rubbing alcohol and put it in a coffee can. Then they light it. It's a good clean burn, Sherry said.

While she's at work, her fiance moves around. Sometimes he walks. Sometimes he rides. He has a monthly bus pass, so sometimes he gets on a bus and just rides and rides. Apparently, the people on the bus don't bother him.

Now that Sherry is working, she figures it won't be long before she and her fiance have enough cash for an apartment. How long? Certainly by Christmas.

In the meantime, the little fire in the coffee can puts out a bit of heat. Not much, but enough. Then the morning comes, and Sherry goes to the fast-food restaurant to stand by the warm grill.

—

RUNAWAY POSES PROBLEMS; POLICE HAVE NO ANSWERS

JUNE 8, 2001

A 12-year-old girl was caught shoplifting at a grocery store in the city Tuesday afternoon. Police were called. They were going to arrest her for petty larceny, but first they ran her name in the computer, and she came up as a missing person. In other words, she was a runaway. So she was taken to the Juvenile Division at the downtown police station on Clark Avenue.

As of Tuesday afternoon, the Juvenile Division had handled 885 runaway cases this year. Still, the detectives notified the lieutenant that this particular child was in custody.

Bring her into my office, he said.

Lt. Daniel Isom is young and soft-spoken. He has a gentle manner that suggests he would rather save somebody than arrest somebody. He likes to put faces to names, so when the detectives bring in a child whose file is known to the lieutenant, he likes to meet the child personally. He was very familiar with this child's file. She is a runner. Seven times this year.

Meet Nicole, said the detective who ushered the 12-year-old into the lieutenant's office.

The lieutenant looked at the child. A pretty kid, but with a look way too worldly for 12. Scruffy, too, but that comes from being on the street. The lieutenant asked her the question he asks all the kids.

Can you read?

The answer speaks to hope or despair. At least let them be able to read, thinks the lieutenant. With everything else in their lives that has led them to this office, at least let them be able to read.

I can read, said Nicole.

He handed her a piece of paper and asked her to read it aloud. It was a police report about her, and it was filled with the language of official-dom, in which a house is a residence, and a tip is information, and officers respond at approximately this or that. Not easy stuff for a 12-year-old, particularly a runner who doesn't go to school.

She read it easily. Smoothly.

Hope then. This child is intelligent and has the potential to succeed. But she is not on the road to success. Already, she is sexually active. She is very promiscuous, say the detectives who know her best, and there is, they say, nothing unusual about that. Sex is the currency by which shelter is purchased. Pregnancy and sexually transmitted diseases are just some of the hazards a young runner faces. Drugs and violence are part of street life, too.

And how does a child find herself in this type of situation?

At birth, Nicole was given to a great-aunt. Perhaps that would have worked out, but the aunt died, and her husband, now in his 60s, is with another woman. She is ill, and Nicole has told the detectives that the couple see her as a caretaker. She rebels by running. At least that is how she tells the story.

The juvenile system is geared for two categories of kids. Much energy is spent on juvenile criminals. Much energy is spent on kids who are abused. Nicole does not fit neatly into either category.

Her crimes are status crimes. That is, they would not be crimes if she were not a juvenile. Violating curfew, truancy, even running. And while her home life is a long, long way from ideal, there seems to be no evidence of abuse. Perhaps you could say that she is just too much for an older couple to handle.

In fact, her uncle has told the detectives that he is willing to relinquish custody. That was good news, as far as the lieutenant was concerned. It would mean that the system could take custody, and maybe do something.

The lieutenant thinks she needs to be locked up in a so-called secure facility – she is, after all, a runner – and there are no such facilities in the St. Louis area for status offenders. The trick, then, would be to get the Juvenile Court to send Nicole away.

The detectives think that's the best idea, too, but at the moment, all plans are on hold. Nicole has run away again.

—

WHEN THE TEAM'S A TROPHY WIFE, HOW SECURE CAN YOU FEEL?

DECEMBER 8, 1999

Are you excited about the Rams? I mean, really excited? Or do you sense something not quite right in the relationship between the team and the town?

If you answered yes to that last question, you're an old-fashioned guy. Deep down in your midwestern soul, you still love the football Cardinals. You think of the Big Red as a First Wife. Big Red was a midwestern girl. Grew up in Chicago. She came here in 1960, and she came here of her own accord. Imagine that. Nobody had to beg her or bribe her. She thought you were a good guy, and she wanted to be with you. She didn't ask you for anything. Nothing material, anyway.

Not that you could have given her anything. You couldn't even buy her a house. Instead, you spent those first years of marriage at the old Sportsman's Park on Grand Avenue. Compared with some of the places she was used to, it was a dive. It had been built for baseball, and the makeshift football field ran from the first base dugout into left field. To provide seating close to the field, you brought in high school bleachers. High school bleachers for your new NFL franchise!

But you know something? She never complained.

You later moved into slightly better digs downtown, but even Busch

Stadium was first and foremost a baseball stadium. She knew that. But still, she accepted the situation.

As football teams go, Big Red wasn't beautiful. More accurately, she wasn't glamorous. Nobody mistook her for a supermodel. But hey, you weren't exactly New York or San Francisco yourself. Nobody was calling you the Fabio of North American cities.

Truth is, you made a nice couple. Solid, reliable old St. Louis and the football Cardinals.

I don't mean to suggest that Big Red was dowdy. She might have enjoyed putting on the feedbag at Pasta House a little too much, but she was fun. There was even a time in the '70s when she lost a lot of weight, and actually looked snazzy. Then she put the weight back on. Just as

well. Look who she married. I mean, come on. Tony Bennett never left his heart in St. Louis, did he?

By the way, you and Big Red stayed married for almost 30 years. Twenty-seven, to be exact. You shared a lot of history, a lot of memories. Some of them were good, and some of them were bad, but in retrospect, even the bad memories were kind of fun.

In the end, though, you took her for granted. She wanted a new house, and you said no. That led to the break-up. She moved to Arizona and remarried.

You were single for a few years, and then decided to get married again yourself. In a fit of megalomania, you even built a big house for your new bride. But nobody would have you. You were shocked.

If you wanted a wife, you would have to buy one. That was painfully clear. You found some young thing in Southern California. You threw money a t her. Whatever she wanted, she got. You acted like a rich old fool, but you tried not to feel bad about it. It was what you had to do. I've already built the house, you told yourself.

The rich old fool act worked. The California babe agreed to come to St. Louis and live in the big palace you had already built. Very reluctantly, though. Like she was doing you a big favor.

The first couple of years were rocky, and your new wife put on some weight. A lot of weight. You found yourself thinking more and more about Big Red. I shouldn't have let her get away, is what you told yourself.

This year, though, your young wife looks great. Everybody is telling you how good she looks. Better even than Big Red in the '70s.

You try to smile and act happy. Maybe you even wear blue and gold paraphernalia. Deep down, though, you're afraid everybody is laughing at you. Everybody knows your second wife didn't marry you for love.

—

TIME AND LIFE UNFOLD QUIETLY FOR WATCHMAKER

Nov. 14, 2004

The watchmaker, as he calls himself, does not really make watches. He repairs them. Clocks, too. He's been doing it for almost 50 years. It's delicate work and cannot be hurried. But hurried for what? In our throw-away culture, a repairman is an outsider.

Just the other day, a young woman came into the watchmaker's small shop on the third floor of the Chemical Building and showed him an in-expensive watch. "How much to repair this?" she wanted to know. The watchmaker thought for a moment. "Ten dollars," he said. "I can get a new one for that," she said. The watchmaker's name is J.B. Watson, but most people know him as Sergeant. He did not start out to be a watch-maker.

He was born in April 1930, the 11th of 12 children. His father worked, when there was work, in a sawmill near Salem, Mo. Then World War II rolled in like a thunderstorm, washing away the old life, and four of the six brothers went off to fight. They survived, but a brother-in-law was killed in the Battle of the Bulge. Meanwhile, Watson stayed home. He could only dream of adventures in faraway places.

He enlisted on the day he turned 17. His mother had to give her ap-proval. The war was over, of course, but the Army did what it was supposed to do. It sent him far away. He spent his 18th birthday in Korea. "We were on red alert," he remembered. But nothing happened, and the unit went to Japan.

There is now, hanging on the wall in the watchmaker's shop, a black-and-white photograph of four young men in uniform. They are sitting at a table staring at the camera. Cans of beer are on the table. The photograph was taken during the interlude in Japan.

The unit then went back to the States. Watson extended his enlistment for one year, and shortly thereafter, in June 1950, the North Koreans invaded the south. Watson and his friends were sent back to Korea.

They were thrown into the thick of things and for a while, they barely held on. Then the tide turned, and the Americans and South Koreans pushed north. Watson was with a cavalry unit less than 20 miles from the Yalu River when the Chinese entered the war. The Americans and the South Koreans were pushed back, and it was during this retreat that Watson was first wounded. Shrapnel from a grenade tore into his hip, leg and face. He was medevaced to Japan in November. After three months, he was sent back to the war.

He was shot in the leg in August 1951, and this time, his war was over. The round tore through his right leg, shattering bone as it went. He was sent back to Japan, and then to the States. He spent a year in a VA hospital, and then another year in rehab. During his time in rehab, friends introduced him to a girl from the St. Louis area. They were married in 1954.

Watson was put on disability. The wound was only part of it. The rest had to do with the effects of the severe cold on his feet and knees. But even a partially disabled veteran has to work. The VA sent him to watchmaking school.

Fifty years ago, watchmaking and watch repair was a healthy business. After working for somebody else for a couple of years, Watson started his own business. He had a little place on Pine Street. About 6 feet wide and 6 feet deep and right on street level. He was there for almost 20 years, and then he moved to the Arcade Building and then to the Paul Brown Building. He stayed there for another 20 years before moving to his present location. It's almost as if downtown redevelopment has been chasing him these many years, and now he has his little spot on the third floor of another building that may or may not have much of a future. He works alone, and lives alone, too, since his wife died about 10 years ago.

He works five days a week, and if you're wondering, yes, he was working on Veterans Day. He was working on a pocket watch. A beautiful timepiece. Very old, too. Just the sort of watch that requires a delicate touch and an unhurried hand. For a man who takes pride in his work, it was not a bad way to spend a holiday.

—

A FARM IN WARREN COUNTY PROVIDED ONE COUPLE WITH A LIFE OF PLENTY
FEBRUARY 27, 2000

In the early years of the last century, William and Lizzie Hanke had a farm near Bernheimer in Warren County. It was not a river bottom farm. It was a hill farm. Very little of the land was flat. So it was much harder to work than a river bottom farm, and the soil was not nearly as rich.

William's back gave out when he was only 48, and he sold the farm and moved to the nearby town of Holstein. That was in 1928. Had he waited another year, he would have been trying to sell during the depression, and that would have been next to impossible. Spared from the rigors of his hill farm, William's health returned. He became a hunter. Squirrels and foxes, mostly, but he gained some renown when he killed two timber wolves in one day. He lived to be 92. Lizzie lived to be 90.

Only one of their six children chose the farm life. That was Cora Marie, their second-born. She was 20 when the family moved into Holstein, and she didn't stay in town long. She married Roy Scharnhorst, a young man with a farm on the Missouri river bottom near Treloar. Her youngest sibling, Bill Hanke, who is now 77 and a successful businessman in Atlanta, remembers one of the family's favorite stories about the wedding.

"Dad told her he wanted to give her a present," he said. "She could have either $100 or a mule he had. She didn't hesitate. She took the mule."

There was – and to some extent, still is – a danger with river bottom farms. The river can rise. For the first six years of their married life, the river took most of their crop. Roy and Cora Marie saved enough to eat, and that was it. They came close to quitting the farm but gave it one more year. The seventh year produced a bumper crop.

Years went by. Cora Marie canned food for the winter. She cooked five meals a day – a big, early breakfast eaten in the kitchen, a lighter breakfast she'd take out to the fields about 9:30, lunch at noon back in the kitchen, a lighter meal, snacks really, that she'd take out into the fields in the late afternoon and, finally, a big supper in the evening.

Their marriage produced no children. They were financially stable but not wealthy. They were solid, dependable people, very much at home with the other citizens, mostly of German descent, who work the small farms and live in the small towns in southern Warren County along the Missouri River.

One day, Roy, who was in his early 50s and seemed strong and healthy, went out to feed the hogs and dropped dead. He had never been sick. After almost 30 years of marriage, Cora Marie was a widow. She was 51 years old. She took a job in the general store in Treloar.

Walter Bierbaum farmed the land next to the farm of Roy and Cora Marie. He was a bachelor. He had been a good friend of Roy's and had known Cora Marie since childhood. Neither Cora Marie nor anybody else had ever called Walter by his name. He was known to everybody as Skinny. He was tall, and very thin.

He was the youngest of the six children of Carl and Louise Bierbaum. Carl had rented land to farm on the Missouri bottoms near Treloar. Of the six children, only one stayed on the farm. That was Skinny.

He was a farmer and a singer. In addition to singing in the choir of the Immanuel United Church of Christ in Holstein, Skinny sang at weddings and funerals. Sometimes when bands would come to town, Skinny would be invited on stage to sing with the band.

Still, he was not the most famous of the Bierbaums. That honor went to his older sister, Thalita. She taught school in Warren County for more than 50 years. She began her career in a one-room schoolhouse. Two of her younger brothers, including Skinny, were among her first students. She never married.

When a decent interval had passed after Roy's death, Skinny began to court Cora Marie. Although neither of them were kids, there was nothing hasty about their courtship. They dated for almost seven years. They were married in August 1966.

The Age of Aquarius was dawning in most of the country. The Beatles were singing "Ob-La-Di, Ob-La-Da," and along the river bottom near Treloar, life went on.

Skinny and Cora Marie went to dances on Saturday night. They went to church on Sunday. They worked on the farm all week. They were fun-loving without being adventurous. They seldom left Warren County. They were not the type of people to take a honeymoon, for instance. In 1979, Cora Marie's brother, Bill, came from Atlanta and put everybody in a van and drove them to Florida. It was the first, and last, time that Skinny and Cora Marie saw an ocean.

They had all they needed in Treloar, and the Treloar bottoms. The couple celebrated their 33rd anniversary last summer, but Cora Marie was already slipping. Her failing health concerned Skinny's friends. All his siblings were gone.

Cora Marie went to the Cedar Crest Nursing Center in Washington, Mo. Before long, Skinny followed.

He died February 17. She died February 18. A joint service was held February 19 at the Immanuel United Church of Christ. They were buried in the church cemetery.

The obituaries mentioned that he was a lifelong farmer and that she was a homemaker.

—

CHAPTER TWO

— THE PATHS WE WALK

SOME CARRY A LOT OF BAGGAGE FROM UNIVERSE TO UNIVERSE

APRIL 1, 2002

I was walking east in the 2000 block of Washington Avenue on Easter morning when a fellow sitting on the curb hailed me.

"Hey, Hobo. You got a light?" He spoke in a very friendly way, and I could tell that he meant no disrespect when calling me Hobo. In fact, just the opposite. It seemed almost like a nickname. Had a third person been around, he or she might have thought that the fellow on the curb and I were friends.

"Sorry. I don't have a light," I said.

"What? You quit smoking?"

Again, he spoke in a very familiar tone, and I was a little taken aback. First, there had been the hobo thing. There are times when I may not look like a clothes horse, but Easter morning was not one of those times. I was wearing my sport jacket. I had made one of my twice-annual trips to St. Xavier College church to be with my family during a service, and then I took off for the newspaper. So if ever I did not look like a hobo, it was right then. And now there was the smoking thing. Most people of quality don't smoke. What made the fellow on the curb think I had?

"Yes, I quit," I said. "Quite a while ago."

"Good for you," he said.

I took a closer look at him. He seemed like a homeless person of the upscale variety. If he had a substance abuse problem, it was not obvious at the moment. I was quite sure I had never met him. At least not in this universe.

As regular readers know, I am a believer in parallel universes. We are the same people in these other universes, but we have made different decisions, and/or different things have happened to us. In another universe, for instance, you might have slept in on the morning in which you met your wife in this universe, so in the second universe, you're either single or you married somebody else. And on and on it goes. You can be a big deal in one universe, and an absolute failure in another.

I figure this present universe – the one in which I am writing this column – is about as good as it gets for me. In fact, it's not too difficult to imagine a parallel universe in which my friends call me Hobo, and on a good day, my substance abuse problem is not too obvious. Could this fellow on the curb be a universe-hopper, one of those rare individuals who can move from one universe to another?

Somewhat shaken, I moved on. As I continued east, I came to The Power House Church. It is one of those Church of the Second Chance places. Restoration churches, they call them. A husky fellow with long hair was standing in the doorway.

"Here for the service?" he asked as I approached.

"Just out for a walk," I said.

"Meetings on Monday and Thursday nights," he said as I walked past.

That made me feel better. The fellow on the curb was not necessarily a universe-hopper. I just look like a fellow who needs a second chance.

Later in the morning, I went to the Greyhound Bus Station. My daughter had taken the Greyhound to Texas for spring break, and when she arrived home Saturday night, her luggage was not on the bus. No one was sure what had happened. The best guess seemed to be that during a layover in Houston, her luggage had been put on a bus heading in the general direction of St. Louis, and with any luck, it would get here sometime.

"You see those boxes," said a baggage handler, as he pointed to a couple of cardboard boxes that had been removed from the Houston bus. "If nobody claims them, we'll put them on another bus. That's what will happen to your daughter's things."

It was not a comforting thought. My daughter's luggage would slowly move from station to station, and, if nobody ever claimed it, it would eventually arrive in St. Louis. It seemed like a system devised by someone like me, a person who believes in parallel universes. "Hey, in some universes, you'll see your luggage again."

And that works for me. Like I said, for me, this universe is as good as it gets. When I checked at the station Sunday morning, her luggage was there.

—

FUNERALS WERE HIS BUSINESS, AND HIS WAS QUITE AN EVENT

JULY 10, 1998

My father taught me not to preach long funeral sermons," said the Rev. Herman Gore Jr. "Because every day of our lives, we write our own funeral sermons." There were a few "Amens" shouted to second that notion, but there was also, I thought, a slight sense of unease among the crowd of mourners. It was true that the service had been going on for more than three and a half hours, and it's true that we all write our own funeral sermons, but still, much was expected of this particular eulogy.

After all, it was the funeral of Charles Stanley Wilson Jr., and he had selected Gore to deliver the eulogy.

In fact, Wilson had choreographed the entire funeral, and for the first three and a half hours, it had been a grand funeral indeed.

That wasn't surprising. Funerals were Wilson's business.

He left St. Louis to go to Boston University almost 30 years ago, and he did extremely well. After graduating from college, he could have had his pick of professional schools, but instead came home to help run the A.L. Beal Mortuary, which was founded by his great-grandfather in 1913 and is the second oldest black-owned business in all of Missouri.

At first, Wilson worked under his grandmother, the legendary Birdie Anderson Beal. She had taken over the mortuary upon her father's death in 1929, and she had been running it for almost half a century when Wilson came home from Boston. She had her own ideas about running a funeral home, and was not easily swayed from those ideas.

So it's possible, maybe even likely, that in his early years at the mortuary, Wilson thought about all that could have been, and it's possible that he wondered if he had done the right thing.

But as the years passed, he came to love funerals. We know this because he did almost 250 of them in the last year, and the truth is, he had no need to work that hard. That's because the A.L. Beal Mortuary was one of four funeral homes that received a contract a year ago to rebury the remains of those poor souls who were interred at the Washington Park Cemetery just east of the airport, and whose not so final resting places were therefore smack in the path of progress.

It is a contract so lucrative that only a person who loved funerals would have continued to do them at such a frenetic pace.

Wilson died last week at the age of 45. He had a history of high blood pressure and had complained recently of shortness of breath. While his death was a terrible surprise to his many friends, an even greater surprise was in store. It turned out that he had planned his own funeral.

It was held Tuesday at the Central Baptist Church.

The church was packed, which wasn't surprising. Wilson had many friends. There were a great many ministers in the crowd, and that wasn't surprising, either.

Ministers are the lifeblood of a funeral home. After all, when tragedy strikes, to whom does a family turn for help and advice? And so funeral home owners and ministers – practitioners of the two oldest professions in the black community – often become good friends and, truth be told, business associates.

In a final nod to this relationship, Wilson had selected more than a dozen ministers to speak at the funeral. The first was Bishop Michael West, the pastor of Saint Michael's Temple of the Expanded Mind. West also serves as vice president of the mortuary.

"I'm happy on one hand, and sad on the other," he said, and the happiness, of course, had to do with the place of many mansions where Wilson was already. Before West was through, some of the mourners were shouting and clapping, and the general mood of the affair had been nicely set.

"Baby brother, so long until tomorrow," West said in conclusion.

"We're on the road now," said the Rev. Ralph Jackson, who, as interim pastor of Central Baptist, presided over the service.

Of the 27 speakers, more than half were men of the cloth, and most made mention of the great honor it was that Wilson, who loved funerals and knew ministers, had included them on the speaking list. And no wonder he had included them, I thought. All of them seemed like gifted speakers, and all could praise the Lord.

A number of them also mentioned that Wilson had been a funeral home owner who knew how to treat preachers, and several spoke of envelopes he used to drop off at the various churches.

I couldn't help but wonder if some of this wasn't directed at Carol Wilson, Charles' sister, who has announced her intention to commute from Atlanta and keep the funeral home in the family. She is an executive in the health-care industry, which may work a lot like the funeral home business, albeit with a little more subtlety.

It would be unfair to single out any particular preacher – although a number of mourners later remarked that for a Roman Catholic, Father Maurice Nutt could surely praise the Lord – but I thought the service really began to cook when the Rev. Darryl Rainey spoke. He's the associate pastor at the West End Mount Carmel Full Gospel Baptist Church. Like so many of the others, he was talking about Wilson's generosity

– "He was a giver!" – when the Holy Spirit seemed to overtake him. He began shouting, and the Spirit seemed to jump from the reverend to a number of ladies, dressed all in white, from the aforementioned St. Michael's Temple of the Expanded Mind.

There were secular speakers, too, including Ida Goodwin Woolfolk. To my mind, that cemented the notion that this was a real happening. Woolfolk is to the black community what Jack Buck and Mike Roarty are to the white community. That is, she is much in demand as a master of ceremonies.

As is her style, she had a little fun before sharing her memories of Wilson. In this instance, she cited the remarkable powers of her good friend.

Who else, she wondered, could have folks shouting at Central Baptist?

It turns out that Central Baptist is generally considered a rather staid institution, as far as Baptist churches are concerned.

No discussion of this funeral would be complete without a long nod to the music. Denise Atty Blount did a wonderful, bluesy version of "I'll Always Love You," and the Higher Heights Christian Church choir had even me tapping my feet when they sang.

But the musical highlight had to be Michael O'Hara's rendition of "Blessed Assurance."

O'Hara, incidentally, is a big-time lyricist who wrote a song for which Anita Baker won a Grammy. More to the point, though, he was a lifelong friend of Wilson's. They grew up together on Windemere Place, which was, at the time, the street for African-Americans who were moving on up.

I listened to O'Hara, who has definitely moved on up, and wondered if Wilson, though he loved funerals, still thought of what might have been.

"Charles could have been whatever he wanted to be. There were opportunities all around him," said Steven Roberts, the speaker who preceded O'Hara.

I was still thinking along those lines when the Rev. Gore began his long-awaited eulogy. He started kind of slow, but soon he really got going, and he wisely opted to ignore his father's advice about short funeral sermons.

He talked about heaven, and the clear, sweet water that runs right through the middle of the place, and how there's good housing on both sides of that particular river, and the organist was playing chords each time he'd slow down, and pretty soon it was like we were in that beautiful place.

But my mind had fastened on something he'd said before the Spirit got hold of him.

"Funerals are getting expensive," he'd said. "It's getting so you can't afford to die. But the Beal Funeral Home would bury you - if you had money or if you didn't. We all knew that."

I'd heard that, too, and it made me realize that Charles Stanley Wilson Jr. had done the right thing when he came home to help run a real family business.

—

IN DRUG CASES, THE RICH HAVE 'MEDICAL ISSUES'

Nov. 6, 2005

Josh Marino and Charles Crispin came to St. Louis from Illinois in March 2004. They had come to buy cold remedy products containing pseudoephedrine, which is used to make methamphetamine. Because authorities are aware of the connection, a person can buy only a limited quantity of the cold remedy products. So a meth cook will hire a couple of people to drive around and buy small quantities from lots of stores. It's called smurfing.

An off-duty police officer who was working security at a store in Brentwood saw Marino and Crispin arrive together, split up, make their purchases and reunite at their car in the parking lot. He called the local police. (It is against the law to possess pseudoephedrine with the intent of manufacturing meth.)

The local police called the county police, who have a small unit – the Methamphetamine Precursor Diversion Task Force – set up for just this ıd of case. Sgt. Tom Murley and Detective Sue McClain responded to the call and confiscated the pills. There were about 1,000 of them. The case was referred to the U.S. attorney's office, and a federal grand jury returned indictments this May.

Why a delay of more than a year? The pills had to be tested in a lab. That can delay things for a few weeks. The real problem is one of volume. The criminal justice system is swamped with drug cases.

I thought about that Friday morning when I picked up the newspaper and read the latest story about Thomas Noonan, an attorney and the deputy mayor of Kirkwood. He was arrested in a drug sting Tuesday after he allegedly gave a woman $2,400 to buy oxycodone. Police said he had 400 milligrams of the drug in his possession when he was arrested. He hired Scott Rosenblum, the most prominent defense attorney in the area. Rosenblum was quoted in Friday's story. He said that Noonan had a "medical issue."

As regular readers know, I believe we ought to legalize all this stuff. Regulate it and tax it. The really bad stuff we ought to just give away. If you want to be a junkie, go ahead. We can't stop you, anyway. Instead of spending all our money chasing druggies, prosecuting and incarcerating them, we ought to spend a chunk on education and a chunk on rehab clinics for people who want help. The rest of the savings can go into general revenue.

We'd also get away from the terrible hypocrisy of the present system. If you're an addict with money, you have a medical issue. Otherwise, you have a criminal issue.

A lot of people in St. Louis had a criminal issue Friday morning. I called the circuit attorney's office to see if there were any drug sentencings. I had a choice of five divisions. I stopped in at one of the courtrooms. A deputy checked the docket. "We've got marijuana and cocaine," she said.

I wandered over to the federal courthouse. Marino was about to be sentenced. He's 28 years old. He's been an addict since he was 12. He has no money. He was wearing an orange jumpsuit, a sign that he had not been able to make bail. He was represented by an attorney who had been appointed by the court. Marino gave a wave to Murley, the man who had arrested him.

"He's a good guy," Murley told me. "He's really funny."

The federal guidelines called for a sentence of 110 to 137 months, but the government had agreed to let the judge give a shorter sentence. Assistant U.S. Attorney Sirena Wissler said her motion in that regard was sealed and she could not comment on it. Except for the agreement to lower the sentence, the case is typical, Wissler said. Judge Rodney Sipple sentenced Marino to 55 months.

Later that afternoon, Crispin was sentenced to 84 months. He, too, is poor. No bail. No private attorney. And like his fellow smurfer, his addiction was not a medical issue.

—

MATH PROFESSOR'S HIGH EXPECTATIONS REALLY ADDED UP

JUNE 11, 2000

Edward Z. Andalafte, a professor of mathematics, was walking across the UMSL campus a week ago Tuesday afternoon when he had a heart attack and died. He was 64 years old but seemed to be in remarkably good shape. He was tall and thin, and he walked several miles every day. As far as anybody knew, he was also a careful eater. Every school day, he ate a turkey breast and low-fat mozzarella cheese sandwich with carrot sticks on the side. He brought that lunch to school in a brown paper bag. Some people claimed he used the same brown paper bag for years.

In that way, and in some others, Andalafte was an eccentric character. Not wildly eccentric, but professorially so. He was a bachelor mathematician who looked like a mathematician. He wore tweedy clothes. His pocket protector was his chief fashion accessory. His hobby was choir. He was a member of the choir at First Presbyterian Church in Ferguson and the Bel Canto Chorus of St. Louis. Just as there is a certain purity in mathematics, there is a purity in harmony. The notes and chords come together like numbers in an equation. There is beauty in the simplicity of it. Before arriving at UMSL 36 years ago, Andalafte earned his doctorate at the University of Missouri at Columbia. Before that, he did graduate work in Europe. Although he had been on campus since 1964, few people knew much about him.

"He was my mentor and my best friend," said Shahla Peterman, a senior lecturer in the mathematics department. "He came by on my first day 18 years ago to welcome me aboard. He loved the school and the students. He knew their life stories."

What about his life story? Did he ever come close to getting married?

"In some ways, he was very private," she said.

The obituary that was printed in this newspaper mentioned only one survivor, his mother. Friends say she suffers from Alzheimer's disease and has not recognized her son for some time. Although he had no children of his own, he was a teacher, and teachers, especially good ones, have many survivors.

Meighan Steever, for instance, is 23 years old. She graduated from high school in Washington, Mo., in the spring of 1995 and began at UMSL that fall. She took her first course from Andalafte in the first semester of her sophomore year. She was, and is, a young woman with high expectations. Her mother is a high school chemistry teacher. Meighan was newly married, had a baby and was working part time when she took Calculus II from Andalafte.

"I did three hours of homework for his class every night," she told me. "I barely pulled a C."

But still, she liked him. He was, in a very dry way, a comic. He sometimes referred to himself by his initials. "I'm E.Z.A.," he'd say, "but I'm not."

Not by a long shot. In a time of grade inflation, Andalafte believed in failing students. You either knew the material, or you didn't. No one could fake it through one of his classes. On the other hand, he was always available to help.

His favorite expression was, "Sideboard tomorrow." That's what he would say when somebody asked a good question, and he meant that the student should put his or her work on the side blackboard the next day, and he would then go over it. Woe be to the student who had asked a question without having first made an effort to solve the problem. He expected some effort to be reflected on the sideboard.

After earning a C in Calculus II, Steever took another class from Andalafte. It was called Modern Math, and it, too, was exceedingly difficult. Steever earned the second-highest grade in the class. She got a B.

The next year, she took geometry from Andalafte, but the following year – this past year – she didn't take a class from him. That's because she had a baby at the beginning of the school year and, while she figured she'd only have to miss a couple of weeks of school, you couldn't miss a couple of weeks of one of Andalafte's classes. That was true even if you were one of his favorites.

And by then, she was. She was an officer in the math club, and he was the faculty adviser. She'd sometimes bring her kids to his office.

Incidentally, by the beginning of this year, Meighan was also working part time at the Chrysler plant. She's working there this summer, too, and she told me she has been offered a full-time job if she wants it.

But she doesn't. She's going to graduate with a dual major next year – math and education – and she plans to teach math in high school. As a beginning teacher, she won't make nearly as much as she'd make at the auto plant, but she wants to be a math teacher, and she says her husband understands.

"I think I'm going to get a plaque," she told me. "I'm going to put it in my classroom. It's going to say that this is an E.Z.A. class."

Of course, she'll have to explain that to her students, which means that Andalafte's legacy will likely touch students who are not yet born.

—

DINNER, THE QURAN AND GOOD WILL IN WEST COUNTY
JULY 31, 2005

I used to sit next to Greg Freeman, who was as honorable and gentle as a person could be. Sometimes when there would be news of a terrible crime, he would look at me and say, "I hope it's not a black guy."

I would nod sympathetically. I gave little thought to the fact that I never entertained the notion "I hope it's not a white guy."

Those memories have come back in recent weeks. After the first of the London bombings, I thought of some Muslims I met a month or two ago. They were very unhappy with some things I had written, and so they invited me to dinner. Yes, that's right. They invited me to dinner. I initially responded that I would be happy to meet with them and discuss the things I had written, but dinner was unnecessary. The hostess was insistent. You must have dinner, she said.

Her home was in west St. Louis County. There were about 10 people there when I arrived. We gathered in the living room and made small-talk before dinner, and had you been a fly on the wall, you would not have guessed that our meeting had been called because of any grievance against me. Quite the contrary. I was treated as an honored guest. I chatted away with the self-confidence – or the arrogance – of a person who knows that he has the power to define the evening. After all, I was armed with a pen.

The dinner was superb. I cannot remember all the dishes, but I do remember the sense that each was better than the last. I also remember feeling silly. The real reason I had initially suggested a meeting without dinner is that I am, sadly, an unadventurous eater. Middle Eastern food? I'll take a gyro. But this food was wonderful. I had seconds of everything.

All during dinner, the conversation remained light and pleasant. I should mention that these people, who had come from several countries, were as educated as they were gracious. They were doctors, professors, a banker and a businessman. Like most Americans, I am vaguely intimidated by cosmopolitan people. I remember being at a gas station in Saudi Arabia somewhere north of Dhahran – a gas station is the modern equivalent of an oasis – and the manager was from India. He chattered away in Arabic with some of his customers, and he spoke conversational English with me. I figured he must speak Hindi and who knows what else. In my world, he'd be a linguist. In his world, he ran a little gas station in the desert.

But back to my dinner. After we finished eating, I finally broached the matter that had brought us together. I know you're unhappy with me, I said.

The unhappiness stemmed from a couple of columns I had written after Newsweek published and then retracted allegations that interrogators at Guantanamo Bay had desecrated the Quran. I had been flippant about the allegations. "Even if the story were true, so what? We are dealing with fanatics who will fly airplanes into buildings and would gladly deliver a nuclear bomb into one of our cities and sit on that bomb as it detonates. These are men who believe that if they die while waging war against us they will ascend to paradise. Good food, virgins, the whole deal. This is the message they get from the Quran. We're supposed to treat it with reverence?" And more in that vein.

My dinner companions wanted to know how much I knew about Islam. Very, very little, I said. Had I ever read the Quran? Not a word. Then how could I make such comments? And why would I preach such intolerance? Did I not understand that this is a time for people of good will to reach out to each other?

I parried their questions as best I could, and I resisted making any kind of an outright apology. But had someone been scoring the conversation as a debate, I would not have done well.

Sometime later, I saw one of the men who had been at the dinner. He said, "I am about as religious as you are."

I knew what he meant. We are so much more than our race, our religion, our nationality. These things are part of us, but just a part. But the world wants to define us in the simplest possible terms. I thought of Greg and the way he would shake his head. "I hope it's not a black guy," he'd say.

—

SHARED LIVES, CHERISHED MEMORIES AND PERFECT ENDINGS

JANUARY 26, 2003

I visited Bob and Annemarie Lauenstein on January 17, and wrote about them for last Sunday's paper.

Their daughter, Ingrid, had already told me their story. They met in Germany in 1945. Bob was an American soldier. Annemarie was a German girl. They fell in love, and Bob stayed in Germany after his discharge. When President Harry S Truman signed the bill authorizing GIs and former soldiers to bring their German fiancees to this country, Bob and Annemarie hopped on a plane and flew to New York, and then to St. Louis. Because Annemarie was the first of the German war brides to come to this country, the Lauensteins got a ton of publicity. Throw in the fact that Bob was a good storyteller, and Annemarie's father had died in a Nazi prison, and it's easy to see why the press really took to the couple.

Then life settled down, and years went by. Last month, Annemarie got pneumonia. She nearly died. Ingrid flew in from North Carolina to be with her mother. While she and her father were in the waiting room of the intensive care unit at St. Anthony's Medical Center, he mentioned to his daughter that he had a lump on his collarbone. Get that checked out, Dad, she said. He did, and it turned out to be cancer. He was given four months to live. He did not want to tell his wife until she regained her strength, but he took a sudden turn for the worse, and was rushed to St. Luke's Hospital. He was told he had days to live, not months. Maybe hours.

He was going to have to tell his wife by phone.

But doctors and administrators at the two hospitals got together, and Bob was transferred to St. Anthony's, and put in his wife's room.

Both Bob and Annemarie were in good spirits when I visited. Annemarie was no longer on a ventilator. Bob seemed strong, and was very candid about his condition.

"I'm terminal," he told me.

Still, he had no trouble telling the old stories one last time. How he met his wife on the banks of the Elbe River. How he eventually smuggled her to Berlin behind some cases of beer. (The authorities were hoping to prevent a huge influx of refugees into the city.) How he told her that his unit was about to ship home, and she suggested he stay in Germany. Which he did.

Bob was 80 as he told these stories, but the young man was not far from the surface. It was easy to see him as a handsome, resourceful

GI. And if a fellow could be described as robust on his death bed, that description could have fit Bob. Perhaps the telling of the stories gave him strength, as if the memories were a time machine of sorts. Perhaps that is exactly what they are. At any rate, he talked effortlessly, and I felt privileged to listen. There are times when newspapering is the best of trades.

Annemarie did more listening than talking during my visit. But what a life she has lived. The Gestapo came for her father on a Christmas Eve, she told me. He was accused of anti-Hitler utterances. This had to do with a poem, she said. He was given a three-year sentence, and he died in prison. Sometime after his arrest, their house was hit in an allied bombing raid, and she and her sister and mother moved to another place. It was bombed, too.

"Some of her hair had been burnt off when I met her," Bob said.

He was still fine Saturday when the early edition of the newspaper came out. Ingrid brought him a copy. He liked the story. He lost consciousness Sunday, and he died Monday. He did not seem to be in any pain, Ingrid said, and he was surrounded by love. His daughter cradled his head in her arms. It's all right to leave, she said. It sounded like a perfect ending to a good life.

And it must have been a good life because I received a number of messages from people who had known him. A kind man, somebody said. A wonderful sense of humor, somebody else said.

After Annemarie recuperates, she will live with her daughter and grandchildren in North Carolina.

—

GRACEFUL COMPETITOR KEEPS COMPOSURE THROUGH LEUKEMIA

AUGUST 30, 1999

A warrior and a gentleman.

The doctor at Barnes-Jewish was very straight with his 22-year-old patient, Tyrone Williford. The chemotherapy is not working, the doctor said. The leukemia has not gone into remission. The only hope is a bone marrow transplant, and even if we find a compatible donor, the odds are not good.

Williford remained so calm and composed that the doctor was not sure the terrible news had registered. Later, as things went from bad to worse, the doctor came to realize that Tyrone Williford was unflappable. "No matter what the news is, he doesn't flinch," the doctor later told me. "It's an inner strength, a faith. I don't know. We're used to dealing with people who are just devastated with bad news, but that's not Tyrone."

That was back in April. Williford eventually received the bone marrow transplant, but it couldn't save him. He died Tuesday. I went to his wake Sunday, and while the place was crowded, I found myself thinking about all the people whose lives Williford had touched who weren't there.

Regular readers might remember the story. Williford was an athlete, and a darned good one. He was captain of the basketball team at North Technical High School for three years. He was one of the top rebounders in the state. But North Tech is not considered a big-time athletic school, and Williford was not recruited. He did not play college ball. Not in a literal sense, anyway.

During his three years at North Tech, he had developed a friendly rivalry with a fellow who played basketball for Block Yeshiva. That fellow was Shimmy Stein, who then went to college at George Washington University in Washington. He organized his fraternity's intramural basketball team. Before each game, he would give his team a talk. He would remind them to conduct themselves the way an old competitor of his, a young man named Tyrone Williford, used to conduct himself. He played like a warrior, Stein would say, but he was always a gentleman.

Williford, of course, knew nothing of this. He was working at a fast-food place, and he probably would have been astounded to know that far away, a bunch of kids on a fast track toward success were being urged to model themselves after him.

He never would have found out except that Stein's father, Rabbi Zalman Stein, ran into North Tech coach Mike Boyce at another North Tech-Yeshiva game. In the course of their conversation, Boyce mentioned that Williford had been diagnosed with leukemia. The rabbi then mentioned it to his son, and Stein wrote Boyce a letter, explaining what Williford meant to him.

Boyce, by the way, immediately understood. Williford was the perfect sportsman. He played hard. He always respected his opponents. He didn't gloat or taunt or complain about calls. He was gracious in both victory and defeat.

I wrote about this relationship between a rabbi's son and a Baptist preacher's son. (Williford's mother, Mildred Young, is a teacher and the youth pastor at new Mount Gideon West Baptist Church.) But more than just writing about it, I talked to my kids about it. To have a competitor feel this way about you, well, it's better than winning a championship. Tyrone Williford had it exactly right.

When Stein, who is back in Washington, heard that Williford had died, he sent Boyce an e-mail.

"Our community has lost a gem, and our generation a true leader," he wrote. "I will do my best to make sure that Tyrone, and all the lessons I learned from him, live on."

Boyce feels the same way. You can be sure that he'll pass the story on to future North Tech teams. And some of Stein's friends will become fathers, and I like to imagine that someday, one of those fellows will be coaching a kids' team, and he'll gather his players around him.

"I want to tell you a story," he'll say. "Once upon a time, there was a young man named Tyrone Williford . . ."

—

SHE'S MOVED ON, BUT SHE'S TAKEN A PIECE OF DAD'S HEART

SEPTEMBER 15, 2002

Approximately 1 million years ago, I wrote about walking my daughter to her first day of school. The column was really about the women in my family.

Mary was my grandmother. She was born in Belfast and came to this country as a child. She married a streetcar conductor. One day he left for work and didn't come back. Mary was left with two small children, a girl and a boy. She got a job in a candy store, and supported those kids. The girl's name was Mildred. Like Mary, she was smart as a tack. The young man who delivered groceries to Mary's apartment fell in love with Mildred. She eventually married him. His name was Art, and he and Mildred had two children – my sister and me.

My sister was like her mother and grandmother. She went to Knox College and graduated Phi Beta Kappa.

That column from so long ago ended like this: "The father walked home, and he pulled out an old photo album. Mary, Mildred and Mildred's daughter smiled out at him. Another one into the world, he said to the photographs."

Another one into the world, indeed. Three weeks ago, I drove my daughter to college. She is attending the University of Illinois in Champaign-Urbana. I was once enrolled in that very university, and if there were such a thing as family cumulative grade averages, my daughter would be on probation.

But she is like her mother, and my wife is very much like the women of my childhood – my grandmother, mother and sister. In other words, my wife is smart, and so is my daughter.

She is taking a heavy dose of science and math classes. I tried to stick to history, and English, and other such subjects in which the ability to write a coherent paragraph could overcome a lack of knowledge. Never take a class in which a professor can accurately measure how much you know. That was my thinking. Not that it worked.

We carried my daughter's possessions up to her dorm room. A lot of it was new stuff, and unfamiliar to me. That added to my sense of disorientation. I had known, at the moment she first disappeared into the school building so long ago, that the outside world would thereafter have a certain claim on her, but my claim was the greater. She lived with me. But now I was carrying strange things into a strange room -- my daughter's new life was taking form.

I started to cry, and walked into the hallway.

In my family, the women are stronger than the men, and while my son tried, with some success, to stifle his own tears, my wife and daughter consoled me.

"It's OK, Dad," my daughter said.

"Pull yourself together," my wife said.

The very last thing I wanted to do was embarrass my daughter in front of her new dorm-mates, and I could sense that a few of them were looking at me. There was a time when an occasional tear was considered the mark of a sensitive man, but now, wimps are from Loserville. Sixty percent of the public thinks we should invade Iraq. Cool people drive SUVs.

"I'm fine," I said.

I wasn't, of course, and I'm still not. I obsess about my daughter. How is she doing? Oh sure, I talked with her last night, but how is she doing now? When I'm not obsessing about her, I'm obsessing about my son. Someday he'll leave.

And I wonder about my parents. They always seemed so casual. When I left for college, it didn't seem like a big deal. They wished me luck, and away I went. Their immature son was leaving home, and they didn't seem worried. Even when I went into the service, they didn't seem terribly concerned.

My mother was strong. I understand that. I come from a family of strong women. It's my father I wonder about. He must have been an emotional wreck at times – I had to inherit this from somebody – but he came from a generation of men that knew how to hold it together. I wish he were around. I could use some advice.

—

DOG WANDERS AWAY, TEACHING A LESSON OF HUMAN KINDNESS

JULY 30, 2003

Kent Maclean runs a woodworking shop at 18th and Chouteau. He takes his dogs to work. They are a mixed group. Zen is a large dog, mostly Labrador. Joy is of middle size and of completely indeterminate lineage. Dixie is a small, furry creature.

Then there is Mona. She is a miniature Yorkshire terrier, and not an everyday visitor to the shop. Mostly, she stays home with Kent's wife, Beth, and their two daughters. In fact, Mona, who is 7 months old, was Beth's birthday present.

Mona paid one of her visits to the shop last Friday. Somehow, she got out. Kent was at lunch when one of the workers called and told him that Mona was missing. Kent rushed back to the shop and began a frantic search.

Everybody in the shop – Kent has six employees – joined the search. So did a neighbor. A canvass of several hours developed the following information: Five people had seen the dog. Two of these people had seen a man leading the dog away.

This was not good news. Mona was wearing her collar, and she had a phone number on her name tag. If the man was a good Samaritan, he'd have called the number.

That night and the following day, Kent printed fliers with Mona's photograph, and posted them in the neighborhood. He sent faxes to every veterinarian in the phone book. "Please scan all Yorkie terriers," he pleaded. Like all his other dogs, Mona has an embedded chip.

He went to the Peabody housing project near his shop. Some of the fellows hanging out asked if he were interested in buying drugs, but he said, no, he was looking for a dog. He gave them fliers, and told them he would pay $500 for Mona's safe return.

He got a couple of phone calls very late Saturday night. We've got your dog, the callers said, but Kent, worried about rushing out with a bunch of cash, asked questions about the dog. One caller hung up, and the other couldn't describe the animal.

It was enough to make a guy lose faith in people.

Monday afternoon, Beth called the shop. We have a message on the answering machine from a woman who says she has Mona, said Beth. She added that the woman sounded, well, good. Beth said the woman had ended the call by saying "God bless."

Kent called the woman, and she told him that Mona had a knobby, little tail. Which is true. Kent rushed to the woman's house, and when she opened the door, there was the dog.

Kent explained that there was a $500 reward, and he said that it would be money well spent because his two little girls were going to be so happy to get their dog back. The woman said she didn't want any money, but she would love a photo of the two girls with their dog.

I know about losing somebody you love, she said, and she pointed to a photo of a son who was murdered six years ago. So Kent got his dog, and the woman was insistent that she would take no money.

Her name is Rochelle Sherrell, and she lives in the 4100 block of Folsom Avenue. She is on Social Security disability. She has diabetes, and she suffers from seizures. She grew up in the old Pruitt-Igoe housing project.

She told me that she saw a young man leading the dog past her house Friday night, and she could tell right away the dog didn't belong to him. He was leading it with a shoestring. "You could tell that dog was somebody's baby," she said. She stopped the young man, and he claimed he had bought the dog for his sister. She told the young man that if his sister didn't want the dog, she did. Sunday night, he came by with the dog.

She was happy to reunite the dog with the little girls, she said. I told her it was awfully unusual to meet somebody who didn't want money, and she laughed, and said her mother always told her she'd die of kindness some day. Then she said the one thing she did want was a hug. "I'm a hugger," she said. And for a moment, so was I. It was an honor.

—

ODD, GENTLE MAN ON BICYCLE WAS NOTICED, WILL BE MISSED, BY MANY

SEPTEMBER 21, 2005

"Bicycle Bob" Sprandel did not show up to work Thursday morning, and that was most unusual. Sprandel had worked at the St. Louis City Water Division for almost 25 years and was not one to miss work. Fourteen years ago, he was riding his bicycle when a driver struck him. Sprandel went through the guy's windshield – his head and shoulders inside the car, his legs dangling outside – and he was out of work for weeks, but because he never missed work, he had enough sick time to cover his absence.

Sprandel rode his bicycle to work. Every day. All sorts of weather. He was 58 years old, and he did not drive a car because of his epilepsy. When he didn't arrive at work Thursday morning, somebody called his house. No answer. At about 10, co-worker Tim Kelly drove to his house on Hampton.

Kelly checked the back porch. Sprandel's bicycle was there. Kelly opened the kitchen window and started to crawl in. Caspar, the white cat, went after him. The cat was almost as much of a character as Sprandel, but while Sprandel was odd and gentle, the cat was odd and mean. Sometimes it would slip out the front door. The people in the bar across the street would watch as Sprandel tried to catch it. He'd finally get it, but the cat would tear into him and escape. Finally, Sprandel would give up and go inside. With the game over, the cat would go up on the porch and meow at the front door.

On Thursday morning, the cat hissed at Kelly and then walked into the bedroom. Kelly followed and discovered Sprandel's body. Indications were, and are, that he died from natural causes.

Sprandel was single, never married, but his sudden death caused ripples in several ponds.

At the water division, of course. "He was eccentric. He hated disorder even though he was the definition of disorder," said Kelly. Supervisor Darrell Lewis nodded. "He was organized chaos."

The biking crowd was stunned. Charlie Marvin, a retired police officer, met Sprandel years ago at South Side Cyclery on Gravois. "Bob was one of those people you meet who are a bit different, a bit odd and not in a bad way," Marvin recalled. "He was known as Flat Man, a take-off on the old Bat Man theme. When you ride any length of time on city streets, you get flats, lots of them."

Tony Blackwood, the owner of South Side Cyclery, remembered the night Sprandel was struck by the car. It was the night of the Moonlight Ramble in 1991. The route went down Gravois, and Blackwood set up a refreshment table. Sprandel volunteered to help pass out water and snacks. Afterward, Sprandel rode away, and that's when he was struck.

"We thought he was dead," said Blackwood. "The driver had no insurance, and Bob got nothing. He was dealt some bad cards, but he never complained."

Perhaps the worst of the bad cards was the death of his fiancee several years ago.

She was a diabetic and had undergone a kidney transplant. One evening, she and Sprandel went for a walk, and as they returned home, he picked her up and carried her. A passer-by saw him carrying her into the house and called the police.

"The next thing you know there were squad cars pulling up and people running around," said Manny Delgado, who works at Area IV, the bar across the street from Sprandel's house. Delgado is a retired police officer, and he was able to straighten the matter out.

Although Sprandel was not a big drinker, he visited the bar almost every night. In fact, several years ago, when Sprandel's boss wrote him a letter of commendation, Delgado hung it in the bar.

Sprandel was a frequent visitor at a number of South Side bars. He particularly enjoyed karaoke. He was known as an enthusiastic, if not overly talented, singer.

Plus, of course, he was a small part of the lives of many people who never met him but who saw him on the city streets. He often wore a pink helmet with polka dots. For a bicycle rider, it pays to be noticed.

—

TWO MORE LAY DEAD, AS PROHIBITION-ERA THINKING RULES DAY

JUNE 18, 2000

Police said Ronald Beasley, 36, was not a target in the investigation but died mainly because he was near Earl Murray. Beasley's death, the lieutenant said, "was unintended, not a mistake."

This unintended death that was not a mistake occurred six days ago in the parking lot of a busy fast-food restaurant on North Hanley Road when members of an undercover drug unit attempted to arrest Earl Murray. According to the cops, Murray was a drug dealer. At least he allegedly sold drugs to the undercover agents on two previous occasions. But at best – or maybe at worst – he was a very low-level drug dealer. His relatives told reporters that he sometimes sold $20 rocks of crack cocaine. The cops say they found about a quarter of an ounce of cocaine under the seat of his car. That was after they shot him. According to the cops, a DEA agent and a detective from Dellwood fired into the car because they thought that Murray might run over them.

In a legal sense, this could mean that the shooting was justifiable, even though neither Murray nor his passenger, Ronald Beasley, was armed. If a reasonable person would feel that his or her life was in danger, then self-defense can kick in.

But step away from the legalities, and there is a Fearless Fosdick quality to the case. I'm reminded of the time the cartoon cop fired into a crowd as he tried to arrest an unlicensed balloon vendor. So it is with a "multijurisdictional task force" that sets up a drug buy, and a potential shootout, at a busy fast-food restaurant shortly after school gets out. Who would approve of such a plan?

Especially when you look at a best-case scenario. What if the arrest would have gone perfectly? At most, Murray would have caught a little jail time. A very low-level drug dealer would be off the streets.

The streets, though, would have remained the same.

Not long ago, I was chatting with a judge at the federal courthouse. He had just sentenced a big-time drug dealer to a ton of time, but he had a sense that nothing had been accomplished. That's because the federal agents had told him that this drug dealer had replaced a dealer that the

judge had sentenced to a ton of time a few months earlier. What's mo
the judge had noticed that this dealer had the same attractive girlfriend
as the previous dealer. It was as if she came with the franchise.

"I have to send people to prison for cocaine," the judge told me, "but
I find it increasingly difficult to do so."

We had this conversation – this very conservative judge and I – during
the did-he-didn't-he flap concerning George W. Bush and cocaine. You
probably remember that one. Reporters would ask Bush if he had ever
used cocaine, and he would respond with a non-answer. I'm not going
to play that game, he'd say. Or, When I was young and foolish, I did
foolish things.

The message, I suppose, was it didn't really matter. And hey, to people
like me, it didn't, and doesn't. Of course, Bush and I are from the same
generation, the generation that tried most everything. People forget that
at their peril.

Like the time John Ashcroft, during his days as governor, declared war
on casual drug use and then stood back in dismay when the first casualty
of his war was his personal "coordinator" for the state's war on drugs.
It turns out the guy used drugs on a regular basis back in his college
days.

Sadly, the humorous stories about hypocrisy are few and far between.
Most of the tales from our long-standing war against drugs are tragic.
I've written about cops who have been shot and killed by the dealers
during raids, and dealers who've been shot by the cops. Occasionally,
it's cops shooting cops by mistake, and often it's dealers shooting dealers. This last variety is reminiscent of the gangster wars during Prohibition. After all, that's what the War Against Drugs really is – another
version of Prohibition.

I have long agreed with the Libertarians that we ought to legalize
drugs. If people want to be junkies, they're going to be junkies. We can
make all the arrests we want – heck, we can bring down the Medellin
Cartel and Pablo Escobar – but supply will somehow meet demand. We
can even cross the line morally ourselves, and it doesn't help. I think
here of Andrew Chambers, the feds' superstar informer who regularly
committed perjury to put druggies in prison. We dirty ourselves and still
don't accomplish anything.

Why not take some of the money we spend on our failed effort to stop supply and spend it to lessen demand? We're spending billions on interdiction, and arrests, and trials, and incarceration. Spend it on education. The most recent statistics I saw said that 60 percent of federal prisoners were in for drug offenses. More than one-third those in state prisons were in for drug offenses. If you add the number who committed crimes to support their drug habits because the War Against Drugs has artificially inflated drug prices, no telling how high the number would be.

In fact, Friday afternoon I called the spokesperson for the Missouri Department of Corrections to see if he knew what percentage of our prisoners are in for drug offenses. He was out of the office. He was at the ribbon-cutting for the newly opened South Central Correctional Institution in Licking. It's not just us. The prison population in this country hit the 2 million mark earlier this year. We can't build prisons fast enough.

Still, we soldier on. Two men were killed Monday in a fouled-up sting set up at a busy fast-food restaurant in the middle of the afternoon. One of the men who was killed wasn't even a suspect. His death, we're told, was unintended, but not a mistake.

As usual, I'd like to give the cops a break. It's the war I want to indict.

—

TO A RESPONSIBLE JOURNALIST, WORDS ARE A SACRED TRUST

DECEMBER 18, 1998

The Gateway Strikers U-12 soccer team has had a fine year, and I'd **testify** to that. I've watched almost all of their games, and on a **prior** occasion, I had to **stifle** a desire to write about an **engrossing** finish to one of their matches.

In that game, the Strikers held a **meager** one-goal lead. It had been a long, hard-fought game, and the lads were suffering from **fatigue**. "Don't let up," **admonished** Coach Randy Miscop.

But with just over a minute to play, a **diminutive** but lightning-quick forward from the other team broke through the defense, and his kick eluded the Strikers' goalie. The **multitudes** on the other side roared in **ecstasy**.

I stood there in a **daze**. My son is the Strikers' goalie. Perhaps only parents of goalies would understand me when I say that in an ideal world, all children would be forwards. A forward scores, or he doesn't. He's a hero, or he isn't.

A goalie, on the other hand, had better be **humble**. He is always an instant away from donning the horns and **raiments** of the goat. Sometimes a goal is **obviously** his fault, and while he can **affect** an air of nonchalance as he digs the ball out from the back of the net, inside he's dying. As a goalie's father, I know this.

Although this particular goal did not fall into the blame-the-goalie variety – it was high and into the corner – it was still a late goal, and had turned an apparent victory into a tie.

I **cast** around for something to say to my son. Generally, I try to **compliment** him. Nice game, I'll say. But in this instance, such a comment would sound **inane**. Sometimes I'll opt for a good-natured **slur**. Good thing this isn't hockey or you'd have sunburn on the back of your neck from the red light going off, I'll say. But again, this seemed like a bad time for a joke.

What to say to a son you **adore**? A **vexing** problem, indeed.

But the late goal seemed to **revive** the Strikers. Patrick took the center ball and knocked it back to Eric. He touched it to Walker, who passed it ahead to Davor, who kicked it to Brett, who one-timed it to Peter, who took off for the enemy goal.

He raced down the left side. He maneuvered past a **hulking** defenseman and stormed toward the goal. With only seconds remaining in the game, he kicked the ball.

I **avidly** watched its **ascent**. Would it be high enough to get over the goalie? Would it be too high?

It was perfect.

The Strikers had won in the closing seconds. A sense of **rapture** enveloped the Strikers and their fans. Especially me. On a victorious team, there are no goats. Again, this is something parents of other goalies would best understand.

Knowledge that is **unique** to us, you might say.

At any rate, I nearly wrote about it, but didn't.

The other day, several of the Strikers approached me after practice. We have a problem, Mr. McClellan, they said. We're in sixth grade at Immacolata School, and our teacher, Mrs. Grainne Bennett, has given us a list of words we have to find in the newspaper. Could you, maybe, do us a favor?

I **loathe** the notion of being so irresponsible. I had been planning to write something about Lt. Gov. Roger Wilson taking a part-time job in private industry. He's a **conceited cur,** I was going to say, but then I thought about the kids' request.

If I wrote something about Wilson, I would be **inundated** with complaints from his friends.

Besides, if I were to grant the kids' request, I would look like a big shot in their eyes. Heretofore, my main claim to fame has been that I know the soccer **icon,** Mark Moser.

I sorted through the **turmoil** in my mind. If I were to devote a column to the sixth grade at Immacolata, make it **teem** with the necessary words, would I be violating, perhaps even **mutilating**, the responsibility I have as a journalist?

Even if it were **acute** column, it might seem **trivial.**

At least, my **antagonists** would say so. They'd say it was nothing but **drivel.**

THIS SWAN LAKE IS PART FAIRY TALE, PART SOAP OPERA

DECEMBER 1, 2000

Willie came to St. Louis almost 15 years ago, and got a place in Lafayette Square. He lived in the lake in the southeast section of the park. Willie was a swan.

He was a wonderful addition to the neighborhood. After all, Lafayette Square has a Victorian flavor with its row houses and their painted fronts. It's one of the oldest neighborhoods in St. Louis and was home to steamboat captains and other notables. In the right light – or viewed through the right eyes – it still has an elegance that hearkens to a time long past. What better place for a swan? "I moved here several years ago," one resident told me. "I visited the park on a February morning. It was cold and misty, and suddenly I saw this swan gliding by. It was like a dream."

A recurring dream, actually. The earliest photographs of Lafayette Square are circa 1870, and there in the lake are two swans.

Apparently, it was this history that brought Willie to St. Louis. Not that he knew anything about the history, but the residents did, and these are people who appreciate the past. Neighborhood lore has it that one of the residents was doing some work at the Busch Gardens in Williamsburg, Va., and had the chance to acquire a swan from the gardens. She brought Willie to Lafayette Square, where he joined a few other birds that called the lake home.

In those days, people fed the birds, but it was an unorganized thing. One day Ethel Bell noticed a couple of dead ducks. She took them to a veterinarian. She wondered if there was a disease going around. It's an old one, the vet said. It's called starvation.

From then on, Ethel fed the birds. Every day, she and her husband, Albert, would take corn to the birds. The birds went through about 400 pounds of corn a month – field corn, cracked corn, occasionally even canned corn as a treat. Ethel and Albert soon knew the birds, and the birds knew them. At least, the birds that lived in the lake did. There have always been just a few resident birds, but they are often joined by migrating birds. Ducks, geese, even herons visit the lake.

Willie was the most glamorous of the resident birds, but he was not the Bells' favorite. Truth is, Willie was something of a crank. His presence gave the lake a fairy-tale quality, but Crazy was the nicest of the resident birds. He was a white goose. He lost his mate a couple of years ago, and then evolved into a grandfather-type character. Most recently, he behaved as if he were the nanny for some Canada geese that stopped by for a short stay.

Last month, the city drained the lake to do some repair work on a retaining wall. That's not terribly unusual. The lake is drained three times a year for cleaning, but on those occasions, it is only drained for a day or so. The repair work, however, is going to take a while.

Ward Buckner, the chairman of the neighborhood association's park committee, thought that the birds ought to be taken to a private lake somewhere until their lake was restored. But do you know how hard it is to catch a duck, or a goose, or a swan? Besides, arrangements would have to be made.

Two days after the lake was drained, some dogs attacked the birds. The birds tried to escape into their lake, but it was really just a sea of mud, and the dogs followed them. Willie was killed. So was Crazy. The Humane Society had to come out and get a couple of the dogs out of the mud and back up on to dry land.

Ethel called a private organization that takes care of domestic waterfowl, and the organization took the surviving resident birds to a sanctuary.

The lake right now is mostly mud and very shallow water. It does not look like something out of a fairy tale. It will again, I'm sure. But somebody else will have to feed the birds.

Albert Bell died in October, and Ethel told me she did not think she could ever go back to the lake.

—

POLISH CHURCH VOTE RECALLS
SOLIDARITY, UNION MEETINGS

JANUARY 10, 2005

There might have been no good way for the Archdiocese of St. Louis to try to wrest control of the property and funds of St. Stanislaus Kostka church from its lay board of directors, but the hard-line approach – the loud talk about parishioners "hijacking" their church, the removal of the priests, the threats of penalties against the directors – certainly seemed less than effective Sunday when parishioners voted 299-5 to reject the demands of the archdiocese.

Maybe a little tenderness would have worked better. A little less shouting, a little more love.

To an outsider, this has always seemed a complex matter. St. Stanislaus has had its lay board since 1891, and much of the 8 acres the church owns on the city's near north side was acquired by the parishioners themselves. On the other hand, none of the other churches in the archdiocese is controlled by a lay board of directors. And isn't the archbishop supposed to be in charge of the archdiocese?

So there it was. One side saying, this is the way we've always done it. The other side saying, no one else does it this way.

Early last month, it looked like the two sides were going to reach an agreement. The board had met with archdiocesan officials – but not the archbishop – and everybody seemed optimistic. There was talk that parish assets could go into an irrevocable trust. Here was the headline that ran in this newspaper: "Attendees are upbeat in St. Stanislaus talks."

But several days later, Archbishop Raymond Burke sent a letter to parishioners and in the letter, he reminded them that the Vatican was on his side and not theirs. Talks broke down. The parishioners found a Polish priest to celebrate Christmas Mass at the church. That seemed an act of rebellion. The archbishop hired a new spokesman, Jamie Allman, and he accused the parishioners of hijacking the church. The archbishop threatened the directors with the penalty of interdict, which is similar to excommunication. And in this overcharged atmosphere, the parishioners voted Sunday. "Should we turn over all property, funds and parish control to the Archdiocese of St. Louis?"

The mood at the church Sunday was defiant. Many of the cars sported bumper stickers: "Save St. Stan." People inside wore red buttons with the same message. The atmosphere was more that of a union hall than a church, and I was reminded of workers gearing up for a strike vote, and perhaps that analogy was in a lot of minds. These are, after all, Poles, and it was their makeshift union, Solidarity, that stood up to the Soviet Union 25 years ago. That's a heritage people don't forget, especially people who grew up hearing "Polish jokes." There were people at the church who had firsthand knowledge of Solidarity. Greg Koltuniak, a parishioner, spent 2 1/2 years in prison for his union activities.

By the way, one of the saddest things about this whole deal has been the rift in the Polish community. There are good people on the other side, even other Solidarity people. For the most part, they have left St. Stanislaus. Of course, others have returned. I spoke to a number of people who once attended St. Stanislaus, and then moved and joined another parish, and have come back now because of the fight. They were not allowed to vote Sunday. The board decided months ago that it would accept no new parishioners until after the vote.

Stanley Maslowski, for instance, grew up in the church and then left. His dad came here from the old country and was the janitor and bell-ringer. Stanley's sister has returned, too. Her name is Ann McKeever, and she is 83. She took her first Communion at St. Stanislaus, and she was married in the church. When the vote was announced Sunday morning – "You have spoken!" said one of the directors – the crowd rose to its feet. McKee-ver, who was sitting in a wheelchair, began struggling to her feet. Someone noticed her struggle and pulled her up, and there she was, standing, one hand holding her wheelchair for balance and the other hand raised as in victory.

I saw that, and I thought, these were not people to bully.

—

TROUBLE PILES UP FOR MAN WHO LIKES TO COLLECT STUFF

MAY 9, 1999

Too much of a good thing can lead to trouble, and I thought about that when I visited Mark McCue in the county jail. He believes in recycling, which is a good thing.

"I don't remember when I got started," he told me. "I saw a videotape of landfills getting filled up." He is a precise man, and precision, too, is a thing that can be overdone. In McCue's case, he insists on recycling things exactly the right way. An aluminum can has to be smashed flat. Its tab on top has to be removed. It must be checked with a magnet to make sure that it contains no tin. Paper has to be separated by type and color. Same thing with glass and plastic.

Naturally, this all takes time, and even if McCue did not have a compulsion about saving things – an aversion, actually, to letting go of things – there would be a problem. It would be easier to collect things than to prepare them for recycling.

In other words, stuff would pile up
.
That is exactly what has happened. I visited McCue's house Wednesday morning. I peered inside the windows and could see nothing but junk. Stuff piled everywhere. It's a two-bedroom house with a full basement, but the place is so crammed with stuff that only one room is livable, and that's where McCue and his dog, Missy, are usually found.

Unfortunately, when there is no room for stuff inside the house – the garage has long been filled – stuff begins to pile up outside.
I spoke to a next-door neighbor.

"He is a very nice man," said Marci Yasein. "He doesn't really bother anybody. The only problem is his property has become an eyesore. He needs help. I'm not sure that jail is the right answer."

It isn't as if the village of Bel-Ridge wanted to put him in jail. Officials just wanted him to clean things up.

"This is a truly sad case," said Michael McAvoy, the attorney who works as the village prosecutor. "Mr. McCue has been in court charged with the same thing about a dozen times since 1985. He has been found guilty and sentenced to jail two different times, but was placed on probation each time. He violated probation each time, but his probation was extended and he avoided jail.

"This last time, I asked the judge to put him in jail but he didn't. Instead, he gave Mr. McCue three more weeks to clean things up. Unfortunately, Mark didn't."

So he got 10 days in jail.

"I guess I'm not surprised," McCue told me. "On the other hand, I didn't think I'd end up in here."

The road to the county jail began in Florida more than 40 years ago. McCue was in third grade with Joe Dahlem. The two youngsters were best friends. McCue was two years older. In these enlightened times, he'd be considered a special needs child, but in those days, he was lumped in with everybody else and simply held back when he couldn't do the work.

Dahlem was a bit of an outcast himself. His mother was single.

"We'd play all day," Dahlem told me. "He was the perfect playmate. We once played a game of Monopoly for nine months. The same game! We had different boards kind of wired together."

Incidentally, McCue was a collector even then. Once a week, residents would put stuff on the curb to be picked up by the local municipality. Before the truck could arrive, McCue would be on patrol, inspecting the throwaways and selecting what he wanted.

Dahlem went away to college while McCue was still plugging away in high school, but the two remained close friends. In 1978, Dahlem decided to open a computer business, and he decided that St. Louis was the place to do it.

He started a company called High Technology. It was a distributorship. McCue was his first employee.

The business did well, and Dahlem sold it in 1983. McCue, who had been given stock, walked away with about $80,000. He used some of that money to buy a house on Natural Bridge in Bel-Ridge.

Ken "Philip" Sliger, who had worked at High Technology, helped McCue move. He remembers that McCue brought a lot of stuff with him, but it was not unmanageable.

"It was a beautiful house. Stained windows, really cute. I remember sitting in the living room with Mark and talking about his model trains. I said that I thought he could set up a nice track there in the living room," Sliger said.

It was not to be. Stuff began to pile up.

There was, for a long time, an unofficial arrangement between Sliger and Thomas Cissell, the village inspector. When things would begin to get really out of hand, Cissell would call Sliger, and Sliger and a number of friends – Dahlem, Bill Bommarito, Jim Vajda, Rich Behrens, Bill and Carla Seiter – would come over and clean up. That worked to a point.

"It was really stressful for Mark when we'd throw things out," said Sliger. "About five years ago, we had a really big cleanup. We filled a huge Dumpster. We walled in the garage. We painted the porch. It was too much for Mark because when we left, he crawled into the Dumpster to dig things out."

At any rate, McCue's friends were able to keep things under control, but barely.

"It was an ongoing problem," Cissell told me.

A couple of weeks ago, Sliger drove past McCue's house and saw that things were looking pretty bad. He stopped at the village offices and asked for Cissell. He learned that Cissell had retired, and when Sliger said he had come to inquire about McCue, the clerk told him that McCue was in trouble. He'd probably be going to jail.

Sliger and a friend accompanied McCue to night court.

"Everybody was kind. We prayed that the God would give the judge wisdom, and I think He did," said Sliger, who is a born-again Christian.

The judge gave McCue 10 days.

The sentence was up on Friday, and before he was released, McCue told me he intended to really clean up his place. Sliger said he had already gotten the volunteers together, and Randy Cerny, one of the owners of FRI Resources, a printing distributorship that sometimes employs McCue, had already supplied a Dumpster.

McCue told me that after the house is clean, he'd like to sell it and move some place where things would be less restrictive.

"We'd like to find maybe an acre or two of ground with a trailer in the middle," said Dahlem.

———

STORE SHOWS ENOUGH SUSPICION OF ME TO MAKE ME HAPPY

August 7, 2000

Something went wrong with my daughter's computer, and whatever it was, it was so complicated that neither my wife nor daughter could fix it. Fortunately, though, the computer was still under warranty, so my wife took it to the Best Buy store where she had bought it. Sometime later, we got a call informing us that the computer had been repaired.

I was sent to get it. Well, fine. When you're not handy around the house, you have to do whatever you can.

I arrived at the Best Buy store Saturday afternoon and was directed to the appropriate counter. My name is McClellan, and I'm here to pick up a computer, I said.

The young man behind the counter nodded and then went to get the computer. He came back in a couple of minutes. He asked if I had the rec eipt or the ticket of whatever it was that my wife had been given when she dropped off the computer. I said I didn't. The young man said he couldn't give me the computer. I could give it to your wife, but not to you, he explained. It's in her name.

She's my wife, I said. She's the one who sent me to pick it up. If you called her, she'd authorize you to give it to me, I said.

The young man explained that he couldn't do that. Maybe I was divorced and was trying to take property that wasn't mine. If he were to give me my ex-wife's property, the store could get sued.

That made sense. Everybody is afraid of getting sued. We have to conduct our lives as if there's a lawyer hiding behind every tree. Still, I wanted to accomplish my mission. I asked if I could speak to the young man's boss.

He left and returned with the store manager. The store manager smiled and shook hands with me. He asked if I had a problem. I explained that I was trying to pick up my daughter's computer, and I didn't have the paperwork I should have, and worst of all, the repair order had been in my wife's name. I said I understood the concerns about a potential lawsuit but again suggested that a telephone call could perhaps solve things. After all, my wife's number was on the repair order – we had gotten a

Bill McClellan

call telling us the computer was ready – and if the manager were to call that number and ask for my wife, she could explain that she had dispatched me to pick up the computer.

There's a problem with that, the store manager said. I'm not accusing you of anything, he said, but how do I know you haven't set up something? You could have somebody there to answer the phone, he said.

I nodded. The store manager was absolutely right. I could have set up something. I'm capable of it. I really am.

For a long time now, people have been treating me like a has-been. A couple of years ago, for instance, I spent a couple of days in Mexico with an old pal from the service. He's of Nicaraguan heritage. As our car approached the U.S. border, we kidded each other. Good thing we're not in a hurry, we said. They'll probably want to search our car. A Latino and a gringo. We could be smugglers. Maybe spies. Up to something.

The border guard glanced at us and waved us through. Like we were too old to be up to something.

I noticed the same kind of attitude when I was in Atlanta for the last Olympics. In the days following the bombing in the park, I wandered the streets. There were all kinds of cops around, and they were scrutinizing the crowd. They'd glance at me, and that was it. Like I was too old to bear watching.

Same deal if I go to a place with bouncers or security. I get no more than a glance these days. You'd think I was wearing a sign – "Perfectly Harmless."

That's not the way I see myself. I might be middle-aged and a little heavy around the middle, but I'm still capable of anything. I really am.

Best Buy is going to get a lot more of my business.

BILL SIGNING IS A FRESH START FOR MAN FREED AFTER DNA TEST

JULY 3, 2006

The ceremony was ready to start in the rotunda of the Old Courthouse, and Steve Toney was nowhere to be found. I was worried. If life were a movie, he'd have been hit by a bus. And more often than not, life is a movie. I looked around and saw Police Chief Joe Mokwa, but before I could ask if he'd make a call to find out whether a bus had hit anybody in the last hour or so, in walked Toney.

He's a slight, middle-aged guy. Short, thinning hair and a short, neatly trimmed beard. He was wearing a white cap, a sports shirt and blue jeans. He gave me a wave and then sat down with two of his friends, the Rev. Milt Stohs and Rebecca Stith. Stohs has been a godsend of late, a solid friend. And if it weren't for Stith, Toney would probably still be in prison, doing time for a crime he didn't commit. Back in 1996, Stith successfully convinced a federal appeals court that Toney, who 13 years earlier had been sentenced to life for rape, should have a DNA test. That science was not available when he was convicted. The test exonerated Toney, and he was set free after serving 13 years and 10 months.

I met him shortly thereafter and was surprised at his apparent lack of bitterness. I was also surprised at the lack of support offered by the state. In fact, there was none. He was treated essentially the same as a fellow who gets released after finishing his sentence. He was given good wishes and bus fare home.

In those early days, he used to go job-hunting with his honorable discharge from the Army. He'd done an infantry tour in Vietnam. He figured that might mean something. Plus, he had a high school degree. But not much in the way of a work record. He'd gotten in trouble after the service and had done a short stretch in prison. Then he was convicted of the rape he didn't do.

He got a job with a car rental company at the airport, but when 9/11 put the squeeze on the travel industry, he lost that job. Then there were a series of low-level jobs. He didn't keep any long. He was on the edge, I thought, of homelessness. He sometimes had to borrow to pay his rent.

Several years ago, the legislators began talking about compensating people who were exonerated by DNA testing. It was a national movement, really. All across the country, men were being exonerated and freed after years in prison. Many states decided these men were owed something.

There were a number of false starts in Missouri, and then a couple of years ago, a bill established compensation, but it lacked a retroactivity clause. Also, there was a financial consideration. Compensation meant money, and there is always great competition for state money. You can count the exonerees on the fingers of one hand. In other words, they are not exactly a powerful interest group.

But now and then, right trumps everything. Connie Johnson, a Democrat, led the fight in the House. Mike Gibbons, a Republican, led the fight in the Senate. They got it done. They passed a compensation bill that would give a man who was exonerated by DNA testing $50 for each day he spent wrongfully imprisoned. The money would not come in a lump sum. A person could receive up to $36,500 a year. To Toney, it represented the middle class.

Gov. Matt Blunt came to St. Louis Friday to sign several bills that had been sponsored by St. Louis area legislators. Among them was the DNA compensation bill. Gibbons spoke. He said the Old Courthouse was a fitting place to talk about doing the right thing. Then he introduced Toney.

There were several dozen people at the ceremony. Except for Stith and Stohs, none of them were there for the DNA compensation bill. But when Gibbons introduced Toney, the crowd rose. They gave Toney a standing ovation. A sustained ovation. He looked perplexed, and then he waved.

Life is a movie, I thought.

—

DOCUMENTATION ALLOWS EMPLOYEES TO FIRE THEMSELVES

MAY 7, 1999

Put a real name on that sheet, advised Chuck Daniels. He was leading the "How to Legally Discipline and Fire Employees for Attitude" seminar that was held last Friday at a local Holiday Inn.

Our seminar materials contained a "Confidential Action Plan" with which we could plot an actual firing. We were also free to use this work sheet and make copies of it, Daniels told us. That courtesy came with the $155 fee. Whose name should I put on the sheet? Which of my colleagues has an attitude problem?

Truth is, gentle reader, I had a wealth of choices. You are considered an oddball at my shop these days if you don't have an attitude.

I selected John Michael McGuire. He is a feature writer. He has worked at the Post-Dispatch for 32 years.

First, I had to document that he has an attitude. That was easy. A couple of days earlier, I had been making fun of one of the junior bosses who walks around with his cell phone in his ear. There are probably 200 phones in the newsroom, but this guy makes a point of walking around chattering away on his phone. Like he's important.

"I overheard him the other day," I said. "No, I don't want to order a pizza right now. I just wonder what sizes you have, and what ingredients you've got. Just talk to me for a while, OK?"

McGuire chuckled.

There! If guys like McGuire didn't enjoy my anti-management jokes, I wouldn't tell them. In a sense, then, he encourages me to stray from the path of righteousness.

"Let's hear what you've got so far," said Daniels. My cohorts enthusiastically responded. "An independent thinker. Wants to do things his way." "Does the minimum. Not a team player." "Doesn't like change, an agitator."

This last one seemed to get Daniels' attention. An agitator, a subversive, he said. A mini-terrorist working against the company.

That sounded a little strong for McGuire, but on the other hand, he has been less than enthusiastic about change recently. Part of our new management philosophy involves employees applying for their own jobs. Resumes, letters of reference, samples of work and so forth.

"I've been here 32 years," he said to me recently. "Where am I supposed to get letters of reference?"

At the time, it seemed an innocent remark. But now, under Daniels' mentoring and with my Confidential Action Plan in front of me, I wondered. Was McGuire trying to make light of change, trying to discourage the rest of us from going along with the latest management theories? "Mini-terrorist," I wrote down.

The next section of our action plan involved behavior style – Aggressive, Nonassertive, Passive-Aggressive, Assertive.

To understand your target's behavior style, it's best if he or she has taken a psychological profile test. One of the best-known is the Myers-Briggs test.

Not surprisingly, Daniels is a big believer in these tests. In fact, he told us that when his sons brought girls home from college, those girls would be asked to take a Myers-Briggs test right at the dinner table.

It is, of course, important to know your target's behavior style so you can anticipate how he or she will respond to your moves. How will he or she respond to counseling? How will he or she react at the termination interview? Will your target become angry, or go into denial, or plead for one more chance?

Most common is the last. The plea-bargainers, Daniels called them. Oh, give me one more chance! I have a family!

You have to be strong. You have to be very clear that you are not accepting an invitation to the pity-party.

Daniels told us a story about a boss who fired an employee, but not with enough clarity, and then went on vacation. (The boss did not feel bad because you never actually fire somebody. They fire themselves.) When the boss came back, the guy was still at his desk!

"What are you doing here?" the boss wanted to know.

"I'm trying to improve. Just like we talked about," said the plea-bargainer.

As Daniels put it, the boss got to fire him twice. "Double your pleasure," Daniels quipped.

At any rate, I did not know what personality grouping McGuire would fall under. I figured he would try to hold a pity-party.

Something to remember, though. Because attitude is difficult to define, it is also difficult to document. Fortunately, attitude leads to certain behaviors and those are what we document.

"Encourages others to make fun of bosses. Discourages others from taking seriously the latest management strategies," I wrote.

Then Daniels led us through the minefields of employment laws. Title VII of the Civil Rights Act of 1964, the Pregnancy Discrimination Act of 1978, Family and Medical Leave Act, Age Discrimination in Employment Act, Americans with Disabilities Act, Uniformed Services Employment and Re-Employment Rights Act. On and on.

It's important to know, Daniels told us, that 85 percent of all cases that are investigated come to nothing. Of the few that go to court, employers win the great majority. So be concerned, and be careful, but don't be intimidated.

The only law I had to worry about with McGuire was the Age Discrimination in Employment Act. He's over 40. Way over.

The trick is documentation. He might try to say he was fired because of his age, but my job is to shine the spotlight on my documentation, and say, "It's got nothing to do with age. It's this and this and this."

While it's important to document the employee's failings, it's also important to document your efforts to "help" the employee. Daniels had a good tip for us. Give him a self-help book. Put that down in your log - "Gave McGuire a copy of The One-Minute Manager on 5-7" - and two weeks later, call him in and ask him some questions about the book. When he admits he hasn't read it, log that in. What have you accomplished? You've documented two counseling sessions, and you've shown that you tried to help him keep his job, but he wouldn't go along with you. Powerful evidence.

A hint to employees: If your boss ever gives you a self-help book or suggests that you read one, understand what's going on. When the boss asks you a couple of weeks later what you thought of the book, never say that you didn't read it. Instead, say something like, "I thought it was philosophy for morons. Did you like it?"

What I'm trying to tell you is that you might as well have some fun. If these people want to get you, they'll get you. They're mean.

Daniels even told us a story about an 80-year-old man who years earlier had been given a contract for a lifetime job by the company's founder. Then the founder died, and his son took over. Could he break the contract?

No need to, Daniels explained. The contract doesn't say anything about job conditions or pay. We'll make it four hours a day in the closet at minimum wage, and we'll see how long he can take it.

Good grief!

Daniels had a lot of good lines and a lot of good stories, and naturally I have selected the worst of them – or the best of them – for these columns. Well, a lot of the worst of them, anyway. He did tell us that if we were too squeamish to fire somebody, he'd come with his truck – "Toxic Employee Removal Service, You Hire, I Fire."

"Wait till they see that in the parking lot," he quipped.

At the end of the seminar, right after he explained that you can tell if a person is lying because a right-handed person will look to his right before he lies and a left-handed person will glance to his left before he lies, I went up and introduced myself.

I'd ask if you ever feel guilty about any of this, but I guess you don't, I said. Your theory is that employees fire themselves.

That's right, he said.

Which is my message to Lynn McGuire. I'd ask for your forgiveness, Lynn, except that your husband fired himself.

HAPPY ENDING ELUDES MAN HATCHED
FROM MOTHER GOOSE EGG

JUNE 22, 2003

In the spring of 1977, the Jefferson College baseball team featured a 35-year-old pitcher. Everybody else on the team was in their teens. Jefferson College is a two-year institution. The pitcher was such an oddity – and such a character – that the Globe-Democrat devoted a "Sports Special" page to him. His name was Ron Sporich.

Sportswriter Joe Castellano was enthralled with Sporich, and wrote about the way this over-age kid entertained his younger teammates with a combination of jokes and tall tales. "He seems more than a baseball player," Castellano wrote. "He wasn't born, he was hatched from a Mother Goose egg. For starters, imagine a guy with Jim Bakken's face, build and intensity, Dizzy Dean's imagination, Casey Stengel's magnetism, Satchel Paige's endurance, Ted Williams' analytical power and Huckleberry Finn's boyhood charm."

An amazing fellow, clearly. But for the next 26 years, no more was written about him. And then, this month, he was back in the news. He made the crime report.

"Ronald Sporich, 62, of Maplewood, was charged Tuesday with shooting at four police officers. The incident started when firefighters were called by neighbors to investigate an odor Monday morning and found Sporich barbecuing a cat, officials said."

Ronald was the only child of Mike and Ethel Sporich. Mike was the son of an Illinois coal miner, and he got as far away from the mines as he could. He became a merchant marine. He was seldom home. He and Ethel divorced when Ron was a child. Ethel was a schoolteacher in the St. Louis Public Schools. She taught business education, but her real love was writing. She was a poet.

"She was brilliant," said Clint Horn, Ron's cousin.

As for Ron, the sportswriter had it right about the Huck Finn charm, according to Horn. Ron was funny, and charming, but always a little odd. Women liked him, and he may have been married years ago, but if so, it was a brief marriage. If Ron had much of a work history, his cousin is unaware of it. "Ronnie wasn't a big worker," Horn said.

As the years went by, Ron went from being a little off-center to way off-center. He sometimes said the FBI and the Mafia were after him. If he was in the back yard and a plane flew overhead, he'd go inside to make it more difficult for his enemies to spy on him. Still, he was a wonderful fellow, according to Horn.

"If he had money, he'd be called an eccentric," Horn said. "He should have had money."

A final thought from Horn – Ron seemed to go downhill after his mother died. She died a couple of years ago.

Sporich was not a police character. That is, he was not one of those fellows who gets arrested on a regular basis. In fact, the only Maplewood officer who had had much contact with Sporich before the big blowup is George Ross, who handles ordinance violations.

"When the grass gets long, we send a letter," Ross said. "If they don't cut the grass, they get a summons. If they don't show up in court, then there's a warrant issued. He never went to court, so I arrested him."

He was not belligerent on that occasion, but he was strange. He told Ross that the FBI and the Mafia were after him.

There was one other prior contact with the police. The morning his mother died, Sporich spoke with a neighbor. She asked about funeral arrangements. Sporich explained that he had put his mother in the van. The van was in the yard, in disrepair, going nowhere. The neighbor called the police. It's against the law to store a corpse, but the prosecutor declined to prosecute. After all, the man's mother had just died. He was probably too distraught to think straight.

On the morning of the blowup, a neighbor called in a possible fire at the Sporich residence. When firefighters and police arrived – police are dispatched to block off the street if there is a fire – they found Sporich on his back porch. A dead cat was burning on the barbecue grill. Sporich threw a cup of straight vodka in the face of the police officer, and then rushed into his house. It was a little before 9.

The cops and firefighters left. Throwing a drink in an officer's face does not constitute a felony, so there was no cause to forcibly enter the house and arrest Sporich. Approximately 2 1/2 hours later, there was a report of shots fired from the same location. Detective Sgt. Mike Martin led the response team. They heard a shot as they arrived at the house. Martin went around to the side of a neighbor's house. Three other officers went into the alley. Sporich fired three shots at the officers in the alley. Two of the rounds struck the tree behind which two of the officers had sought cover. Looking around the side of the neighbor's house, Martin had an opportunity to fire a shot at Sporich, but he didn't think it was a sure thing, and he didn't want to fire wildly. Sporich turned and saw him, and fired a shot that whizzed past. Then Sporich retreated back into the house. The Maplewood police called the county police, which sent a TACT team.

After a five-hour standoff and a barrage of tear gas, Sporich came out of the house and was arrested.

Radio and television reporters were all over the story on that first day. They were especially interested in the fact that a cat had been on the grill. Was this an animal abuse story? Probably not, said the cops, but they were exasperated. Somebody had fired a high-powered rifle at them, and the reporters were interested in the cat.

By the way, the police figured there was no animal abuse because Sporich seemed to love animals. He had four dogs – they were all docile – and approximately 10 cats. An exact count was impossible. The cats scattered.

Sporich was charged with four counts of first-degree assault and four counts of armed criminal action. Also, some weapons charges, and the misdemeanor assault on a law enforcement officer.

I visited Sporich in the county jail last week. He told me he had been cremating his cat when the cops first came. He said the cat had been dying for two days, and he'd been with it every minute. He denied shooting at anybody. He said the police were making the whole thing up.

"I'm a political prisoner," he said.

He said the case was really about drug-running, and lawsuits, and truckloads of weapons that date to Iran-Contra. He is, at least at the moment, acting as his own attorney, and he said he did not expect the case to make it to trial. Too much information would come out, he said. They will probably try to do a "mental thing" on me, he said.

I asked what he had been doing for a living the past few years. He said he had been his mother's bodyguard.

Then I asked him about the Jefferson College baseball team. He stood up and took off his shirt. "I'm still in good shape," he said, and I agreed that he was. He told me he thought he could still pitch, and, in fact, he thought he could pitch better now than ever before, and as he said it he grinned, and for that brief moment, I caught a glimpse of what Castellano had seen a quarter of a century ago.

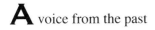

A REVOLUTIONARY MEETS SUCCESS, AND ALL GIVE THANKS

APRIL 8, 1998

A voice from the past

The man who used to be Stokely Carmichael was expected any minute. He is now Kwame Ture, and he is gravely ill with prostate cancer.

He was once a fiery civil rights leader. He was an anti-war activist, too, but he framed his opposition to the war in terms of the civil rights struggle. "Why should I be mad at the Vietnamese?" he asked. "They never called me nigger."

As that tumultuous decade drew to a close, Carmichael dropped off the radar screen, at least as far as white, middle-class America was concerned.

Last week, my colleague, Greg Freeman, wrote that the former Stokely Carmichael would be coming to town. A local businessman, Mike Roberts, was going to hold a luncheon tribute for him. The money raised at the luncheon would go toward Ture's medical bills.

I was shocked. In our celebrity-driven culture, it seems almost impossible to be famous and poor.

Even the disgraced can expect a payday. The president's family-values guru, Dick Morris, gets caught with a prostitute and a second, albeit unofficial, family? No problem. He gets a $2.5 million book contract.

Carmichael was legitimately famous. He was historically significant.

Now he's living in Africa. He has no health insurance. What an odd development.

The night before Monday's luncheon, Roberts held a private reception for Ture at his home on Lindell Boulevard.

The setting was elegant and spoke of money and good taste. The crowd, predominantly African-American, was largely of the professional class. As I waited for the guest of honor to arrive, I listened to the polite chitchat of successful people.

I wondered what Carmichael would think. Not the middle-aged Kwame Ture, but the young Stokely Carmichael.

He had worked in the South in the early '60s. Poverty was the reality. Opportunity was a dream.

He will look at this house, this crowd, and he will realize he won, I thought.

He finally arrived. He was wearing an African robe called a boubou. The cancer has aged him, and he looked older than his 56 years. He sat in a chair facing the crowd, and he spoke softly.

I'm not sure exactly what I was expecting, but I was unprepared for the depth of his intellect. I tend to lump most of the firebrands from the '60s together - Fonda, Rubin, Hoffman, and, yes, Carmichael - and dismiss them as media-savvy but essentially shallow.

The man in the chair was anything but.

"We are winning," he said, in a way that suggested the battle was far from over. "We will win. The march of humanity can be slowed, but it cannot be halted."

He is a socialist, and when he mentioned the ills of capitalism, he made a joking apology to his host, who is, of course, one of this city's most successful capitalists.

Bill McClellan

That was another strange thing. Ture was, and is, a self-described revolutionary, and the crowd he addressed Sunday night is doing just fine, thank you, within the system. But they believe, obviously, that they would not be where they are if it weren't for the long struggle that Ture and others waged.

After Ture spoke, Akbar Muhammed, an official in the Nation of Islam, auctioned off some pieces from Roberts' collection of African art.

The idea was that the auction would jump-start the fund raising.

Retired Army Gen. Ernest Harrell bought one of the items. Harrell, who is now the president of the Board of Public Service, served two tours in Vietnam at about the time the young Carmichael was raging against the war.

Then again, Harrell became a general, and maybe that wouldn't have been possible if it had not been for the movement.

At the end of the auction, Ture, the revolutionary without health insurance, thanked the crowd of successful people, but they shook their heads, and said, thank you.

—

EVEN WITH A DEAD BODY INSIDE, CAR ISN'T A TOTAL LOSS

MARCH 10, 2002

Jeanne and Frank are a young married couple who live in St. Louis. On a Monday evening in January, they bought a new car. It was the first new car that either of them had ever owned.

"We started out looking at used cars," Frank said. "But you know how that goes." Of course. If you want a fairly new used car, you're going to have to spend a lot of money. For a little bit more, you can get something new. And then you look at something new but modest, and you realize that for a little more, you can get something snazzy. Jeanne and Frank finally decided on a Chevy Malibu with a V-6 engine.

"I just decided to go for it,'" said Jeanne. You see, this was going to be her car. Frank, who had been bicycling or taking the bus to work, would inherit the Saturn that Jeanne had been driving.

Jeanne had her new car for one day. She drove it very carefully, and when she parked it in front of her house on Tuesday evening, the car had gone a total of 20 miles.

It was stolen Wednesday morning. Jeanne went out to start it, and then went back into the house. Within a minute, the car was gone.

Fortunately, she had insurance. Full coverage. It came from AIG Specialty Auto, which has its headquarters in Georgia. She had purchased her policy from a local broker. She called him to report that her car was stolen, and he told her to call the insurance company directly. She did.

"They had me do a recorded statement, and they sent me a bunch of forms. They said we'd just have to wait to see if it was recovered. If it wasn't recovered in 30 days, it would be declared a total loss, and I'd get the Blue Book value," Jeanne told me.

The car was recovered. Jeanne got the call two and a half weeks later. The police had found her car in an alley. That was the good news. The bad news was the front was dented, the rear was dented, and there were several bullet holes in the car. One more thing. There was a body in it.

The body was that of Shamar Walker. He was 17 years old. He was found sitting behind the steering wheel. He had been shot at least eight times in the head and chest.

There was more bad news. The car had been driven more than 1,400 miles. It had had a flat – maybe the result of an accident – and the original tire had been replaced with the spare, a little doughnut tire. It's impossible to say how long it had been driven on the replacement tire.

Jeanne and Frank called the insurance company's claims office in Kansas City. We think we ought to get a new car, they said. They based their argument on two points. First, there was no telling what damage had been done to the engine. You're supposed to be very careful with a car the first few hundred miles, and quite obviously, that had not been the case here. Second, a young man had been murdered in the car. That ought to count for something.

Well, no. If the car was repairable, it would be repaired. Jeanne talked to a claims agent, and then a supervisor. No luck. The estimate for repairs came out to about $7,000. The interior would be cleaned, not replaced.

I called the Kansas City office, and left messages, but nobody returned my calls. I then called my own insurance agent, and asked what he thought.

"I feel for this young couple," he said, "and I wish I could tell you that we'd get them a new car. But we wouldn't. Most companies are the

same on this. If the damage is less than 75 percent of the value of the vehicle, it gets repaired. It just comes down to numbers."

Jeanne thinks it's all unfair.

"That's why you have insurance. For worst-case scenarios," she said.

The car is now being repaired. Jeanne is making payments on a car that she drove for only one day. She has written a letter of complaint to the Missouri Department of Insurance.

Meanwhile, the cops say they have identified a suspect in the shooting. He has not yet been arrested.

—

HALF-CENTURY OF BULLETS AND BASEBALL BIND OLD FRIENDS

JANUARY 9, 2000

Can you imagine us years from today /Sharing a park bench quietly? How terribly strange to be seventy.

"Old Friends" by Simon and Garfunkel

Fifty-five years ago, they were young men rushing across the Luden-dorf railroad bridge, which was, at that time, the last standing bridge across the Rhine. The Battle of the Bulge was over, and the end of the war was in sight, but still, the Germans fought on. But that was long ago. On Thursday, the two old friends met for lunch. Naturally, the conversation soon turned to the war.

"That was 100 years ago," one said, and the other laughed, and then said, "You know, it's funny. I can walk into a room now and forget why I came in, but some things I still remember in such detail. Like the hedge rows in Normandy . . ."

There was a silence for a moment and then the first one spoke again.

"Have you seen that 'Private Ryan' movie? They walked along like it was Sunday in the park. It wasn't like that at all."

The second one nodded. "Yeah, and did you notice that the officers were wearing insignias?"

"Yeah, and how about the way they threw a mortar round against a tank? And it exploded?"

The two shared a chuckle.

One of the men had brought a book along. It was about the size of a yearbook, but instead of commemorating a high school class, it commemorated the wartime exploits of the 9th Infantry Division. I had invited myself along for the lunch, and I asked to see the book. I wanted to see the copyright date.

The book had been published in 1948. Timing is always such a problem for historians. You wait too long and records get lost and memories fade. But if you move too fast, you lose a certain perspective.

"You in this, Frank?" I asked the man who had brought the book.

"No, no," he said, and he waved his massive hands, as if to dismiss the thought that a history of the 9th Infantry Division would include the likes of him.

Yet, had the writer waited until 1950, he almost certainly would have included Frank Borghi. That was the year that Borghi was the goaltender for the U.S. team that upset England 1-0 in a World Cup game in Brazil. The Brazilian fans carried Borghi off the field. So what if the United States lost to Spain and Chile in its other games? It had pulled off one of the greatest upsets in soccer history. So in 1950, Borghi was probably the most famous veteran of the 9th Infantry Division.

Borghi's friend started reminiscing about the days right after the war. He was stationed in Germany then, playing on the division's fast-pitch softball team.

"We had this pitcher named Slim LeBar," he began, and Borghi uncharacteristically interrupted.

"I knew Slim!" he said.

It turned out that he and Slim had shared a foxhole one night, and the Germans had attacked and Slim had shot one of the attackers right between the eyes.

That was the way the conversation went. A little war, a little baseball. That's not surprising, because Borghi's companion was Cardinals announcer Jack Buck. Besides, it was baseball, not combat, that brought the two together. When the war ended, both fellows went out for the division's baseball team. Both went out for first base. Borghi got the position. Buck then went to play first base for the fast-pitch softball team.

In 1954, Buck moved to St. Louis and began working as a Cardinals announcer. One day, he went to a soccer game – "I used to go to any sporting event I could find," he said – and he thought he recognized one of the goalies. He went down at halftime to talk to him and found out that it was Frank Borghi, the guy who had beaten him out for the first baseman job. Small world.

In 1975, Buck was the emcee at a CYC soccer banquet, and Borghi was at the head table, being honored because it was the 25th anniversary of the World Cup game against England. The two men were chatting. I know you were in the 9th division, Buck said, but what company were you with? K Company, said Borghi. So was I, said Buck. What did you do? I was a medic, said Borghi. Were you at Remagen? Sure, said Borghi, and he explained that he was the only medic for the company at Remagen, the other having been killed a little earlier.

Which is how the two men realized that they had met before the division baseball tryouts. Borghi had treated Buck when Buck was hit by shrapnel a week and a day after the division had crossed the bridge into Germany.

The two men see each other fairly regularly now. Sometimes they'll meet for lunch. During the baseball season, Borghi will sometimes be Buck's guest at a game.

Borghi worked for years at the Calcaterra Funeral Home on the Hill. First, he was a driver, and then he ran the place. He retired about three years ago. He'll be 75 this year.

Buck, of course, still does home games but no longer travels with the

team. He'll be 76 this year, and he is aging as gracefully as a guy can. Parkinson's disease has given him a little bit of a tremble.

"A young guy came up to me not long ago and told me that his mom had just been diagnosed with Parkinson's. He told me she was devastated, and he wondered if I could say anything to boost her spirits. I agreed to do it," Buck said. "I told her you can live a normal life with Parkinson's except you can't play on the offensive line. You're always moving before the snap. Also, you better be careful about going to auctions."

A world-class storyteller, that Buck is. Still, there were times Thursday when Borghi would do the talking. An unassuming man, a solid guy. A good man to have lunch with.

Which reminds me of something. If you're out there, Slim LeBar, a couple of your old friends would love to have lunch.

—

Bill McClellan

CHAPTER THREE

-YOU WIN ... SOMETIMES

STORM STIRS UP NORTH VS. SOUTH POWER STRUGGLE ON MY STREET

JULY 24, 2006

We are a region divided. Some of us have power and some don't. Neighborhoods are divided in the same fashion. Even streets.

My street, for instance. Those of us on the south side have power. We were out for a couple of hours Wednesday night. Very quickly, our power was restored. The people on the north side of the street have been without power since the storm struck.

At first, it was fun. I would walk on to my porch and I'd be wearing a sweater. "It's cold inside," I'd yell to my neighbors across the street. They were sure to be outside, by the way. The heat had made the inside of their homes unbearable. They had pulled furniture out on to their porches or in their yards, and they sat there sullenly, the have-nots staring across at the haves. They could see the lights on in our houses, the television lights flickering. They could hear the steady hum of our air conditioners.

"Any extra blankets?" I'd yell at them. "I like to crank the A.C. up on these hot nights, and the rest of the family complains."

The first night, some of my neighbors seemed to chuckle. By the second night, they didn't respond. Their moods had become as dark as their side of the street.

One of them approached me one evening and asked for ice. He said the stores were sold out.

"I'd love to help," I said, "but if I give you any, I'd have to give some to everybody. Then what happens if my power goes out? I'd be caught short. Sorry."

He shook his head and returned to his side of the street.

My wife developed a form of survivor's guilt. She didn't enjoy sitting on our porch with our porch light blazing. Although we couldn't see our neighbors across the street, we could feel their eyes. They were watching us. I felt like part of the oligarchy in a Third World country.

Sometimes neighbors from the south side of the street -- the good side of the street -- would come by and we'd laugh and chat. Always, though, we were aware of the people on the other side of the street staring at us out of the darkness.

"I like to think we'd be a little more gracious if this were reversed," I said to one of my neighbors. "I can just feel the resentment from those people on the north side. I like to think we'd be better sports about it. I can tell you that I wouldn't constantly be asking for ice or cold beverages. That gets old in a hurry."

My wife had a different attitude. She wanted to give ice away. She wanted to invite people over. Maybe they could even spend the night. We were just lucky, she said, and we should be willing to share our luck.

"Luck has nothing to do with this," I said. "We pay our bills promptly, and I suspect that's why AmerenUE has treated us well. I wouldn't be surprised if some of those people on the north side are behind on their bills. That probably explains it."

Actually, I had just thought of that, but I liked the sound of it. I repeated the theory to several of my neighbors from our side of the street, the good side, the side that pays its bills promptly.

"You think that's it?" one asked me.

"I'm quite sure of it," I said. "I doubt that Ameren wants to go public with this, but I don't believe luck plays much of a role in who has power and who doesn't."

That put a different spin on the resentment we were feeling from the north. Why were they blaming us for their own shortcomings? They had a lot of nerve. If nerve were electricity, their lights would be blazing.

Still, I've tried not to say much. Oh, I've speculated aloud to some of my south side neighbors about which of our north side neighbors are behind on their bills. "It's often the ones you wouldn't expect. Maybe the ones with the fanciest cars." But mostly, I've said nothing.

Have I resented the resentment from the north? Yes. It's made me uncomfortable, but I bear it in silence. After all, everyone will have power soon enough, and the region and the neighborhoods will come together again.

—

BEING THE GRANDSON OF THE BEST DOESN'T MEAN MUCH HERE

APRIL 21, 2002

The violin-maker's father was a newspaperman, and not just any newspaperman. He was Dickson Terry, perhaps the finest writer ever to work at the Post-Dispatch.

He worked on this newspaper for 30 years. He retired in 1972. For most of his career, he was a feature writer on the Everyday magazine. In those days, that assignment meant star status. The news section was largely a rewrite operation. Reporters would phone their information to the rewrite men. The rewrite men would ask questions – "What color shirt was he wearing? Did he say anything when the verdict was announced?" – and then the rewrite men would hammer together the stories. It was an anonymous gig. Neither the reporters nor the rewrite men got bylines. The feature writers did. They were considered the best writers on the staff, and Dickson Terry was widely regarded as the best of the best.

His writing was unpretentious. One of his colleagues once wrote of his style: "Dickson's copy covered ground so comfortably that it was a temptation to say he wrote at a loping pace. That would be a technical inaccuracy because the lope is not a gait much associated with the thoroughbred."

He was also an old-fashioned newspaperman. That is to say, he drank a bit. He did not have a college degree. He talked of writing novels, but he never got around to it. Instead, he wrote his newspaper stories. He had seven children. Six of them were boys. Their house was filled with newspapermen and drinking and story-telling.

Dickson Terry died in 1978.

In the first few years after his death, he was mentioned in the newspaper on numerous occasions. Reporters searching the files would run across his stories and would write that Dickson Terry once said this or that. As the years went by, he was mentioned less and less. For one thing, the reference department became computerized, and the computers did not go back to the days when Dickson Terry worked here.

One of his sons became a violin-maker. The violin-maker had a son who aspired to journalism. The young man went to a very good college, and the violin-maker called the newspaper. He spoke to a woman about an internship. Later, he wrote me an e-mail about the conversation.

"She said he must apply. I said OK, but I thought maybe he could get on the fast track, given the history with the paper of his grandfather, Dickson Terry. She laughed aloud. She really, truly laughed at me over the phone. I was crushed and humiliated."

It was a sad story, but not really shocking. As smart as they are, a lot of women don't understand the father-son thing. Suffice it to say that you should never laugh at a man when he invokes the name of his father.

Even to a grown son, a father can be a mythological figure. Which, come to think of it, Dickson Terry really was. On the other hand, whoever the woman was – and the violin-maker did not know – she probably had never heard of Dickson Terry. After all, he retired 30 years ago. She certainly had never met him.

For that matter, I never met him, either. He died before I got to St. Louis. Nor have I met the violin-maker. Still, I'm glad he sent me the e-mail. It was like meeting the ghost of Christmas Future. Although I have never been called the greatest writer in the history of the newspaper, I have convinced my children that I am a big deal. I know Ted Drewes. I know Jack Buck. I could go on and on in this vein, and often I do.

I can easily imagine one of my kids calling the newspaper someday in the distant future, invoking my name, and being rebuffed with a laugh. This is, I'm afraid, that kind of business. Transitory to the max. By tomorrow morning, this column, and this newspaper, will be in the recycling bin.

Meanwhile, the cycle begins anew. Dickson Terry's grandson has a job lined up with another newspaper. That's not surprising. I hear he writes like his grandfather.

—

VIETNAMESE MAN TAKES SQUALID SPACE AND MAKES A HOME

JULY 19, 1998

In a corner of America that Cuong V. Pham never envisioned when he left Vietnam, he now makes his home. He lives on the top floor of an abandoned public housing project on the outskirts of downtown St. Louis.

He has no electricity and no running water. He was discovered recently by a couple of city cops who sometimes go into the ramshackle building to peer down, unobserved, at the flourishing drug traffic in the housing project across the street.

"The dealers over there have plenty of lookouts. Old crackheads usually, and there's no way to get close to anything. So sometimes we come up here and watch," one of the cops told me.

It was during one of these excursions that the cops discovered Pham. They had slipped quietly into the building when they heard a hammering sound.

There isn't much left to steal – anything of any value has long since been stolen – but the cops figured somebody must have found something. Hard to believe, but that had to be it.

So the cops quietly climbed the stairs, and discovered Pham. He was building a chair.

The cops were stunned. It wasn't so much that Pham was living in the building - they've discovered bums flopped out in there before – but the way he was living. He had made a home.

That is, he had cleaned up the place. He had ripped the carpet out and sanded the floor. As far as furniture was concerned, he had a cot, and that was about it. But everything was clean.

To appreciate what Pham has done, you'd almost have to see the rest of the building. There's junk and garbage, and the pipes have been ripped out of the walls. Saying it's a mess hardly describes it.

But Pham's place looked good.

It was primitive, of course. With no bathroom fixtures – stuff like that was taken long ago – he had a small hole in the bathroom floor. His water had been carried in and was stored in plastic milk bottles.

He told the cops that he got food from one of the downtown shelters.

Technically, the cops should have thrown him out, maybe busted him for trespassing.

On the other hand, his place was definitely better than a shelter – at least he had so decided. And the cops figured he wasn't bothering anybody. Maybe the best way to handle this would be not to handle it.

A humane decision, I'd say.

I visited Pham Friday afternoon. He is 34 years old, and he has been in this country since 1989. His English is very poor. He told me he used to work as a cook in a Chinese restaurant, but he got tired of it and now doesn't do much of anything.

He said that everybody in Vietnam had wanted to come to America, the land of great wealth.

In a way, it was true, but in another way it wasn't.

"For 500 American dollars, you can live two, three years in Vietnam," he said. "Here, maybe a month."

Unless, of course, you live like Pham. Then you need practically nothing.

He said he never married and his mother and father still live in Vietnam. He wishes he were there, too, he said.

I left his apartment, and as I walked to the car, the lookouts across the street watched me carefully. Graffiti covered much of the building behind me.

"RIP Willie," said one of the messages, and I knew it referred to the death of Willie Richie. He was on the wrong side of one of the turf wars that regularly flare up across the street. He was 24 when he was killed in February, and his death was notable - at least among those who note these things - mainly because he had shot the first three hit men who were sent out to hit him. Finally, his rivals resorted to subterfuge, and Willie was done in by a 23-year-old woman.

Happened right outside Pham's secret apartment, which is, as I mentioned, in a corner of America he had never envisioned.

—

FROM HELLISH SEASON TO THE BENCH: WHAT HAPPENED TO WARNER

SEPTEMBER 15, 2003

There are all sorts of theories about what happened to Kurt Warner. You remember him, don't you? He's the second-string quarterback for the Rams these days, but not so long ago, he was the best story in sports. He came from nowhere – OK, a grocery store – to become the greatest quarterback ever to throw a pass.

He had the highest pass rating ever. In his first year as a starter, he led the team to a Super Bowl victory. He was the Most Valuable Player in the regular season, and the MVP of the Super Bowl. He led the team to the playoffs the next year, and in his third season, he was again selected as the league MVP as he led the Rams to another Super Bowl.

Three great years, and then, boom. Last year was awful.

There were a number of theories, mostly centered around injuries. Maybe it was his thumb. Yes, that had to be it. How else could you explain that the greatest passer of all time suddenly looked like a fellow who couldn't have been a college star, let alone an NFL star? But then you had to stop and think about that. Because you know something? He wasn't a college star. He played at Northern Iowa, which is not exactly a football factory, and he wasn't a starter until his fifth year. What were those college coaches missing? How could the greatest passer of all time spend all those seasons on the bench at Northern Iowa?

Before we could really wrestle with those questions, we were into a new season. Last year was a fluke, we were told. But in the first game of the new year, he fumbled six times. He looked lost. It could have been George Plimpton out there.

He was injured again, we were told. But he was cleared to play in Sunday's game against San Francisco.

He didn't. Marc Bulger, who performed so ably in Warner's absence last year, led the team to victory, and has become, almost certainly, the new starting quarterback for the Rams.

So what happened to Warner?

I think it might be the devil. I wouldn't normally think of this – I see very little of the spiritual in football – but Warner keeps bringing it up. In fact, he spoke about the devil last year.

"Over the last few years, the enemy's been trying to attack me physically. And this year, I've seen that switch, where it's basically like . . . now he's trying to get to people around me. He's trying to use words, and use situations, and twist things, and turn things, to get other people to fall off the bandwagon."

Personally, I thought it was the sportswriters and the talk-radio guys who were doing the twisting and turning, but I know very little about the metaphysical. The one thing I have heard about the devil is he likes to buy souls. That's second-hand information. Apparently, he doesn't feel the need to make me any offers. It wouldn't be that way with Warner. From everything I've heard, Warner is a truly good man.

I can imagine old Beelzebub staring longingly at Warner as he stocked grocery shelves. The devil would know about his dream, of course. Warner wanted to be a great quarterback. So the deal would be straightforward – three great years and then you're on your own.

It's easy to imagine a truly good man rationalizing the deal. Could I still witness for God? Whatever you want to do, the devil would say. So might a good man, a selfless man, not think: I could use my success on the field to save so many souls that it would be a good deal. A thousand souls for my one.

And so for three years, the former bench-warmer from Northern Iowa could do no wrong on the football field. He'd fling that ball into coverage without hesitation, as if he knew that it would somehow find its way into the right hands. Oh, how the Wily One must have laughed as Warner credited God for his success.

Now the three years are gone, and so is Warner's success. Or maybe not. This is, like I said, just a theory.

———

Through the Glass Darkly

AFTER HITTING JACKPOT ON SLOTS, WOMAN'S LIFE COMES UP ALL LEMONS

MAY 8, 2002

Last Wednesday, Cassandra Leonard woke up feeling lucky. She and her roommate, Regina Spinner, went to the President Casino on the Admiral. They arrived about 11 a.m.

The two women went downstairs to play the nickel slot machines. Cassandra parked herself in front of a machine called "Catch-a-Wave." As the morning turned into afternoon, Cassandra drank beer and fed nickels into the machine. She won two $150 jackpots, but she kept putting those nickels back in the machine. By three in the afternoon, she was down about $125. She was just about out of money and time. She worked as a short-order cook at a tavern on Gravois, and she had to be at work by 5. Then came the lucky nickel. At exactly nine minutes after 3, Cassandra hit a jackpot worth $1,500. Lights flashed. Bells rang. A casino employee came over to confirm the jackpot. For jackpots over $1,200, a winner has to fill out tax forms.

"I didn't win. It was her," said Cassandra, pointing to Regina.

The casino employee was suspicious. Maybe it was because Cassandra had cashed in the two smaller jackpots from the same machine. The employee said that it was against the law for a person to claim a jackpot that she had not personally won, and she explained that the casino had surveillance cameras. Cassandra then admitted she had won. She had no identification, she said, and that was why she had been less than honest.

Incidentally, Cassandra usually has a drivers license, but as Cassandra was leaving a different casino not so long ago, the cops in Maryland Heights got her for DWI and speeding. She surrendered her license until her court date.

Cassandra gave the employee her name and date of birth, and the employee went into an office. When she returned, she had very bad news.

"You've been banned from this casino," she said.

It was only a one-year ban, argued Cassandra, and it should have expired by now.

As Cassandra tells the story, she had been drinking beer and playing slots about 15 months ago when she got into a very heated argument with a fellow playing a nearby machine. One thing led to another, and the security people gave her a choice – get arrested or get banned. She signed something, and left. She thought it was a one-year ban. As the casino officials tell the story, there is no such thing as a one-year ban. A ban means forever, unless the general manager personally rescinds it.

In reality, the argument about the length of the ban was irrelevant. The importance of the ban was this: You need a card to enter the casino, and Cassandra's had been taken when she was banned. That meant she had used somebody else's card Wednesday. Therefore, she had entered illegally, and the casino was not going to pay her for the jackpot. Furthermore, the illegal entry meant she was trespassing. The casino people called the police.

The cops took Cassandra to the station on Jefferson Avenue. But not to worry. They weren't going to book her on trespassing. They were going to let her go. First, of course, they had to run a quick record check.

Remember those traffic charges from Maryland Heights? It turns out Cassandra had missed a court date. There was a warrant on her. She was taken to Maryland Heights where she spent the night. In the morning, Regina came up with $300 and bonded her out.

More bad news. Because she had missed work without notifying the manager, she was fired.

I went to the casino this week to see if I could help get her the money. After all, it seems kind of chintzy to let a person gamble until she wins the jackpot, and then discover she's banned. But the casino officials said the Missouri Gaming Commission forbids paying people who have entered a casino illegally.

I called Cassandra to give her the bad news. She said she was thinking of checking into the hospital for stress. Sounds better than going to the boats, I said.

———

CHOOSE YOUR WORDS CAREFULLY; YOU MAY REGRET WHAT YOU SAY

SEPTEMBER 25, 2000

Last week, some smart aleck – probably a teen-ager, probably a teen-ager I know very well – wrote "Wash Me Please" on the dirt and grime on the back of my car. I was tempted to give my kids a lecture.

"When I was your age, I had too much respect for my father to write things on his car." But that kind of lecture doesn't work. It sounds as if I'm telling them about how I used to walk to school in the snow. More to the point, I'm always giving them lectures about speaking carefully. Don't say mean things. Don't fire off a snappy reply just because you think of one. You never really regret things you didn't say, but you spend sleepless nights about things you did say. Don't accuse somebody of something if you aren't sure he or she did it.

So how could I accuse them of writing "Wash Me Please" on the back of my car?

Besides, I had a free ticket for a car wash.

I have always been philosophically opposed to professional car washes. It seems to me that a man ought to wash his car himself. It's the least he can do. Or, in my case, the most he can do. I'm not very mechanical.

But even I can wash a car. Unfortunately, it takes a bit of time, and I have been awfully busy of late. And I did have a free ticket. It was from Gas House Express on Forest Park. I stopped in on my way home from work.

As I pulled into the lot and headed toward the entrance to the car wash, there was a sign that said, "If you want a wash, you need a ticket." No need for me to worry. I had my ticket. A coupon, actually. As I approached the entrance – why do these things always remind me of the Tunnel of Love? – I saw something that looked like an ATM. Auto Cashier, it said. There was a place to "Make Payment," and a place to get a bill changed, and a place to enter a code. A code? I was glad I had a ticket!

I pulled up to the entrance itself. I guided my wheels onto the ramps, or whatever those things are called. A sign said, "Take your foot off the brake." I took my foot off the brake, and I roared through the Tunnel of Love. Really. I roared through. I was out the other side in about six seconds. My car wasn't even wet. Sensing that something was wrong, I parked and went into the snack shop that serves as the office.

"Did you have a ticket?" the girl asked me.

"Yes, here it is," I said. "It's a free coupon."

She looked at me with a mixture of amusement and scorn. She took my coupon and gave me a ticket. It had several numbers on it. These numbers, she explained, were my code numbers. I was to punch them in at the Auto Cashier. I thought I heard her whispering to other customers as I left the office.

I went back to the Auto Cashier. I punched in my code numbers. I approached the Tunnel of Love and put my wheels on the ramp. I took my foot off the brake. I roared through again. Six seconds later, as I emerged into the sunlight, my car was wet, but barely, and I could see the water shooting out of jets behind me. I had done something wrong again.

This was one of those moments when life takes your measure. I could do the easy thing, and go home and wash my car. Or I could go back in the snack shop. I went back to the snack shop. Either the car wash isn't working today, or I'm doing something wrong, I said.

"OK," she said. "You punched in your code. You got your wheels positioned right. You put your car in neutral."

Neutral! Of course!

"Actually, it may not have been in neutral," I said.

"You mean you drove through the car wash?" she said.

I was going to point out that it's a drive-through car wash, but it's like I tell the kids, just because you think of a snappy put-down doesn't mean you should say it.

———

PAINFUL PATH LEADS MAN TO REWARDING WORK WITH CHILDREN

MARCH 15, 2006

Pat O'Donnell is a blue-collar man. He spent his early years in a four-family flat on the city's south side. His family then moved to Lemay. He graduated from Mehlville High School in 1964 and went to work.

He got a factory job. That factory closed and he got another factory job. He would keep it for 31 years.

In 1971, he got married. He and his wife, Kathy, had two daughters. O'Donnell spent a lot of time with the girls. They didn't have the money to go on fancy trips, but they did a lot of fun things. As they were leaving the Zoo one day, he noticed the Channel 2 television towers. "Let's take a tour," he said, but when they went into the station, the receptionist said they didn't give tours for three people. You need 10, she said. So the next week, O'Donnell rounded up seven kids along with his two daughters and they all squeezed their way into his car and went to the station. They got their tour.

Except for a few zany things like that, O'Donnell lived a conventional life. He was a regular churchgoer. He did his best at work, but he did not have a particularly fulfilling job.

The ordinary nature of his life took a sudden jolt on a late summer day in 1992. A tow truck was towing another truck in the westbound lanes of I-44 when a wheel came loose from the truck being towed. The loose wheel rolled across three lanes of traffic, struck the guardrail, went airborne and landed on the roof of an eastbound car. That car contained five teenage girls on their way to the Zoo. Two of the girls were killed, including O'Donnell's youngest daughter, Bridget. She was 16.

O'Donnell never again looked at life quite as he had before.

Two years later, his wife's father died. The next year, her mom died. Kathy inherited some money. It wasn't a huge inheritance, and O'Donnell didn't immediately think of quitting his job. By this time, he was warehouse manager. But a few things happened at work – the sort of minor irritants that workers usually shrug off – and O'Donnell decided to quit. Because he and his wife lived simply, they didn't need his paycheck. He was 50.

Bill McClellan

He thought about doing volunteer work at a hospital, but a friend, Sam Bommarito, whose wife had gone to Notre Dame High School with O'Donnell's wife, had another idea. Bommarito was a Title 1 reading instructor in the Jennings School District, and was working on a project he intended to use for a Ph.D. dissertation. The project involved tutoring young readers, and Bommarito needed another tutor.

O'Donnell agreed to give it a try. He wasn't much of a reader, but he had taught religion classes at the parish school and he liked kids. So 10 years ago, he went to Woodland School.

He has been there ever since. He tutors on Mondays and Wednesdays.

He does not have an office, just a desk in the hallway. He begins tutoring at 8. He works with one student at a time. Each class is half an hour. He takes a half-hour for lunch at noon and continues tutoring until school gets out at 2:30.

"His space is in the hall near my office, and I can hear him working with the kids," said Kay Blodgett, a school counselor. "He's just wonderful with those kids."

"I get more than I give," he told me.

The other day, he was at a convenience store near the school. A young man carrying a trombone case stepped up to him. "You tutored me when I was in second grade, Mr. O," he said. "I'm in eighth grade now and I'm getting A's and B's."

Sometimes the lessons are about more than reading. One youngster's brother died. "I'm sad that I can't talk to my brother anymore, Mr. O," the youngster said. The boy's classroom was in a trailer outside the school. O'Donnell was walking him back to his class and he waited until they were outside. He didn't want to talk about God in the school. As soon as they got outside, O'Donnell said, "He made it possible that when somebody we love dies, we can still talk to them. I know."

———

CITY JUSTICE SYSTEM STRUGGLES TO DEAL WITH BROTHERHOOD

APRIL 16, 2003

Wayne Mitchell turned 46 last month. He is a stable citizen. He'll celebrate his 20th wedding anniversary this summer. He has never been in trouble. That is not something you can say about his brother, David.

In December, a friend who works at the St. Louis Workhouse called Wayne to tell him that David was locked up. That was unhappy news, but the worst part was this -- David was locked up as Wayne. That was bad news but not startling. Three years ago, brother Marvin got locked up as Wayne. It is not difficult to figure out why an arrested person would use a name other than his own. If a person on probation or parole gets arrested, he faces some serious – and almost immediate – trouble.

Because Wayne had been through this before, he knew he had to get things straightened out. He went to police headquarters on Clark Avenue and explained that David had been arrested on a drug charge and had used his name. The cops listened to his story and promised to try to correct the problem.

The problem did not get straightened out. When another family member went to visit David, an employee at the Workhouse said there was no David Mitchell in the institution. "How 'bout Wayne Mitchell?" "Yes, we have a Wayne Mitchell."

So the real Wayne called the courthouse and found out when his brother had a court date. The real Wayne showed up.

"I'm Wayne Mitchell," he told the judge.

"Do you have a public defender?" the judge asked.

"Wait a minute. We have Wayne Mitchell in the hallway," said a deputy.

After some initial confusion, the matter was settled. So Wayne thought. That was in January.

But before things were sorted out, a girlfriend put up bond for David. As Wayne. Not surprisingly, David skipped bond. That is, he did not show up for court. Wayne did, and he explained things to David's public defender. Don't worry, said the public defender.

"The next thing you know, a bounty hunter shows up at my dad's place, looking for me. My dad called, and I explained things to the bounty hunter, and he asked if I'd go down to court with him and straighten it out. I said I would," Wayne said. "We got to court, and the judge had left for the day. I was arrested and taken to the Workhouse."

The mistake was quickly discovered. First of all, Wayne's friend at the Workhouse saw him and told the deputies they had the wrong man. More proof followed. As a safeguard to make sure that the wrong person is not released, inmates are given bracelets with their booking photos attached. The booking photo for Wayne Mitchell was actually a photo of David.

"We do have the wrong guy," everybody concluded. But nobody knew quite what to do. Who had the authority to release him? Wayne called his wife, Rose, and told her to contact David's public defender. Rose was unable to reach him. Not surprising. The public defenders are busy with their own clients, let alone a client's brother.

After three days, Rose hired a private attorney, Wesley Bell.

"It was strange. I got the impression that everybody realized the wrong man was locked up," Bell told me. A judge quickly signed a release order.

But Wayne wasn't released. He was transferred to the city's Justice Center to face some traffic charges of which he knew nothing. He spent four days in the Justice Center before appearing in video court and explaining to the judge that he, Wayne, has a 1979 truck, and not a black Mustang. That would be the car that David was driving.

So Wayne was finally released. That happened late last month.

Earlier this week, Wayne heard that David had been arrested, and was back in the Workhouse. Wayne said he hoped that things were finally straightened out.

I called the Workhouse Tuesday afternoon to confirm that David Mitchell had been arrested. We don't have a David Mitchell, said the woman who answered the phone, but we do have a Wayne.

———

FIXTURE AT BALABAN'S LEFT BEHIND
FRIENDS -- AND A GREAT GUMBO

MARCH 4, 2001

Gaslight Square is just a memory. It was, they say, an unusual place that attracted some real characters, people who were over the top and on the edge. Charles Perrine was comfortable with that kind of crowd.

He was known as Lady Charles, or, more simply, Lady. He was born 67 years ago, and grew up in Flora, Ill. His father was a foreman in a shoe factory. After Perrine graduated from high school, he worked a year in the factory. Then he joined the Army. He did just fine in the service, which seems odd when you figure that he was openly gay – flamboyantly gay! – long before it was common for gays to be open about their sexuality. Then again, there was something about his openness that seemed to disarm people.

Not all people, of course. During his days in Gaslight Square, he used to get in some fights. He hung around in bars, and he sometimes drank too much. He had long hair before that was fashionable. He had a mouth, too. That is, he had a penchant for devastating one-liners, and he directed them at strangers as well as friends. Throw in the fact that he sometimes wore a dress, and you can see how the occasional fight was inevitable.

He worked as a bartender in a number of the Gaslight Square saloons – Jacks or Better, Left Bank, the Dark Side, Flakey's. He drank Budweiser and he smoked pot, and this was in the late 1950s and early 1960s before marijuana use became widespread.

In fact, he was busted for pot once. He was arrested with a friend, Chris King. King is dead, but his son, Ed, knows the story.

"The judge told my dad and Lady that one of them was going to go to jail, and he didn't care which it was. 'You choose,' he said. Lady said he'd go."

He did a year.

When Gaslight Square shut down, Perrine migrated to the Central West End. He worked at the Pleasant Peasant, a restaurant-bar on Euclid Avenue that was known as much for its collection of fancy porcelain cups as its food. The cups were displayed on a rack above the bar. The young man who lived in the upstairs apartment had a pet monkey, and one night the monkey got loose and came down to the restaurant and began throwing the cups at the customers. Shortly thereafter, the restaurant closed.

Herb and Adalaide Balaban opened another restaurant – Cafe Balaban's – in that space in 1972. Perrine was their first chef. The restaurant, which was wildly popular from the start, suited Perrine perfectly in that it attracted an offbeat crowd. In fact, there's a plaque in a corner of the restaurant honoring its very first customers, Victor and Edmund. They sat at that corner table every Saturday night for years. Victor was quiet and could have been cast as a bookkeeper. Edmund reminded people of Liberace. If Perrine was sitting at the bar – and he was often sitting at the bar – he and Edmund would trade insults as Edmund and Victor were escorted to their table.

One reason Perrine was often at the bar was he lived in an apartment upstairs. He lived with his spiders – he kept tarantulas – and he raised crickets to feed the spiders. He had very little furniture. Just a bed and a table and some easels. He was a painter of considerable talent. Although he was a chef, he never cooked for himself. He went out for all his meals, and his circle of restaurants was rather small. They had to be within walking distance. He never drove. Never owned a car. Never had a drivers license.

"I'm just an old pioneer woman," he'd say.

His friends were a remarkably mixed assortment of people. He was friendly with bikers. He had friends who were successful business people. Not only were many of his friends straight, but some of them were people not normally comfortable with gays.

Frank Mormino, for instance. Mormino owned the Europa bar on Euclid. He was a gruff fellow, a man's man. He served in the Marine Corps during World War II. He was a former minor league baseball player, a big sports fan. Some of the local Bohemians likened him to Archie Bunker, but he and Perrine were great pals. It was hard to figure, except that there was something genuine about Perrine, a total lack of pretense.

But mainly, his life revolved around Balaban's. When Herb and Adalaide sold the restaurant in 1986, Herb mentioned Perrine to one of the new owners.

"You'll take care of Lady, won't you?" Herb asked.

"Of course," said Tom Flynn, who had started work there as a busboy in 1976 and understood that Perrine paid no rent and more or less came with the place.

As the years went on, Perrine worked fewer and fewer shifts. He was in semiretirement. He'd work a service bar, filling drink orders for servers – he was a terror! – and he'd make soup. His specialty was gumbo. It was his own recipe. He shared it with no one.

He became ill last year, and was diagnosed with pancreatic cancer. He wanted to die at home, and his friends said they'd take care of him. He last left his apartment in December when he came down to the kitchen to make gumbo. Sometime thereafter, he gave his recipe to chef David Timney, Flynn's business partner. Also, to Selina Ford, who has also worked at Balaban's since the beginning.

During these last few weeks, Jimmy Howe, John Newhouse, Rob Scheer, Ed King and Timney took turns watching Perrine. Of that group, only Howe is gay. By the way, the fellows wanted me to mention Nino Giovanni, a nurse from BJC Hospice Care. He was a huge help, they said.

Perrine died Monday. His will stipulated that he be remembered at a party at Balaban's, and that's scheduled for Wednesday night. Friends only, of course, but still, Timney figures to have to make a lot of gumbo.

—

ST. LOUIS SIGNED ITS NAME WITH A LIPIC FOUNTAIN PEN

NOVEMBER 13, 1998

Leonard Lipic, 86 years old and dapper, sat in the Jack Buck Grill at the Missouri Athletic Club and ordered a cup of coffee.

"Let me sign for this," he said with the kind of enthusiasm you would expect from a man who enjoys putting his signature on paper. He was,

Bill McClellan

I thought, the very portrait of an old-fashioned gentleman. The sleeves of his white shirt extended just the right length beyond the sleeves of his jacket, and I could see that the shirt's cuffs were monogrammed. He wore cuff links that were solid gold replicas of pen points.

Not just pen points, but nibs. A nib is the business end of a fountain pen, and a fountain pen, Lipic would tell you, is the ultimate fashion accessory for a gentleman.

"It's a mark of distinction, certainly," Lipic said. "Watch me sign."

He signed the bill the waiter had placed in front of him.

"You can sign with character. You can shade things," he said, and sure enough, he signed his name in such a way that some of the lines were narrow and some were thick. No question about it. There was a style to his signature.

As well there should be. Lipic is president of the Joseph Lipic Pen Company, which is in the 2200 block of Gravois, and he is something of a legend in the world of pens.

And yes, there is such a world, and a magazine called Pen World caters to it. The magazine is published in Kingwood, Texas, and the receptionist there told me she couldn't disclose circulation figures, but it is enough, I think, to know that there is such a magazine, and that it featured a two-part story about Leonard Lipic in 1990. The writer, Bevy Jaegers, began her story this way:

"It is sheer excitement to meet a man who almost literally cut his teeth on pens as a child, and grew up in a world bristling with Duofolds, eye-droppers, Dorics and piles of golden nibs."

It's all true. Leonard Lipic grew up with pens.

His grandfather was George L. Berg, who opened a one-room pen-making shop down by the river in 1863. Berg was 18 when he went into business.

By virtue of its riverport status, St. Louis was, in those days, the great commercial center of the Midwest, and with no computers, typewriters or mimeograph machines, the burden of this commerce rested entirely on the pen. Berg made the best.

Actually, what he did was invent a pen that required less-frequent dipping, and he produced gold nibs that were more flexible than the old metal ones, and therefore more responsive to stylish writing.

In 1904, Berg's son-in-law, Joseph Lipic, a baker before his marriage, joined the company. Lipic turned out to be a brilliant penman. He invented a self-filling fountain pen, and under his leadership, the company began to grow. This growing company needed a name, and so it became the Joseph Lipic Pen Company, and it was one of the finest success stories in a town filled with them.

The Joseph Lipic Pen Company had customers all around the world, and its retail outlet in downtown St. Louis was the largest pen store in the country. Leonard, one of Joseph's five sons, went to work there in 1930.

"We had nine girls doing nothing but selling pens all day," he recalled. "There were times when there were lines to get in."

Ah, the heyday of pens.

Then the world changed. The ballpoint pen was invented.

"I didn't think they'd make it," said Lipic.

Goodbye to shaded signatures, but goodbye also to the need to fill a pen with ink. Style fought convenience, and convenience won.

And typewriters were soon in wide use, and computers, and, worst of all, disposable pens.

"We didn't get on that bandwagon like Bic did," Lipic said, and there was both pride and sorrow in his voice.

Before long, parents were no longer giving their kids quality pens for graduation. The downtown store closed, and the Jospeh Lipic Pen Company was mostly selling disposable ballpoint pens to companies that wanted their names on the things. Darned near novelty items.

Oh sure, there are still some customers who want solid, durable pens. The St. Louis Police Department, for instance. Those black, disposable pens the cops carry come from the Joseph Lipic Pen Company.

Although Leonard Lipic is still the president of the company, his son-in-law, Wayne Hoover, pretty much runs things. I asked Lipic whether Hoover is a pen lover or a businessman.

"I'd say he's a businessman," said Lipic.

After the company's downtown store closed, Martin Lipic, Leonard's nephew, opened a store on Hampton Avenue. Mostly, the store sells to large accounts, but there is still a small retail outlet in the front. I visited it Thursday morning.

I was glad to see a portrait of George L. Berg on the wall. Also, a photograph of Joseph Lipic, and another of Emil Lipic, Martin's dad. I stood in the store for a moment, looking at the cases filled with quality pens. A young man came out of the back room to wait on me.

That's not a fountain pen in your pocket, is it? I asked.

"No. It's a Bic," he said.

Then Martin came out, and he said that yes, fountain pens were making something of a comeback. Not a tidal wave yet. Just a bit of a groundswell.

Even so, the news would be heartening to Leonard Lipic, an old-fashioned man who understands that a gentleman is defined by his signature.

—

A GAME OF GOALS – AND OF FATHERS AND SONS

NOVEMBER 13, 2005

Soccer was not a sport in the Chicago of my youth, at least not in my neighborhood. It was a game played in parks near downtown, played by boys from homes in which English was not spoken. It was as foreign as squash.

That changed for me here in St. Louis. My son began playing when he was 5. Soccer became to him what baseball had been to me. That understates it. Unlike baseball, soccer was not seasonal. The outdoor season gave way to the indoor season. Jack was often on two teams at once, sometimes three. We spent Saturdays driving from one game to another. When the St. Louis Ambush won the National Professional Soccer League Championship in 1995, I took Jack, who was 7, to the airport to greet the team.

Mostly, though, soccer was played rather than watched. The Lightning, the Raiders, Our Lady of Lourdes, the Gateway Strikers. Each name has its own memories. Most are sweet. Triumph, disaster, heartbreak -- all were woven into soccer. He was, for a time, a goalie, and my torment as the enemy approached his goal is something I would not wish on any father.

In high school, he became a defenseman. He was a marking back, a sweeper, and then again, a marking back. That meant he marked, or guarded, an opposing forward. Along with Andrew O'Neal and Ethan Knoll, he was a captain of the Clayton High School team.

When he was a child, I would look at the opposing team and always think, "Those boys are giants!" They weren't, of course, and when I would see them come off the field, they would be as young and as small as Jack and his mates. In high school, though, they all look like young men, and it's a sobering thought that some of them perhaps are a year away from Iraq.

As Jack's senior season wore on, I became more and more aware that this was it for me as a soccer dad. The sport that had defined my son's childhood was nearly over for the two of us. What a fine season it was. No. 1-ranked Priory had outscored its opponents 38-4 when it played Clayton in late September. Clayton lost 4-2. Jack marked Jimmy Holmes, the top scorer in the area, and held him to a single goal. The two boys chatted briefly after the final whistle. I watched almost in awe. Never had I been such a warrior on the athletic field.

Districts began the first of this month. Clayton beat Cleveland, and then Affton, and then played Trinity for the district championship. Trinity was ranked third among the area's small schools. If Clayton were to get to the state tournament and keep the season alive, it would have to beat Trinity on Trinity's home field.

Trinity carried the play in the first half, and had two or three scoring chances, but Clayton goalie Alex Neil was on his game. After 40 minutes, there was no score. Clayton did better in the second half. Max Leabman, another senior, has an uncanny ability to impose his will on the ball. You will go in the direction I want you to, he seems to say, and sure enough, he and the ball emerge from a crowd. He brought it near the Trinity goal. Andrew O'Neal, who scored so many big goals this year, got off a shot -- and hit the top of the crossbar. Another shot went wide. The second half ended in a scoreless tie.

The overtime was fiercely contested, too, and then Matt McCluskey of Trinity, deep in Clayton territory, got loose in the corner and fired a crossing pass in front of the Clayton goal. Jack McKenna, with perfect timing, headed the ball into the goal. My son, who was marking McKenna, stood on the field motionless for a long moment. Then he consoled his teammates, congratulated the opposition and walked over to me. He gave me a hug.

"We've got some soccer memories, Dad," he said.

—

DON'T EXPECT MUCH ADORATION FROM YOUR WIVES AT ELECTION TIME
DECEMBER 4, 2000

I recently wrote a story about Bobby Reynolds. He got started in the sideshow business 60 years ago as a child magician with Professor Roy Heckler's Flea Circus. Shortly after that story appeared in the paper, I received a letter from Robert W. of Florissant.

Dear Bill McClellan: I was glad to read your article about a legitimate flea circus. I saw one in 1959 in Tivoli Park in Copenhagen. My wife still won't believe me. They harnessed them to miniature carts and wagons just like you said. I saw one on a tight rope. I think it had an umbrella. I swear I wasn't drunk. Even with you writing about a legitimate flea circus, my wife remains a nonbeliever. Robert W.

I read that letter several times. I don't mean to sound like a pop psychologist, but it was clear to me that the letter had little to do with flea circuses. Instead, it was about husbands and wives. It was a cry for help. Excuse me, then, while I put on my counseling hat.

Robert? You out there this morning? I hope so. First of all, let's re view the facts as we know them. You saw a flea circus in 1959. In fact, you saw a flea on a tight rope, and you think it had an umbrella. A tiny, little umbrella, I'll bet. You also saw fleas pulling miniature carts. Your wife has never believed your story.

Robert, why did you feel it necessary to tell me you weren't drunk when you saw a flea with an umbrella? Do I seem like a judgmental person? I don't mean to seem that way, Robert. Truth is, I don't find your story far-fetched at all. Bobby Reynolds told me that he has seen fleas juggle cotton balls. He said that if you put a flea on its back, and then take a tweezers and gently place a cotton ball on its tiny little legs, it will juggle that cotton ball. I didn't put that in my story, Robert, and you know why?

My wife wouldn't have believed it. She'd have laughed at me, Robert. "You believe anything anybody tells you," she would have said. So I heard this wonderful, marvelous story and I was afraid to share it with the readers. How do you think that makes me feel? Of course, your wife wouldn't have believed it, either. After all, you mentioned that even with me writing about a legitimate flea circus, your wife remains a nonbeliever. In other words, she didn't believe my story even though I intentionally left out the most unbelievable part.

Have you ever noticed, Robert, that wives are particularly contemptuous of their husbands during election campaigns? It's true. I think it has to do with the way political wives have to gaze adoringly at their husbands. For some reason, that really bums out other wives. Maybe they instinctively put themselves in the shoes of the political wives and try to imagine how difficult it would be to gaze adoringly at us.

They empathize, Robert. That's what women do.

This year was especially bad. Think about Laura Bush. She was a librarian by trade. She loved books, and that meant she loved words, and she had to gaze adoringly at her husband while he talked with great "dignitude" about "subliminable" messages. The wives empathized with her, Robert.

And what about Tipper? You know what her husband did at all the campaign stops? He'd let her introduce him – would your wife like to have to give you a gushy introduction? – and while she'd be talking, her husband would come "sneaking" up behind her while the crowd cheered and laughed, and then he'd grab her, and kiss her, and she'd have to act surprised and happy. Have you ever tried that, Robert? Sneak up on your wife while she's talking to a group of strangers, and then give her a big kiss?

I'll bet nobody was happier to see this campaign end than Tipper Gore!

I hope you see what I'm getting at, Robert. This is a bad time to talk to wives about flea circuses. But if it helps, Robert, I believe you.

—

STATISTICS ASIDE, SOME CRIMES ARE BEYOND ALL REACH

JANUARY 28, 2005

Keith Wilson is a simple man. The prosecutor made that point in his closing argument. "Do you think he's sophisticated enough, cunning enough, to make this up?" asked Assistant Circuit Attorney Bob Craddick.

Wilson had been the state's star witness in the case against Henry Woods, who was charged with murdering William Robinson in May of 2003. Woods was also charged with assault for shooting Wilson in the same incident. Because Wilson survived, you might think the case was a slam-dunk, but when the state's star witness has a mental problem, it can complicate things.

Wilson is 29. He doesn't work. He gets Social Security disability and he lives with his dad. He rides around his north side neighborhood on his bike.

Woods does not seem a whole lot more complex. He's also 29, and he doesn't work, either. He rides around the neighborhood on his moped. At least, he used to. He shared the moped, by the way, with his girlfriend.

I glanced over at Woods while Craddick was urging the jury to find the defendant guilty of first-degree murder, which carries a sentence of Big Life. That means real life. No possibility of parole. Woods has a long, thin face and he looked mournful as he sat at the defense table. Perhaps he recognized the enormity of the hammer that hovered over his head. Maybe he was thinking about how absolutely stupid and senseless this whole thing was.

I found my mind drifting to the recent stories about crime statistics. A decline in crime is always greeted with a certain pride by police officials, as if departmental policies can have a major impact on crime. I suppose that's true, but there are some crimes that are beyond anybody's power to prevent. For that matter, sociologists sometimes talk about jobs as the solution. The more jobs, the less crime. That, too, is probably beyond debate, but again, some crimes are beyond all reach.

As the state explained this one, Wilson was standing on the sidewalk on a spring day two years ago when Woods' girlfriend came by on the couple's moped. Apparently, words were exchanged. The girlfriend left and a few minutes later, Woods came by. Stop messing with my girlfriend, he said, or words to that effect.

Later that day, Wilson was in a parking lot with his friend William Robinson. He was 27. The two men were drinking. They had a can of beer and a bottle of Cisco wine. Only the wine was open. Perhaps they were saving the beer for desert. Suddenly, two gunmen appeared. Wilson was shot in the mouth and ran into the street. One of the gunmen continued to shoot at him. He hit two cars instead. Meanwhile, Robinson was killed.

Wilson said the man who shot him was known as "Light." He told the police that Light had threatened him earlier in the day. He said he did not know the second shooter's name, only that he was a friend of Light's.

Light happens to be Woods' nickname. An anonymous caller gave police the name of George Morning, and Wilson picked his photo out of a photo lineup.

Morning, who was 19 at the time of the shooting, went to trial in

November and was convicted of first-degree murder and assault. He was sentenced to life in prison plus 30 years.

The evidence was the same – Wilson's testimony was key and was corroborated, in general anyway, by a fellow who saw the two gunmen but could not identify them – so the odds seemed to be against Woods. His lawyer, former prosecutor Douglas Forsyth, made a spirited argument about reasonable doubt and pointed out, as gently as possible, that a fellow like Wilson was, well, prone to confusion.

But in Craddick's rebuttal, he argued again that Wilson was not the type who could, or would, make up such a story. The jury agreed and convicted Woods of first-degree murder and first-degree assault. He faces life in prison.

Robinson and Woods both had family members in the courtroom. So much lost over so little, I thought. An exchange of words on a spring day. Wilson does not even remember what it was he is supposed to have said.

—

STRICKEN FARMER'S NEIGHBORS REAP WHAT HE SOWED

NOVEMBER 1, 1998

Bernie Voytas had been working 28 straight days, and long, hard days they were. That's the way of it, though, for a farmer at harvest time. Especially for a farmer in Randolph County, where the Southern Illinois soil is rich enough for a man to earn a good living, but only if he's willing to work hard for it.

"I'd say the soil's fine, but there's farmers in Central Illinois who wouldn't think it was worth walking across," is the way one Randloph County farmer described it. After 28 straight days, Voytas decided to take a break. He announced his decision to Byron Johnson, a 74-year-old friend who'd been helping him.

"He said, `I'm tired, and you're tired. Let's take a day off.' I figured something was wrong. Wasn't like Bernie to say he was tired," said Johnson.

This day off was last Sunday, and Bernie decided to spend it in the city with Steve Keith, who had invited him to a Rams game. Keith has a small agricultural research firm, and each year he gets tickets to one game.

"I was surprised Bernie agreed to go," Keith told me. "What's the chances of him taking a day off during the harvest?"

As odd as it was for the 44-year-old farmer to take a day off during the harvest, there was something else that seemed even stranger. His speech had become halting. That is, sometimes he'd momentarily stumble on a word, as if he couldn't quite remember the way it was supposed to sound. A little thing, but troubling. Keith noticed it. So did Johnson.

Maybe the day off would help.

In a way, it did. Everybody now figures it was a blessing that Voytas was in the city when he had the seizure.

It happened exactly 27 seconds into the football game. It's funny the things you remember, and Keith remembers looking at the clock, which said that 14:33 remained in the first quarter. His best friend, who seemed almost indestructible, who had been a coal miner and a farmer before the mines closed and he threw himself into farming, was suddenly stricken. His face was contorted. His right side seemed frozen.

Keith rushed to find an usher.

"I'll tell you, they got help there in about three seconds," he said. "I was only gone an instant, and by the time I got back, a doctor in the crowd was already with Bernie."

Voytas was rushed to St. Louis University Hospital. His condition was stabilized. Doctors soon discovered the cause of the seizure. Voytas had a brain tumor.

Very early Monday morning, more than 15 farmers arrived at Voytas' fields. They brought their combines and their trucks. They came un-bidden, a lmost magically. It was not an organized thing.

"How did the word get out?" said Keith, repeating my question. "I don't know. This is a small community. Hard to say how the word gets around. It just does."

There were acres and acres of corn to be harvested. Same with soybeans. There were acres of wheat to be planted.

The farmers got to work. They worked into the darkness, and they were back the next day at 6 a.m. There were too many of them, and Keith, who was more or less trying to keep things organized, had to send some of them home, back to their own fields.

A couple of the fellows who were too old to do the harvesting insisted on doing something, so Keith told them to shuttle meals out to the workers. That is what Virgil Hoffman and Augie Voytas, Bernie's father, tried to do. But truth is, the men were working on the fly, the combines rolling through the fields, stopping only briefly to feed the field loaders, and the loaders rolling to the silos, and the silos being unloaded into trucks, and the trucks heading immediately toward Evansville, where the crop would be sold; and if one man stopped, the whole thing would stop, and so the meals went mostly uneaten.

Wednesday was a replay of Tuesday, and Thursday a replay of Wednesday, and by the time the fellows knocked off in the darkness Thursday after four days of steady work, the end was in sight.

Friday morning, the fellows had mostly returned to their own fields, and only a couple of fellows were needed to get the job done. The last field to be harvested was just outside the town of Eden.

Keith was getting ready to climb into the combine. David Boyd would be handling the field loader. Boyd is 34, and he farms with his dad, and he'd been working Voytas' fields since Monday morning.

Your dad didn't mind? I asked.

My dad was here, too, he said.

This was, the fellows said, something of a farming thing. Neighbors pitching in when help is needed. There's a sense of community when everybody is dependent upon the weather and the soil.

But in this instance, it was more than just a farming thing.

"Bernie is always the first to help anybody," said Keith. "He loans out equipment. He hauls stuff. He does things for you that he doesn't have to do. He doesn't do it for return favors. So everybody wanted to help. It's why we had to turn people away."

As you sow, so shall you reap. We hear that even in the city.

"Our goal is when we're able to talk to him, and he asks about the harvest, we can tell him not to worry. It's taken care of."

Voytas, by the way, is getting better. It's too soon to say when he'll get out of the hospital, but the doctors say he's recovering.

I found that out later, after I'd returned to the city, after I'd left the cornfields that lie just this side of Eden.

—

FIREFIGHTER'S EX-WIFE WATCHES PROCESSION WITH ALMOST ENVY

JUNE 12, 2002

As the funeral procession for Fire Capt. Derek Martin moved down South Broadway last month en route to the Jefferson Barracks National Cemetery, a woman stood at the side of the road. Next to her was a young man in a wheelchair.

The young man's father used to take him to fire houses, and several firefighters in the funeral procession recognized him. They called out his name and waved. Then the procession moved down the road, and out of sight. The woman, whose name is Mary Sims, felt great sympathy for Martin's widow, just as she had felt great sympathy for the widow of Fire Capt. Robert Morrison, who had been buried a day earlier. She also felt something else, something harder to define, something bordering on envy.

Martin and Morrison had died heroes' deaths. Both were survived by beautiful families. A memorial service was carried live on television. The governor spoke at that service. His message was echoed by other speakers. We will not forget these heroes nor turn our backs on their families.

Mary's situation is ever so much more complicated. First of all, she had long been divorced from her firefighter husband, Rick Oldham, when he died last year. Also, he did not die a hero's death. He committed suicide on the night of his 43rd birthday. He had been out drinking with some pals from the department. His girlfriend was also with him. Then he went home and shot himself. He left no note.

Mary was 14 when she met Rick at Cleveland High School. She was 20 when they were married in 1980. On April 1, 1981, she had their first and only child. Jeremy was three months premature. He was not expected to survive his first night. He did, but he was not expected to ever get out of the hospital. He did, and if his survival can be considered a miracle, the miracle has not come without a cost. Jeremy is severely disabled, and confined to a wheelchair. His mind functions better than his body. He understands but has difficulty communicating. He cannot speak, and he does not have adequate muscle control to sign.

Caring for a severely disabled child can strain even a strong relationship. Mary says Rick was a very nice man and a loving father, but the heartaches and stress got to him. At least, that's her theory. They were divorced in 1990.

Rick stayed close to his son. He took him to the fire station. He sometimes kept him overnight. He did not miss his child support payments. He worried along with Mary when they would talk about what would become of Jeremy when Mary was no longer around to care for him.

Mary remarried in 1993. Her new husband forged a fine relationship with Jeremy. You have two dads, Rick used to tell his son. Nice man though this new husband is -- and he intends to adopt Jeremy, which tells you something about the man -- he has not been a huge success in the financial world. He worked at a printing company that went under. Now he works for a remodeling company.

When Rick killed himself last year, his pension went to Jeremy. Also, there was a $30,000 lump sum payment. Jeremy also gets Social Security, and Mary gets disability -- due partly to arthritis that she says she developed lifting Jeremy all these years. So it's not like they're broke, or Jeremy didn't get anything when his dad died.

Still, Jeremy sleeps in the dining room. He's too heavy to carry up and down the stairs. Mary would like to put a small addition on her house, but that doesn't seem to be in the cards at the moment. She worries about other stuff, too. Medicaid covers most medical expenses, but not everything. Diapers, for instance. Or a new wheelchair. The St. Louis Variety Club has helped in the past, but Jeremy turned 21 in April. That will change things, Mary thinks.

She knows that her son is ineligible for assistance that is earmarked for children of men or women who die in the line of duty, but he's still a firefighter's son. That's what she was thinking, she told me, when the funeral procession moved down the road.

—

FOR CUBS FANS, SOMEHOW THE MAGIC ALWAYS HAPPENS

OCTOBER 3, 1999

John Provinzano is a Cubs fan. Always has been, too, even though he grew up in Vandalia, which is solid Cardinals country, its Illinois postmark notwithstanding.

At 47 years of age, John is old enough to recall the lean years of the early '60s. He can remember the Lou Brock-Ernie Broglio trade. He can remember how everything came together in that glorious summer of 1969. Came together, but didn't stay together. Then there were more lean years until the magical year of 1984. A division title. Victories in the first two games of the best-of-five playoff series against San Diego. The first World Series of Bob's lifetime was one victory away. Three straight losses. The Cardinals, of course, just kept chugging along. Pennants, division titles and World Series championships were not unknown.

And still, John kept the faith. Actually, he did more than keep the faith. He passed it on. He took a little Cubs cap into the delivery room when his son, Tony, was born 10 years ago. Despite the difficulties of raising a Cubs fan in Cardinals country -- and the Provinzanos live in Highland, which is even closer to St. Louis than is Vandalia -- John has done his job. Tony is loyal to the team of his father.

Back in May, John went into the hospital for angioplasty. After opening a partly blocked artery with a balloon, a doctor attempted to insert a stent in the artery to keep it open. The artery was cut. Open-heart surgery saved John's life, but there were complications, and he ended up in a coma. His prognosis was uncertain. His wife, Debbie, had to face the possibility that when he came out of the coma – if he came out of the coma – he might not be the same man.

He came out of his coma in July. He tried to talk, but had trouble putting words together. Finally, dramatically, he mouthed a complete sentence.

"Turn on the ballgame, please."

He didn't have to say what game. He has a framed picture of Sammy Sosa on his dresser at home. He has a bat signed by Mark Grace. He wanted to listen to the Cubs. He had taken his first step on the long road to recovery.

The Cubs were coming to town in August. Debbie wondered if there was a chance the team could do something for him. She didn't know what. Anything.

She wrote an e-mail to the Cubs. She addressed it to Whom it May Concern, and she wrote about how much her husband loved the Cubs. She wrote about the teasing he got from Cardinal fans. She wrote about what a wonderful husband and father he was.

She got back a form response. Thanks for the message and we regret that we can't answer all e-mails. That sort of thing.

I heard about it and called her. Regular readers know that I'm a Cubs fan. Like most Cubs fans, I believe in magic and am keenly aware that there is a mysterious curative power associated with the Cubs. At any rate, I talked to Debbie and visited John, and I wrote a column about the situation.

I ended it with the comment that Debbie shouldn't give up on the Cubs. Magic is an old thing. Computers are new. This lack of response to her e-mail message was a computer problem.

Ted Barr read the column. He's in the shoe business. More importantly, he's got a daughter, Michelle. She's a nurse, and she lives in Chicago.

She's good friends with a young man named Dan Falato. He's a sports producer for WGN radio.

So Ted called Dan, and read him the column. Dan was touched by the story, and sent me an e-mail. We'll do something, he said.

Fortunately, he was in a position to do something. Not only does he work for WGN radio, which broadcasts the Cubs' games, he has a roommate. The roommate is Mark Grace, the Cubs first baseman and reportedly one of the nicest fellows around.

No "reportedly" about it. He sent me an e-mail promising he'd do something, and he said that if anybody deserved thanks, Ted Barr was the fellow.

Mark Grace then sent Tony a baseball with a personal message about John. He also sent Tony the cap he had worn in the 1997 All-Star game. He signed it, too. He sent one of his rookie cards, which he also signed. He sent Debbie an e-mail to make sure his package had arrived.

Meanwhile, the team sent a box of things to the hospital. Caps, dolls, a ball signed by the entire team, a Sammy Sosa T-shirt, and so on.

Then Dan Falato called and said to make sure that John was listening to the radio broadcast that day. Ron Santo and Pat Hughes, the announcers, will be wishing him well, Dan said.

Unfortunately, the reception in John's room wasn't good. He couldn't hear much more than static. No problem. Dan sent him a tape.

To say John was moved by all of this is an understatement.

"When I heard Ron Santo mention me, well, it brought tears to my eyes," John told me Friday afternoon. "And Mark Grace? I can't even tell you. He's always been one of my favorite players, and I've always heard that he was a nice person, but still, it's just too much. It's way above what I would have expected."

By the way, John is still in the hospital, but he's doing much better. He's not well enough to get to a ballgame yet, but he'll be making his first trip out of the hospital Sunday to visit relatives. He's certain, he told me, that he'll be going to some games next year.

Debbie told me that one of the doctors said John's recovery so far as been something of a miracle.

A miracle or Cubs magic? There are some things they just don't teach you in medical school.

—

I'M A SUCKER FOR JUNK IN MAILBOX, E-MAIL AND EVEN SALES CALLS

JULY 28, 2003

I have always appreciated junk mail. Years ago, when I was a young man living in Arizona, I had a post office box. I considered it a mark of sophistication. Each day, I would walk the two blocks from my apartment to the post office to check for mail. How unhappy I was if the box was empty.

Once a month, I would get my GI bill check. Occasionally, I would get a letter. But the rest of my mail was of the junk variety. I was on a number of mailing lists because I had once sent away for a copper bust of Abraham Lincoln, suitable as a paperweight. I paid $5 for the copper bust, which turned out to be a penny. The people who sold me that copper bust must have sold my name to other entrepreneurs because I was soon deluged with various offers. I was finally getting mail. I felt like my $5 had been well spent. Then some of my friends from journalism school were unable to get newspaper jobs, and a couple of them landed in the junk mail business. That made me appreciate junk mail even more. I saw it – and still do – as a refuge. A person with a gift of gab can always write junk mail letters to people who might want a copper bust of Abraham Lincoln, suitable as a paperweight. It's sort of like being an editorial writer.

Junk mail on computers is something different, though. Admittedly, I'm not much of a computer guy. I'm strictly in the dead-tree end of the business. But every day, I get an e-mail from our e-mail administrator – a person I don't even know – and this person gives me a list of e-mail messages that were "blocked because they appear to be spam." I'm allowed to retrieve those messages if I want them, and of course I do.

About half of them are from people in Nigeria who want to cut me in on a deal in which I will make millions, and the other half are from people who want to help me enlarge a part of my body. I understand that the people in Nigeria heard about me from the folks who sold me the copper bust of Lincoln, but what about the people who are concerned about my body? How did they get my name?

I'm almost embarrassed to get on the elevator at the newspaper these days. I'm always afraid that one of the people on the elevator is the e-mail administrator, and he or she probably has to suppress a snicker when I climb aboard.

Then there are the telephone solicitors. As regular readers know, I am very much against the no-call lists. Why put telephone solicitors out of business? After all, nobody grew up wanting to be a telephone solicitor. It's generally a bridge job, something to hold you over while you look for something better.

Still, I got a very unsettling call the other day. It was just about dinner time and a fellow called me from Citicard. "We see that you pay your credit card bills in full and on time, and we'd like to give you a little reward," he said. I knew that was a lie because the credit card people hate it when you pay in full and on time, but I pretended to be interested. He then offered me some kind of credit protection. He said it would cost just $3 a month and any time I wanted to cancel, all I had to do was call.

Over the years, I have gotten some dandy books from Book of the Month Club because I am too lazy to send in the form saying I don't want this month's selection, but it's one thing to get a book you don't think you want and quite another to get credit protection. But the solicitor was good, and wouldn't take no for an answer. I finally asked to speak to his supervisor.

I don't want credit protection, I said to the supervisor.

"Do you want to go on the no-call list?" she asked, and it sounded more like a threat than an offer. I had the sense that she was part of the whole network of junk communicators, and a word from her could cut me off completely. So I reversed myself. I ordered the credit protection. After all, I can always cancel, and the monthly charge is less than the cost of the copper bust of Lincoln, which turned out to be such a fine investment.

———

UPON CLOSER LOOK, SOLDIER'S LETTER RAISES UNSETTLING QUESTIONS

MAY 31, 2004

In January 1944, a woman wrote a letter to this newspaper. She said she had just received two letters, one from her husband, who was fighting overseas, and the second from one of his pals. She read the second letter first. Her husband's pal was writing to say how bad he felt that her husband had been killed. Then she read the letter from her husband. He wrote about how much he missed her: "I can hardly wait till I get back – 6 if I ever do."

The woman talked a little about her husband. "He was born in a small town in Arkansas and he was an orphan since he was a small boy. He had no one but me." She said she was 29 and her husband was 34 and they had been married for two years. She said that she was pregnant with their first child. She signed her letter, Mrs. Earl Crumpton. The newspaper published her letter, and the letter from her husband. A reporter tried unsuccessfully to find her. Her letter had not carried a return address. Just "St. Louis."

Sixty years later, another reporter came across the letters and the story while doing some research. He showed them to me, and I decided to try to learn more. A colleague in the research department, Steve Bolhafner, got on the Internet and discovered that Sgt. Earl Crumpton of the Army Air Corps had been killed January 5, 1944, and his remains were returned to this country in 1949. He was buried in a mass grave in Zachary Taylor National Cemetery in Kentucky. His birthdate was given as March 6, 1916. That would mean that he was 27 when he was killed.

I called the cemetery. The man who answered the phone said they had no further information. I asked how reliable the birthdate was. All we know is what they tell us, he said.

A check with City Hall showed no birth certificates issued in 1944 with Earl Crumpton as the father. No marriage licenses with the name Earl Crumpton, either, from 1941 through 1944.

I checked with the National Personnel Records Center here in Overland. Crumpton's records were destroyed in the fire of 1973. The only new information the center had was this: Crumpton had enlisted from Ogden, Kan.

I called information. There was one Crumpton listed in Ogden. Her name is Michelle. I called her and said I was trying to learn about an Earl Crumpton who was killed in 1944. "That's my uncle," she said. I'd like to find your cousin, I said. Earl's child. She said she didn't know anything about such a cousin and referred me to her uncle, Carl Crumpton. Earl was his brother. Carl is 79 and lives in Topeka, Kan.

Carl Crumpton told me about his family. He said he was the last survivor of 10 children. The family lived in Kansas. The father was a farmer and then a blacksmith. There were eight boys and two girls. Six of the eight boys were in the war. Two of them were killed: Earl, who died in a plane crash, and Elmer, who was killed in Germany six weeks before the war ended. Both of the girls' husbands fought, too, Carl said. None of that should come as a surprise, he added. Their father, Edward, fought in the Spanish-American War and their grandfather, Pinkney Crumpton, who lived with them, was a veteran of the Civil War. He was from South Carolina and fought for the South.

I thought about the letter from 60 years ago. "He was born in a small town in Arkansas and was an orphan since he was a small boy. He had no one but me."

Carl said he knew about the letter. Shortly after it was published, somebody from St. Louis sent it to them. Nobody in the family had heard that Earl was married, but whoever sent them the letter, knew who the woman was. One of Earl's sisters, Betty Jane, contacted the woman. The woman and Earl were not really married, Carl said. Betty Jane died last December, and so there was no way to learn the girlfriend's name, Carl said.

Was she really pregnant?

"We don't know," Carl said.

He said that Earl had girlfriends all over. He was tall and handsome, and a boxer of some renown. By the way, the cemetery had it right. Earl was 27 when he died.

"He was quite a rounder," Carl said. "He used to say, 'Why marry one and disappoint hundreds?' That was a favorite saying of his. He probably had girlfriends in London."

So the mystery of 60 years ago remains a mystery. We can only guess at parts of it. Did the woman in St. Louis make up that stuff about Earl being an orphan, or was that a line he used? Was he really in love with her, or was she one of many?

Personally, I like to think he was in love with her. The fact that he was a playboy in his youth – a rounder, as his brother put it – means little. The war could have changed his notions about what really matters in life. He must have talked about her. After all, his buddy wrote to her to tell her of his death. Perhaps the buddy realized that his letter would be the only way she'd learn of his death. The government did not notify girlfriends.

Carl told me he wrote a little something about Earl's death, and it was published in the newspaper in Topeka. It was about the personal effects that the government sent to their mother. One pair of shoes, one pair of shorts, one tie, one belt buckle, one handkerchief, two pairs of socks, two towels, two sewing kits, one soap box, one pair of wings and insignia and one very damaged wrist watch. That was it, Carl said. A few odds and ends to mark a life.

Not quite. In this instance, there was also a letter. Two letters, really. And an enduring mystery.

—

STUDENT GETS BY WITH SOME HELP FROM MOTHER, GRANDMOTHER

MAY 16, 1999

To get to the MetroLink that would take her to the University of Missouri at St. Louis campus, Toya Like first had to take the bus down Vandeventer. That trip took her past the cocktail lounge where her mother once worked, and so it was natural to think of her mom every day as she headed toward school.

Her mother, Marvina Mayweather, was murdered in October 1986. A former boyfriend shot her, and the newspaper account of the shooting stated that Marvina was trying to get a court order to keep the guy away. Toya was 8 years old at the time, so she knew nothing about any problems or court orders, but the night before the shooting, when her mother tucked her in bed, her mother had said, "Even if something happens to me, I'll always be with you." She has been, is what Toya would tell you today, but metaphysics aside, the person who has really been there these last 13 years is Viola Austin, Marvina's mother.

Viola is one strong woman. Her sister Dolly had died shortly before Marvina was murdered, and Viola had taken in Dolly's youngest child. He was a teen-ager. Then when Marvina was murdered, Viola took in her two daughters, Toya and Pauletta, who is a year and some months younger than Toya.

Viola is a seamstress, and a believer in hard work. She passed that on to Toya and Pauletta, but Pauletta got sidetracked. She got pregnant in high school and she didn't get her diploma. She finally got her GED, and then she became a certified nurse's assistant, so she's doing fine.

Toya, meanwhile, became something of a whiz. She graduated from Beaumont High School – she had been on the drill team, and Viola had sewn the team's uniforms – and Toya earned an academic scholarship to the University of Missouri at St. Louis. She was thinking of going to law school someday, but she took "Introduction to Criminology" her first semester, and she was hooked.

This was real-life stuff. Not only did Toya know too much about the impact of crime on victims' families, but she had seen her own neighborhood deteriorate, and while a lot of her good friends from high school had gone on to college, she knew too many people who had "graduated" to prison.

She wanted nothing more than to research all of this. She wanted to understand how crime impacts the minority community. As you'd expect from a bright kid who is enthused and inspired, she did well.

Then she got pregnant.

That could have been the end of Toya's dream, but it wasn't. Viola wouldn't let it be. Then, too, a lot of credit has to go to Toya. She juggled her schedule to include school, work and her daughter, Tamara. The child's father, Tebyron Graham, has also helped, and he and Toya are still together and planning to get married.

Still, when Toya talks about help, she mostly talks about her grandmother.

There was a class, for instance, that was only offered in the evening, and Toya's schedule was such that she was rushing from school to the day-care center and then back to school for the class. Viola was getting home from her job with no time to spare, and the only way the schedule could be worked out was for Viola to come straight to campus and take her great-granddaughter from her granddaughter just as class began, and that's exactly the way the threesome did it for the entire semester. Viola took Tamara from Toya as she rushed into class, and who can say that Marvina, who had once promised to be always be there, wasn't there, and smiling, too?

I visited Toya Friday morning. She lives in a three-family flat. An uncle lives in the second apartment, and Pauletta lives in the third. "Did I mention we were a close family?" Toya said, and she laughed.

She was taking a day off, getting ready for graduation the next night. She told me she intends to continue her education, and she plans to get her doctorate in criminology.

First, though, would come graduation, and Toya said she was going to have a number of people at the ceremony. Family-family and church-family from the Centennial Missionary Baptist Church. Too many names to get them all in the paper, but I agreed to make a special effort to get Viola Austin's name in the story, and, of course, I promised I would mention Marvina Mayweather, who is never far from her daughter's thoughts, and who used to work at a lounge that years later, her daughter would pass daily on her way to a better life.

—

Bill McClellan

CHAPTER FOUR

—— BELIEVE IT OR NOT

SECULAR HUMANISTS NOW FIND OURSELVES ON THE OUTSIDE

MAY 29, 2005

"I'm driving to New Orleans,
got a half a tank of gas,
Got a Jesus on my dashboard,
got a third wife on my (behind). . . ."

I was cruising through the night somewhere between Springfield and Rolla. The big trucks were rolling along I-44. Maybe the truckers were talking to each other. I had only my radio for company. I went from country music to country preaching.

The preacher was talking about the direction north. "North is," he began, but static – the devil's own noise? – interrupted, and the next thing I heard was the preacher saying that the Bible confirms that theory about north. "I'm gonna give you the verses," he said. "You may want to write these down." I heard him say "Isaiah," but that was it. I had this flash: Somewhere out there in the night, people were scribbling down those verses, hands were reaching for Bibles. Another flash: Those are the people in charge.

These are difficult times for secular humanists. You know who you are. You probably profess a belief in God. You may even go to church on a regular basis, but you go as much for the sense of community as for anything spiritual. Do you believe in heaven and hell? Well, not exactly.

Sec-Humes have had things our way for a long time. We own pop culture. Except for the occasional odd duck like Mel Gibson, Hollywood is ours. The media, too. I can tell you from being on the inside of this media beast, we are mostly liberals, but you might be surprised by the number of conservatives in our ranks. But the hard-core religious, the True Believers? Not many of them. If the country is divided between those who talk regularly with God and the rest of us who occasionally ask for a favor, the media is dominated by the favor-askers.

Politics, too. Religion used to be a prop. Being photographed at church was as important as being photographed hunting. That's the way the True Believers were seen – as an interest group. Something like the National Rifle Association, but not as well-organized.

The True Believers and the Sec-Humes get along all right when we mingle. Everybody knows somebody from the other side. But mostly, there was, and is, this sense of mistrust. They question our godless values. We think they're unsophisticated.

They've never had a president before. At least not in our lifetimes. There can be arguments about the Founding Fathers, but in our era, only Jimmy Carter came close, and there was something, well, worldly about Carter. Born again? Yes. But he was a nuclear engineer. He believed in science.

President George W. Bush says he is unconvinced about evolution, and I believe him. I do not think he is playing to his political base. He went to the best schools, the ones that produce the most sophisticated people, but it is as if the education did not take. How many people graduated from Andover, Yale and Harvard and do not believe in evolution? Possibly only one.

Let me quickly add that I am not one of those hysterical people who think that the restrictions on stem cell research will prevent discoveries. The pharmaceutical companies are international entities, and while the research will not be done in this country, any discoveries will be made available to us. All we lose is the research jobs. We may have lost them already. My daughter is a biology major and for one of her classes, there is no textbook. The knowledge advances too quickly. By the time a book is written and published, it is obsolete. So the students read studies and journals. Most of these advances are being made in other countries. But unless you're a research scientist, that will not affect you.

So why, you might ask, are these difficult days of Sec-Humes? Well, we've never been on the outside before. We were always the ones who marginalized the others. Now everything seems to be about faith. Islam? Who gave a thought to Islam before? The evangelical vote? We were more comfortable with soccer moms.

I fiddled with the radio dial and found some more country music. But somewhere in the night, just beyond my understanding, somebody was reading Isaiah.

—

VERDICT IN TANGLED CASE DOESN'T EXPLAIN WHAT HAPPENED ON THAT ROOF

MARCH 18, 2001

The country preacher told me that he sometimes goes to bed Saturday night without knowing what he's going to say in the pulpit in the morning, but he has learned not to worry. God takes care of these things.

I knew the preacher in another life. Back then, he was a detective with the St. Louis Police Department. I didn't know him well, but he seemed like a hard man whose world was a very rough place. Still, he had a soft side, even then. I remember him once talking about street people. He spoke with a sensitivity I had not expected. He grew up in the Bootheel town of Kennett, and when he retired from the police department, he left the city and moved to a place on the Gasconade River. He quit drinking.

He started going to church. Eventually, he became a preacher. He's got his own church now. He doesn't come into the city very often, but he was here last week for the trial of his son, Robert Dodson Jr.

The preacher and I spoke in the hallway outside the courtroom. He told me about the changes in his life. Big changes, indeed. He had not been a churchgoer when he lived in the city. "You wouldn't have expected this, would you?" he said of his new calling.

Absolutely not, but that was the kind of trial this was. Very strange.

By the way, the preacher's longtime partner was a detective named Bill Zipf. I didn't see him at the trial, but his brother, Tom Zipf, is now a police captain, the commander of the 9th District. The captain stopped in at the trial for a short time and stood with the other cops who were there to support Dodson, who was, as you know, accused of murder. Dodson and another cop had gone on to the roof of a pawnshop to arrest two burglars. One of the burglars, Julius Thurman, later died from an injury to his head.

At any rate, Capt. Zipf came in to show his support for Dodson – the son of his brother's partner – and during a break in the trial, chatted amiably with Dwight Warren, the assistant circuit attorney who was prosecuting Dodson. Before he became a prosecutor, Warren had been a cop. He went through the police academy with Capt. Zipf, and because the academy believed in law and order of the alphabetical sort, Warren and Zipf spent a lot of time together.

If Warren felt at all conflicted, he handled it well. He finished his closing argument with a reference to John Kennedy's "Profiles in Courage." Those stories were about people who did their duty, he told the jury. That's what I'm asking you to do, he said. Duty isn't something you always do with relish, but you do it anyway, he said.

He spoke softly, as if he were talking to himself. Perhaps in a sense, he was.

"I thought it was a very effective closing argument," said Devereaux Cannick, an attorney from New York who is representing the Thurman family. We spoke while the jury deliberated. Cannick is a former prosecutor who is now in private practice. His firm – Aiello, Cannick & Esposito – is also representing the family of Amadou Diallo, the West African immigrant who was shot and killed by police in New York City in 1999. The officers shot Diallo when he reached for his wallet, and the officers thought he was reaching for a gun. His family is suing the city for $81 million.

Cannick said he attended the trial in which those officers were acquitted of murder and other state charges. He said he had not been impressed with that prosecution. It had seemed half-hearted, insincere. This effort in St. Louis, he said, seemed genuine.

Of course, the state had a huge problem. Dodson was a cop who climbed onto a roof in the darkness to apprehend a burglar. If he then gets in a fight with the burglar, how can you accuse him of murder?

Furthermore, the only witness against him was another burglar.

But the defense had a problem of its own. The defense was not arguing that Dodson had struck Thurman in the back of the head with a heavy flashlight during a struggle on the roof. The defense was arguing that Dodson had not struck Thurman in the back of the head at all. Dodson didn't carry a heavy flashlight. He didn't carry a nightstick, either. That was the defense position, and it was consistent with the original police report Dodson had written.

Well, SOMETHING happened to Thurman, and the defense would have to deal with that reality.

Defense attorney Chet Pleban tossed out three theories. Maybe one of the other burglars had accidentally struck Thurman in the head with a sledgehammer while they were unsuccessfully trying to break into a safe. That seemed far-fetched. Maybe Thurman had suffered the injury in a fall. Could not have happened, said the state's doctors. Certainly could have, countered the doctors who testified for the defense. The third defense the ory was that maybe the other cop on the roof delivered the fatal blow while helping Dodson subdue Thurman.

Who knows?

The other burglar who was on the roof testified that Dodson beat Thurman after Thurman was handcuffed. On the other hand, that burglar admitted he had previously lied about several things, including how many people originally participated in the burglary. One guy had left before the cops arrived, and the burglar didn't want to give up a friend.

The other cop who was on the roof testified that he had not seen Dodson strike Thurman at all. I listened to him and I wondered - would he, like the burglar, lie for a friend? I've heard combat veterans say there comes a time when you realize that in a way, you have more in common with your en emy than with the people back home. It's the enemy who shares the jungle and the bugs and the darkness with you.

I'm not saying that the cops and the burglars in this case have much in common except that for a brief time on a dark night, they shared a roof. Those of us who weren't there will never know what really happened.

After the jury came back with its not guilty verdict - the right verdict, I thought - I spoke briefly with the country preacher. I asked if he knew what he'd be talking about this Sunday.

Not yet, he said, and he said it like a man who really does believe that God takes care of these things.

MIDNITE BASKETBALL FAILED TO MAKE THE PROPER 'CONNECTION'
NOVEMBER 2, 1998

As the Midnite Basketball trial progresses this week, prosecutor Pat Kiernan will try to convince the jury that Darryl "Pee Wee" Lenard stole money from the league over which he presided, and Lenard's lawyers will argue that the league was so poorly managed that it is impossible to prove that anybody stole anything.

A failed experiment the league was, no matter how you look at it. But let me take you to the early morning hours of February 26, 1994. Friday night had turned into Saturday morning. The clock at the Wohl Recreation Center on North Kingshighway had the time at 2:53. Despite the late hour, the stands were nearly packed.

Sean Tunstall was at the free throw line.

There was, at that moment, a sense of magic in the air. After all, this was the first night of the great experiment. The city's first black mayor, Freeman Bosley Jr., was an enthusiastic supporter of the notion that all things are connected. You can't curb crime unless you can create jobs, and you can't create jobs unless you have better schools, and you can't have better schools unless you have stronger neighborhoods, and you can't build stronger neighborhoods unless you can curb crime, and you can't do anything unless you have everybody working together.

And that's really what Midnite Basketball was supposed to be about.

It was, at its core, an anti-crime program, a way to get young men off the streets and into the gym. But as Bosley envisioned it, the program was going to be so much more. Once the young men were in the gym, then all these other connections would come into play. Players would be required to take computer classes. They'd have to get into a life-skills program. They'd learn about responsibility. The program was aimed at young black men, and it would be funded by the white business community.

And now, on the very first night, at the end of a second overtime in the last of four games, Sean Tunstall was at the free throw line with the game tied.

Oh, such synergy.

You see, Tunstall was exactly the kind of young man this program could rescue.

He had been a huge star at Vashon, where he had led his team to two state championships. He had gone to the University of Kansas and had played on a national championship team.

Then, while at Kansas, he was busted for selling drugs. He went to prison. His life was in tatters. Midnite Basketball was his second chance.

Of course, as we know now, the experiment failed. The jury that is hearing the case will decide whether any criminal acts were involved, but no matter how the case turns out, the program failed. Its failure was instrumental in Bosley's re-election defeat.

In October of 1997, Tunstall was murdered. He had been shooting baskets at the Wohl Recreation Center, and he was standing in the parking lot talk ing to a friend. A gunman walked up and shot him.

The cops figured it was a drug killing. Unpaid debts or something.

A couple of months later, while investigating a different murder, the cops arrested a fellow named Montrell Futrell. The gun he had turned out to be the weapon that had killed Tunstall.

But the cops couldn't put the Tunstall murder on Futrell, and truth is, they didn't think he was good for it, anyway. The fellow they suspected, a friend of Futrell's, was later taken down by the feds for something else.

Futrell, by the way, is scheduled to go on trial for that different murder later this month. He'll be right down the hall from the courtroom where the Midnite Basketball trial is currently going on.

It's like Bosley used to say. All things are connected.

Oh, I almost forgot. Tunstall made the free throws. It really was a grand night.

—

NATURE AS ART MAY TRIUMPH IN CASE OF DEAD TREE

DECEMBER 15, 2003

Betty Wynn is an unusual defendant, and so it is not surprising that the case against her has taken a strange turn. A very strange turn.

Regular readers might recall that Betty is charged with having a dead tree in her back yard. The case has its beginnings more than two years ago when an inspector from Olivette went to a house on Pricewoods Lane to check out a complaint of an unkempt lawn, and discovered that there was more to this than high grass. There was a dead tree in the back yard. You'll have to cut the grass and remove the tree, said the inspector. Betty agreed to cut the grass, but the dead tree had a certain meta-physical value. When did it die? Shortly after Betty had been in a car

Bill McClellan

accident. She survived that accident, and she believed that the tree had died in her place. You don't cut down a tree that died in your stead. You honor it. Besides, AmerenUE had already cut down the taller section that had been up in the wires, and what was left was a 15-foot stump. To Betty's eye, it was more like a sculpture than a stump. So that was her defense. She didn't have a dead tree in her yard. She had a piece of art.

Betty is 89 years old, and she lives with her brother, Sam Lachterman. They inherited the house in Olivette from their brother, Julius. He was an accountant. Betty and Sam are both graduates of Washington University, but neither ever spent much time in the mainstream economy. For years, they have been part of the campus scene, looking like street people, but attending lectures and exhibits. They are especially well known for attending functions at which food is served.

Sam has stayed out of the dead tree case. Betty says he believes the government should not concern itself with dead trees. So Betty has handled the case. She lost at the local level in Olivette, and then appealed that loss. The case then went to court in St. Louis County.

By a stroke of good fortune, the case ended up in front of Associate Circuit Court Judge Michael Jamison. He is a smart fellow, a former assistant general counsel for Anheuser-Busch. He did not dismiss Betty's argument as frivolous. Dead tree as art? He knew that there is a dead tree sculpture at Laumeier Sculpture Park. Of course, the dead tree has been dandied up a little bit. So Jamison called Jeff Pike, the dean of the art school at Washington University. Would any of Pike's students want to look at this dead tree in Olivette and take it on as a project?

Emma Levitt took the assignment. She is in her junior year. She has a double major in sculpture and ceramics. She visited the dead tree, and came up with several ideas. She was going to cover it with clay, and give it glass limbs. She thought about doing something with ceramics. Then she came up with her final idea – a talking tree. Visually, the tree would remain as is, but Levitt would install camouflaged speakers attached to a digital audio player. Every couple of hours, the tree would recite a poem.

Friday afternoon, the judge convened court in an art department studio on Kingsland Avenue. Betty was there with her attorney, Mark Kruger. Olivette was represented by attorney Steve Moore. Levitt first suggested that the dead tree was already art. She said that the essence of art is to provoke socially relevant questions, and this tree had brought us all together to discuss the social values of suburbia. Then she discussed her proposal, which she called the Lorax Project. The Lorax is a Dr. Seuss character who speaks for trees.

Betty seemed to like the idea of having a talking tree in her back yard, but Moore, while polite and respectful, seemed dismayed. A talking tree in Olivette? What would the neighbors say? Might such a thing not invite trespassers?

The judge ended the proceedings without making a decision. As we left, I had the feeling that Olivette might just let Betty keep her stump, as long as she agrees not to let it talk.

—

FATHER'S LOVE UNITES A FAMILY ACROSS OCEANS AND YEARS

JUNE 7, 2000

Kenneth Gaeng was born in 1922. His father was a cobbler. His mother was a cook. They lived on the north side of St. Louis.

Kenneth finished eighth grade, and then it was time to go to work. He worked in a packing plant, and he worked with his father, repairing shoes. By his late teens, he had a steady girl. Her name was Rosemary Crofton, and she was beautiful. She looked like Donna Reed. Then came World War II. As happened with so many young people, Kenneth and Rosemary put their plans on hold. Kenneth went into the Marine Corps. He was sent to the Pacific. He returned to the States in May of 1945, and he came to St. Louis on a short leave. He was done with combat. He was headed to San Diego where he would be a drill instructor.

Before leaving for California, he married Rosemary.

When the war ended, Kenneth and Rosemary returned to St. Louis. They quickly started a family. Their first child was born in 1946. A

Bill McClellan

second was born in 1947 and another in 1949. A fourth was born in 1951. The last child, the eighth, was born in 1960. The family lived in a smallish house in St. Ann.

Kenneth had a shoe repair shop in St. Ann, but even in those early postwar days, we were becoming a throw-away society, and a cobbler's art counts for little when people no longer repair shoes, but simply buy another pair. When Kenneth found it difficult to support a family as a cobbler, he became a groceryman. He opened Ken's Food Mart.

The surviving kids – there are six of them – remember their child-hoods fondly. Their mother was a saint, patient and loving. Their father was hard-working, open and kind. He seldom talked about the war. He told the kids that he had contracted malaria, and he mentioned a couple of islands he'd been on, but even that is a little foggy. Bougainville and Guam. Or was it Bougainville and Guadalcanal? The kids, grown now, aren't quite sure.

The small grocery store eventually fell victim to the chains of convenience stores, and Kenneth went to work as a meat cutter.

He died in March of 1994. Rosemary died in July of 1999.

A month or so after her death, Dan Gaeng, the oldest surviving son, got a phone call from New Zealand. Actually, Dan was asleep, and his wife, Mary, answered the phone. The man on the other end said his name was Micha el, and he was Dan's brother. That is, he was the son of Dan's father. Something about a brief liaison in New Zealand during the war. What's more, the man said he was one of three brothers. This liaison had resulted in triplets. Needless to say, Mary got Dan out of bed.

"I was floored," Dan told me. "The man said he wanted to learn about the family, and I told him that if this were true, I'd help him in any way I could."

After the conversation, Dan pondered the situation. Coming so close on the heels of his mother's death, it had the feeling of a scam. But that made no sense. It wasn't as if there was much of an estate.

Dan and Michael agreed to communicate by e-mail. Michael said that as he understood the story, his father, their father, had spent only a few days in New Zealand and had never realized that his liaison had resulted in children. Michael said that his mother became ill when he and his brothers were very young, and so the boys had grown up in foster homes. One had died at the age of 18. The other two had always wondered about their father, whose name they thought was Kenneth Geange. Finally, after years of searching, Michael had found his way to the military record center and to Kenneth Gaeng of St. Louis, and hence to the Gaeng family.

It was a plausible enough story, but what really convinced Dan were the photographs the man sent via e-mail. As soon as Dan saw the pictures, he knew the man was his father's son. Dan called a family meeting.

"I figured it was something about Mom's estate," said brother Dave. "Then Dan told us about the call and showed us the pictures of the triplets. They looked more like Dad than we do."

On Christmas Eve, the brothers and sisters got together and called New Zealand and then Australia, where, John, the second of the surviving triplets lives. Long talks they were, and good, too, and the two brothers from Down Under agreed to come to St. Louis to meet the family they never knew they had. They'll be arriving this weekend with their wives, and they'll be staying in the house in St. Ann in which their half siblings were raised.

Forget that half sibling stuff. As far as the Gaengs are concerned, their newly discovered brothers are just that. In fact, I mentioned that maybe it was a good thing that this discovery came after Rosemary's death. After all, some wives would have a hard time handling this kind of news.

I made that remark during an interview with several of the siblings at the family home in St. Ann. Jane, one of the sisters, politely dismissed the idea that their mother would have been upset.

"If Mom would have heard about this, she'd have put them in the Christmas drawing," Jane said, and the other siblings laughed in agreement.

"Had Dad known, he'd have wanted to help them," added Dan.
Everybody agreed with that, too, and I realized that while it has taken Michael and John many years to find their family, it is an awfully nice family that they've finally found.

———

D'ARCY WAS TOAST OF THE TOWN BEFORE MORE SOBER TIMES

MARCH 29, 2002

There was a time when the lunchtime crowd at Anthony's Bar would be thick with D'Arcy guys, and each of them would have a bottle of beer next to his plate. They had to. I mean, they had to. Anheuser-Busch was one of the ad agency's accounts, and the agency was strict about supporting its clients. If a fellow worked on the Budweiser account, he had better not be seen having lunch without a bottle of Bud, and it was the same way, of course, for the fellows who worked on the Michelob and Natural Light accounts.

Not that you had to force the ad guys to drink. In fact, if you looked closely at that lunchtime crowd of long ago, you'd see that more than one of the fellows dutifully displayed a beer while drinking a martini. Or three. But that was then, and this is now. The lunchtime crowd at Anthony's on Thursday was filled with ice-tea drinkers, and if anybody in the crowd worked at D'Arcy, there was no way of knowing. And soon, there will be no more D'Arcy in St. Louis.

The agency, now based in New York and known as D'Arcy, Masius, Benton & Bowles, announced Wednesday that it was closing its St. Louis office. That office, incidentally, employs 40 people.

Twenty years ago, there were 10 times that many. The agency had several longtime clients, but none more important – nor more long-standing – than Anheuser-Busch. Mother brewery, it was called. The agency got the brewery account in 1915. It wouldn't be too much of a stretch to say that as far as the agency was concerned, "When you've said Bud, you've said it all."

In fact, the agency did say that. Wally Armbruster came up with that line. He started at D'Arcy in 1940 as an office boy, and he retired in 1984 as an executive vice president. He never attended college. He was a gangly man, and he grunted and scratched and grimaced whenever he thought, and he was all the time thinking. He smoked all the time, too, and he absent-mindedly flicked his ashes any old place. He worked on the account for Milnot, a dairy substitute, and he came up with the line, "If cows could, they'd give Milnot."

As far as job security was concerned, D'Arcy seemed a surprisingly stable place in an industry noted for instability. There was, however, a legend among the lunchtime drinkers that Gussie Busch demanded a body a year. They made it sound like a sacrifice. Once a year, a group of D'Arcy executives would have a meeting with Gussie. Usually, it would be out of town. Gussie would lose patience with somebody, the story went, and Gussie's will could not be thwarted.

"Twenty-one of us went to South Carolina," a lunchtime drinker might say. "Twenty of us came back."

So closely linked were D'Arcy and the brewery that brewery heir James Orthwein became the agency head in 1970. He led the agency into a series of mergers, and the agency seemed to thrive. What happened, then, to cause the agency's demise?

Some analysts might point to the area's shrinking skyline of corporate headquarters. D'Arcy represented Southwestern Bell and TWA and had a chunk of Ralston Purina's business. Maybe it's impossible to be a big-time ad agency if you're not in a big-time town. Then again, Anheuser-Busch is still here, but the brewery pulled the Michelob account in 1988 and the Budweiser account in 1994, and by 1996, the agency had none of the brewery's business.

I thought about all of this as I sat in Anthony's on Thursday. It's no longer a rowdy place at noon. It struck me as I looked around that D'Arcy – and the whole region, for that matter – began to slide just about the time Americans quit drinking at lunch. I really can't explain it. Maybe St. Louisans did better work when we had a couple of shots at lunch. Or maybe the rest of the country did worse after a couple of shots, and we can't compete now that everybody is sober.

It was the kind of topic the guys from D'Arcy would have relished.

—

PETE STUPP'S TRIAL INCLUDED EVERYONE BUT THE MISTRESS

The Stupp family of St. Louis made its considerable fortune in the steel business, but these are bad days for American steel, and worse days for the Stupps. That's what I thought last week when Erwin Peter Stupp III went to trial. He was charged with stealing.

It was a case that owed more to Tennessee Williams than Sir Arthur Conan Doyle. Stupp's two sisters, both of whom seemed unpretentious and not at all like heiresses, testified against their brother. Stupp testified. So did a parade of interesting characters who live on the fringes of legality. But the main character was missing. Neither side called Michelle Hunt. She was the heart of the case.

Pete Stupp, who is 46 years old and married, met Ms. Hunt at a girlie joint across the river. Before long, he had set her up in an apartment in Frontenac. He and his wife temporarily separated. His father, Erwin Peter Stupp Jr., chairman of Stupp Brothers Inc., did not approve of his son's affair. His disapproval grew when federal agents executed a search warrant at Midwest Bank Centre in February of 2000. The Stupp family is the majority owner of the bank, and Pete was its chief executive. The agents wh o visited the bank wanted Pete's computer files. This is not bank business, they said.

No charges were ever filed, and there are a number of stories floating around about what the feds were looking for. All the stories mention Eddie Cotton, which brings us back to Michelle Hunt. Cotton was her special friend. Yes, even as Pete paid her rent, Ms. Hunt had a friend.

At any rate, the father was unhappy with Pete. The father died in September of 2000. To the outside world, nothing seemed amiss. In fact, Pete gave the eulogy at the memorial service. But several days later, when family members and attorneys gathered in the living room of the family home in Ladue for the reading of the will, Pete got the bad news. He would receive one-sixth of the estate. Each of his sisters would receive five-twelfths.

Not that one-sixth was anything to sneeze at. The estate was supposed to be worth around $29 million. If so, Pete would get about $5 million. Plus, the will stipulated that Pete would receive his father's gun collection, all his hunting equipment, and a full one-third share of the personal property. That would include his father's art collection.

Two nights after the reading of the will, the house was burglarized. Some guns and some very expensive artwork, including three paintings by Oscar Berninghaus, were taken. The police thought the whole thing was very odd. There seemed to be no sign of forced entry. More to the point, the thief had known the code to the burglar alarm system, which had been deactivated and then turned back on. Very strange.

When the detectives talked to Pete, he seemed nervous. So the cops talked to Cotton, who knew Pete and seemed like the sort of fellow who ought to be checked out. He said he knew nothing about any burglary.

A couple of months later, Robert Stupp, the late Erwin's brother, was at an art gallery in Scottsdale, Ariz. He saw one of the stolen Berninghaus paintings, "The Overland Mail." Police worked backward, from the gallery to a dealer in Texas, and eventually to Joel Flaaen, a long-haired fellow in the Kansas City area who hung around in cowboy bars and seemed an unlikely aficionado of the arts. Sure enough. He said he bought a whole bunch of stuff from Eddie Cotton. He said he paid Cotton a total of about $19,000. Appraisers say the value of the stolen goods was approximately $800,000.

The detectives brought Cotton in again. Faced with the fact that the property had been recovered, he changed his story. He had taken that stuff from the Stupp house, he said, but he had done so with Pete. It was stuff Pete was inheriting, anyway, Cotton said. Pete wanted him to store it in Kansas City. Cotton said he and a friend, Ray Huffine, had met Pete at the house. Pete had unlocked the door, turned off the burglar alarm and had then told them what to take. The cops talked to Huffine, who gave them the same story.

Phone records showed that Pete had made two calls to Cotton's cell phone on the day of the burglary, and Cotton had called Pete's cell phone that evening. So Pete was arrested.

The state had a couple of major problems at the trial. One was motive. Why would Pete steal guns when he was going to inherit them? Why would he steal artwork, which would have to be fenced at pennies to the dollar, when he was going to inherit a third of it, anyway?

The state's other problem was Eddie Cotton. If all he had done was move some stuff that Pete had inherited, why had he originally lied to the police? Also, his story didn't seem believable. If somebody had inherited artwork and guns, why would he want the stuff moved at night, and why would he want it stored in Kansas City?

Cotton is a husky fellow with short hair and a neatly trimmed beard. He came to court wearing an American flag on the lapel of his sports jacket, but it didn't help. He denied all wrongdoing and claimed to think it was quite logical for a man to store his inheritance at the home of a fence in Kansas City.

The only positive for the state was that Cotton did not strike me as a fellow who could have figured out how to deactivate a burglar alarm. So that was a problem for the defense.

Defense attorneys Art Margolis and his son, Bill, attacked that problem by ignoring it. Instead, they concentrated on the positives. Pete testified that he had no reason to steal anything. He had a receipt showing that he had been having dinner at the time Cotton claimed they were at his father's house. He said he had called Cotton because he was trying to get in touch with Michelle.

In his closing argument, Art Margolis said that Pete was guilty of one thing, and that was Michelle Hunt. The jury must have agreed because on Thursday afternoon, they voted to acquit.

The acquittal did not seem to mend any fences within the family. Pete shrugged it off and said the Stupp family has been feuding for 75 years.

I called Flaaen on Friday. He has pleaded guilty to three counts of receiving stolen property in the case. He has received probation. I told him he was the only person found guilty in the whole affair.

"That seems strange," he said.

By the way, Ms. Hunt and Cotton are now living in Arizona.

—

WRITER'S MUSINGS FORM PRETTY PACKAGE OF PAST AND PRESENT

DECEMBER 27, 1998

As is his habit, the columnist put things off until the last minute, and so it was only this week that he began to think about coming up with a Christmas column.

Actually, there was some confusion about whether he would even have a Christmas column, what with Christmas falling on a Friday. His newspaper, the Montgomery County News, is published on Tuesdays, Thursdays and Saturdays, and his column appears on Saturdays. So he originally figured he wouldn't be doing a Christmas column this year. I mean, you can't write a holiday column after the holiday. Even a young columnist knows that.

Bob Bliss is 87. I visited him at his home in Hillsboro, Ill., a couple of weeks ago. It was like chatting with the Ghost of Christmas Future.

"Do you still interview people, Bob?" I asked.

"My hearing isn't good enough," he said. "Plus, my eyes are so bad I wouldn't be able to read my own notes."

Doesn't matter, I said. Your musings are plenty good enough from what I've seen.

"I dream of interviewing people," he said, and then he told me of a recent dream. It involved a woman who'd been falsely accused of something, and Bob was running around, trying to sort fact from fiction, and as he recounted his dream, I realized that if I live long enough, this would be my future. You write for a newspaper long enough, and eventually you cross an invisible line.

That Bliss would someday dream of newspaper stories was written in the wind a long time ago. A cold wind, too, according to family lore. It was blowing and snowing, the story goes, on the February day in 1892 when Charles W. Bliss, then a middle-aged attorney, left the courthouse, walked down the street and bought the local newspaper.

He was tired of the law, some folks would tell you. His daddy had been a frontier preacher, and Charles wanted his own pulpit, others would say.

At any rate, Charles threw himself into newspapering. He could imagine no higher calling than that of a country newspaper editor. In one of his early issues, he told the readers what to expect.

"The Montgomery News strives to be something more than a mere neighborhood gossip or a Mrs. Grundy, but it realizes the fact that it must and does record a lot of tittle-tattle and piffle in which the readers are interested. This is necessary in every country paper, and we have no apologies to offer for doing so."

So there was tittle-tattle, and there was substance, but mostly, there was fun. In the beginning, the News was using a weather forecast that had been published elsewhere, and when the proprietor of the elsewhere demanded payment, Bliss informed his readers that he would issue his own monthly forecasts.

Did he ever. They were usually more about politics than weather, and if the weather forecasts didn't seem entirely serious, well, Bliss explained that he was doing the best he could do with the methodology available. He used the breast bone of a goose.

"If the bone is white and clear, the winter will be open and mild. If it is discolored and covered with dark shadings, the winter will be severe. . . . The black splotches and shadings indicate just what part of the winter be stormy and cold," he wrote.

But the bone would not work, he wrote, if the goose from which it was taken was more than a year old or if the goose had ever squatted on ice.

Not surprisingly, Charles Bliss was soon getting a lot of attention. The Chicago Tribune wrote about him in 1895, and the Post-Dispatch published a feature story about the Hillsboro humorist in 1897.

He continued writing until his death in 1931, but by then he had turned the newspaper over to his son, Clinton.

Of Clinton I know little. (There was a book, "The Goose Bone Papers," written about Charles.) But Clinton was Bob's father, and Bob once told me a story that I suspect speaks volumes about the kind of newspaperman that Clinton was.

It seems he took Bob to the county jail one day to visit a man accused of murder. The man had told police that he hadn't been anywhere near the murder scene. Clinton went to see this man and took young Bob along.

"I wasn't even there," the man told Clinton.

"My son happened to be out that night," Clinton said, nodding toward Bob. "He saw you out there."

Nothing of the sort had happened, but what the heck, Clinton must have thought. It was worth a try.

"I'm sticking to my story," the man said.

Even though it didn't work, it tells me something about Clinton. A heck of a newspaper guy.

Bob and his brother, Tom, took over the paper in 1934. Tom took care of the business side, and Bob did most of the reporting. He did weddings, court stories, sports and editorials. Sometimes his editorials were slapped on the front page.

Because they were particularly important issues?

"Importance had nothing to do with it," Bob told me. "We'd put them on the front page when we were short of news. It's like my grandfather used to say, 'Any fool can put out a newspaper when there's a lot of news, but you have to be smart when there's not.' "

It looked like Bob and Tom were going to be the last of the family, as far as newspapering was concerned. None of the next generation seemed interested.

One of Bob's daughters, Nancy, had gone to Northwestern to study Russian and Russian culture. She went to the Soviet Union on a student trip. In Leningrad, she met Richard Slepika, who had majored in Russian and English at Stanford.

They came home, and married, and went to a Navajo reservation to work for a dental clinic.

"We finally figured that if we wanted to save the world, maybe we ought to start at home," Nancy said, and in 1971, they came to work at the Montgomery County News.

In 1978, Bob retired, and they took over. Well, Bob didn't actually retire. He became a columnist.

Which brings us back, of course, to the Christmas column. Daughter Nancy decided that her father should do a Christmas column. It would be published on Thursday.

"I'll think of something," Bob told me when I talked with him Monday night. "I had a pretty good one last year."

It was shortly before Christmas 1916. Bob was 5 years old. He'd seen a red bicycle that he wanted very much. Bob lived in a house at the edge of town, and there was a barn, and a chicken coop and all the other outbuildings that you associate with a farm.

Shortly before Christmas, Bob was playing in the barn, and he found his red bicycle hidden in the hay. He said nothing, and come Christmas morning, there it was next to the tree. A gift from Santa.

A timeless story of joy and heartbreak mingled together.

"Maybe I'll do one this year about the time I built a doll house. Blue prints and all," he told me.

But he didn't. He opted for a nice little story about Christmas trees. It began when he was a kid, lying on his belly cutting down a cedar. It ended this year, as his daughter and granddaughter decorated his tree while he sat in the recliner.

Quite nice, I thought. The ghost of Christmas Future bringing Christmas past and present together.

—

YOUR CREDIT HISTORY CAN BE CLUELESS ABOUT THE REAL YOU

OCTOBER 21, 2005

If you don't think the world has gotten too impersonal, let me tell you about Nancy Belgeri. She went to the Sears store in Crestwood earlier this month. She picked out a pair of blue jeans and took them to the counter. She handed her Sears MasterCard to the cashier. The card was issued in March. It expires in March of 08. It says on the card: Member since 1978. The cashier tried to process the sale. The charge was denied. Belgeri was surprised and asked why the charge had been denied.

The cashier said she didn't know, and then asked if Belgeri would like to apply for another card and use the new one. Belgeri said yes, but after a short wait, her application was denied. She then paid for the jeans with a different credit card.

Belgeri is 77 years old. She owns her own home. No mortgage. She pays her bills on time. She wondered about that problem at Sears – she told me she couldn't sleep the night it happened – and she figured that perhaps somebody had stolen her identity and ruined her credit.

The next day, she called the number on the back of her Sears Master-Card. She was bounced around a bit but finally got this word: The original card had been canceled several months ago after Sears learned of the death of Belgeri's husband, Harry. Although Belgeri's name was on her card, Harry had been the primary cardholder. And the denial of the new card? She did not have enough credit under her own name.

Sure enough. She received a letter from Sears a few days later: Dear Applicant, Thank you for your recent request for credit. We regret that we are unable to approve your request at this time for the following reason(s): INSUFFICIENT CREDIT HISTORY. Sincerely, Credit Services.

I called Credit Services, but the woman I spoke with said she could not discuss the case because of privacy concerns.

That's too bad. I would have liked to tell her a bit about Nancy Belgeri. It is true that her husband died in December of 2003. But it's also true that he had been disabled since 1965. From that time on, Nancy was the primary breadwinner for the two of them and their six children. Nancy was well-suited to the task.

She grew up in Pine Lawn. She was one of 15 children. Her mother was a seamstress. Her dad worked in concrete. The family did not have a lot of money. Nancy graduated from high school and enrolled in a nursing program but dropped out at 19 to get married. She had six children in eight years. Her husband was a bartender. She worked as a licensed practical nurse. Her husband developed cancer of the larynx in 1965. He could not return to work as a bartender because of the smoky atmosphere. He occasionally picked up part-time, minimum-wage jobs. Most of the time he watched the kids.

Nancy went back to school to become a registered nurse. She continued working full time as an LPN while going to school. She graduated in 1974. That was the same year her husband's health deteriorated to the point he could not work at all. Nancy cared for him at home until he had a massive stroke in 2001. He spent the last 19 months of his life at a skilled nursing facility.

Although Nancy had pretty much retired to care for her husband, she never really quit working. Even at 77, she still works 10-15 hours a week at St. Joseph Hospital of Kirkwood. She was recently named Nurse of the Year in her unit.

Now it might be that some – maybe most, maybe all – of her credit cards list her husband as the primary cardholder, and apparently that's enough for Sears to deny her credit. But the "dear applicant" with the "insufficient credit history" supported six children and a disabled husband and has been working and paying bills for the last 58 years. In a less impersonal world, that would count for something.

—

MURDERER FORGOES HIS LAST CHANCE FOR SOME REDEMPTION

MARCH 24, 2000

Jim Hampton got his wish and was executed early Wednesday morning.

His final words were, "Take the phone off the hook." Apparently, he wanted to make sure there would be no last-second phone call from the governor. He need not have worried. Despite the efforts of death penalty opponents who argued that Hampton was incompetent to decide his own fate – I guess they had to argue something – there was no way the governor was going to spare Hampton's life. He had been given the death penalty for the 1992 murder of Frances Keaton, a 58-year-old beautician who worked in Florissant and lived in Warrenton. Her two children, both adults, attended the execution.

"He got off easy," said LaVon Bowlin, Keaton's daughter. "It was like he just went to sleep."

Keaton's death had not been so peaceful. Hampton beat her to death with a hammer. It was part of a kidnapping for ransom plan that went bad.

Also in attendance at the execution was a daughter of Christine Schurman, a New Jersey woman who was murdered by Hampton. He shot her after another botched kidnapping attempt.

I visited Hampton a few days before his execution, and I asked if he felt any remorse for either of the murders. He seemed to think the question was off-base. He said he had not intended to kill anybody. Instead, he had decided that if his plans went bad, the people would have to die. The plans went bad. The people had to die. Why would he feel remorse?

I left the interview thinking that Hampton was a bad man. Way to go, Dr. Freud, you might be saying to yourself. How astute. What an unlikely observation.

For me, though, it was unlikely. I've talked to a lot of guys in prison, and I almost always have some sympathy for them. You don't have to be a bad person to do a bad thing. That's the way I look at it.

But Hampton struck me as just plain bad. I asked him if he had committed any murders other than the two for which he had been convicted. Yes, he said. There had been six others during his long career as a criminal. Hampton, you may remember, was 62 years old.

I asked about these other murders. Were they fellow criminals? Killed when drug deals went bad, or something along those lines? Or were they like the two women we know about – innocent citizens?

More like that, said Hampton. They were people who maybe saw something they shouldn't have seen, or heard something they shouldn't have heard. For whatever reason, I thought they were a threat to my personal freedom, he said.

Bill McClellan

More than that he wouldn't say. With a fellow like Hampton, it's impossible to know what to believe. But still, he was a career criminal, a drifter, an amoral man. Other murders were possible, maybe even likely.

I talked to Hampton one last time on the phone. You've got a chance to do something good, something right, at the very end of your life, I said. Write me a letter about the other six murders. Put in enough details so we'll know you did them. Mail it to me, and I'll get it after your execution.

Why would I do that? asked Hampton.

Because there's a chance that somebody is doing time for a murder you committed, I said.

That's very possible, Hampton said. But I'm not going to do it. If I were to write a letter, the state could get ahold of it before I'm killed. If I admit to some other murders, those jurisdictions will want to talk to me, and my execution could be put on hold. I don't want to take that chance, he concluded.

And so he died – went to sleep, as LaVon Bowling described it – without taking advantage of an opportunity to do, at long last, a good thing.

—

STADIUMS AREN'T ONLY THINGS THAT AREN'T FOREVER

OCTOBER 2, 2005

Most of the official tributes to Busch Stadium will have to do with important victories or significant events – historic home runs, no-hitters and so forth – but for most of us, the memories are much more personal. For me, they are intertwined with my children.

Especially my daughter. I raised her as a Cubs fan. I tried to raise my son that way, but Jack turned on me. Too much peer pressure, too much Ozzie Smith. So any life lessons I could impart to him – and they fall heavily into the "Do as I say and not as I do" category – would have to come outside of baseball. For Jack and me, Busch Stadium has been a place to share good times, and that's it.

For my daughter, it has been something more. Lorna is a senior at the University of Illinois. She had to be at school in late August, but she came home for Labor Day weekend, in part because the Cubs were in town. We went to the game that Monday.

I am sentimental but slow. The realization did not immediately hit me that this would be our last game at Busch Stadium, the stadium where she had seen her first game, the stadium where we had lived through so much heartbreak.

Not that it was all heartbreak. It wasn't. In the early years, I used to show her off. For instance, when a Cubs pitcher would start throwing in the bullpen, I'd say – and always loudly enough so that the people around us would hear – "We've got somebody up in the pen." Lorna, barely past the toddler stage, would glance at the bullpen and say something like, "It's Bob Scanlon, Daddy." It was like a parlor trick. We watched so many games together on television that she knew all the players. People were astounded.

But that was early. As she got older, we got more serious. There is a Zen-like quality to Cubdom. One learns the virtue of suffering, the inevitability of things going wrong. Ronald Reagan was a Cubs fan – he used to announce Cubs games from a ticker-tape machine – and it was that Cubness that steadied him through the tough times. Iran-Contra? That's nothing. Cubs fans remember listening to Lou Boudreau on the radio: "Ernie Banks hits a long one! It's going, going, going, caught at the wall."

That sort of thing toughens you up. One day I turned on the radio and the announcer was not Lou Boudreau but Charley Grimm, who had been the manager the previous day. Mr. Wrigley, who owned the team, de-cided they should change places for the rest of the year. I never figured out with whom he had been unhappy – the announcer or the manager.

These were the sort of stories I told Lorna between innings.

In July 2002, we were at a game and the Cubs scored two runs in the first inning and four more in the second. We shouted. We stomped our feet. The Cubs still led by five going into the ninth. The Cardinals came back and won. Going, going, caught at the wall.

On Labor Day, Lorna wore a Cubs jersey that had been autographed by Ryne Sandberg. (Years ago, he came to town to autograph copies of his book. Lorna carried in a jersey for him to sign.) "Should you really be wearing that?" I asked. "I mean, he's in the Hall of Fame." Lorna shrugged. "If I can't wear it to a game with my dad, when can I wear it?"

Makes sense, I said, but I thought, "Yikes. A game with her dad. Stadiums aren't the only things that aren't around forever."

A couple of rows down from us was a father and a young daughter. They were both decked out in Cubs blue. It was the Ghost of Christmas Past. My heart was very full.

The Cubs trailed for most of the game. They were down by four going into the ninth. Then they rallied. They loaded the bases with nobody out. The next batter walked. They were now down by three with still nobody out and our best hitters coming up.

The little girl a few rows in front of us was jumping up and down. Lorna looked at me. "She's too young to know it always ends badly," she said.

One batter and one out later, Derek Lee, our best hitter, bounced into a double play to end the game. Somehow, it seemed right. Lorna and I walked out of Busch Stadium for the last time. I miss it already.

—

Through the Glass Darkly

WHEN A FATHER OF 18 WAS SLAIN, A GRANDSON POINTED FINGERS UNTIL A FINGER POINTED AT HIM

JULY 4, 1999

Melvin Willyard raised peacocks.

He owned three of the birds. They lived in a coop on a vacant lot next to the family home, which was located in the 3900 block of North 20th Street. That's right by Hyde Park on the near North Side. The 5th District, in police talk. Not so many years ago, the neighborhood was populated by working-class whites. Mostly Polish. Gradually, the Poles moved out and were replaced by blacks. The whites who stayed tended to be tough, hard-scrabble people. By most lights, Melvin would be included in that number. He and his wife, Martha, raised 19 children. Eighteen of them were their own, and one was a grandchild. This grandchild was not the youngest of the family – he was older than one of his aunts – and Melvin and Martha raised him as a son. The other kids who were close to him in age thought of him as a brother.

Melvin was a mechanic. He repaired and sold cars. He and Martha also ran a grocery store. That store was in the front of the house. The family lived in the back. There were plenty of makeshift bedrooms but only two bathrooms. It sounds rough, but as the grown kids remember it now, it wasn't so bad.

"It wasn't like we were poor. We'd ask for something, and Dad would see that we got it," Brenda Grant told me Wednesday afternoon. At the time, the jury was deliberating the fate of James Willyard. He is the aforementioned grandson who was raised as a son.

He was charged with first-degree murder. The state contended that he had murdered Melvin.

The murder happened on Oct. 25, 1997. Melvin was shot twice. James told the police he had witnessed the shooting. It happened right in front of the house, he told the police. It looked like a robbery. Three black guys.

Two days after the murder, James called the police. I'm looking at one of the guys who shot my dad, he said. Get over here quick.

Bill McClellan

The cops came, and James pointed to a young man on the street. A juvenile. He's one of the three guys, James said.

The cops took the youngster to juvenile detention. He was in custody for 10 days before he agreed to be interviewed. He told the cops he had an alibi for the night of the shooting. He had been to the Soldan Homecoming Dance. The alibi checked out. The youngster was released.

Not long after that, James called the cops again. He'd found another of the three men. He was 100 percent sure this time. The cops talked to the man James had fingered. He had an alibi.

By this time, the cops were taking a hard look at James. He was, frankly, the sort of fellow who invited suspicion. Five months before Melvin's murder, James had pleaded guilty to conspiracy to commit murder. The state was recommending a five-year term. James was awaiting sentencing.

Three homicide detectives – Ken Hornak, Gerald Young and Phil Wasem – brought him in for questioning. We think you're making up the story about the three black guys, they said.

James broke down. You're right, he said. I made that up. I did it to protect my mother. She shot Dad.

The detectives talked to Martha and quickly figured she had not shot her husband. It had to be James. Why else would he be accusing everybody else, including his mother? But there was no evidence against him. The cops arrested him for hindering prosecution – inventing the story about the black guys – but they didn't have enough for murder charges. The chances of this case ever getting to court seemed remote.

In May of 1998, Martha died. She was 73.

The next month, Billy Hayes went to the police. He was, and is, as strange a character as any ever invented by Elmore Leonard. Another resident of the near North Side, Billy is 40ish, heavy, an alcoholic and a homosexual. The word "gay" seems wildly inappropriate for Billy's lifestyle. He drinks a 12-pack a day on those days when he can afford to. The letters "CSA" are tattooed on his neck, and stand for an organization that cannot be mentioned in a family newspaper. According to a pretrial deposition, he used to get some kind of disability, but when the government tightened the eligibility rules, Billy was among those dropped from the rolls.

He told the cops and later testified that he and James had had a relationship and that he had been outside the Willyard home on the night of the murder. He had seen James run to the peacocks' lot and pick up a gun that was hidden there. James then went back to the house and shot Melvin, Billy said.

Based on this new evidence, James was arrested and charged with murder. He went to trial last week.

It was an odd case even before it officially began. Normally, the defense wants black jurors. Conventional wisdom says that black jurors are more skeptical of authority, more willing to believe that a defendant has been wrongly charged. But in a case in which the defendant himself wrongly accused two black men of a crime, conventional thinking is out the window. All the defense strikes were used on blacks.

"I had reasons other than race for all my strikes," said Clinton Wright, the court-appointed defense attorney.

Opposing Wright was veteran prosecutor Dwight Warren. So there were two very capable attorneys, but the real stars seemed to be the Willyard clan. At least, they attracted most of the attention. They filled 2 1/2 rows in Judge Sherri Sullivan's courtroom. They discussed the case, sometimes loudly, in the hall.

Two of the sisters testified, one for the defense and one for the prosecution. Brenda Grant testified for the defense and told the jury that Martha, on her deathbed, indicated that she had shot Melvin. Velma Pugh, testifying for the state, said their mother had done no such thing. After court that day, there was a shouting match in the hallway between the factions. A Jerry Springer moment, some of the courthouse wags called it.

"We all get along. We're just loud, and we argue," Brenda told me.

She seemed to have that right, too. The next morning, as the family awaited the verdict, the arguments of the previous day seemed forgotten. Everybody seemed sympathetic toward James.

"He has some real problems," Sheila Williamson said. "We all do. We all have a temper, and problems reading. We were never tested. Mom thought you could work your problems out. With James, though, he has the most problems. He can't carry a board in each hand and walk. I mean that. We tried to have him do it once, and he fell down."

The general feeling among the family was that James should be acquitted.

"I'm not saying he did it, and I'm not saying he didn't do it," said Timmy Willyard. "I'm just saying they didn't prove anything. How could they? Both sides were up there just lying. How can you base anything on that?"

As far as Timmy was concerned, he distrusted Hayes. The family's distrust of Hayes was heightened by the fact that he had testified several years earlier in another Willyard murder trial. Dewayne was the defendant then. He was convicted and caught a life sentence. First Dewayne and now James, and Billy Hayes both times. Too much of a coincidence is what the family thought.

The jury deliberated all day Wednesday, and all morning Thursday before reaching a verdict Thursday afternoon.

James is 26 years old. He was thin and pale, and looked uncomfortable in a white shirt and tie as the jurors marched into court. He blinked rapidly as the clerk read the verdict. Guilty of second-degree murder.

The courtroom was packed with sheriff's deputies. Obviously, there was some concern that the family would react emotionally to the verdict. But the Willyard family reacted with dignity. There were no outbursts.

Later, the family stood outside the courthouse and talked among themselves. They'd be meeting at Timmy's place in Cahokia in a couple of days like they do most weekends, but nobody seemed to be in a hurry to go home.

"I'm still not knowing," Velma said. "We're going home the same we were the night Dad died. And that's not knowing."

Then the talk turned to Melvin. What a fine father he was, they all agreed. He was always whistling and singing, somebody said. He sure did love animals, too, somebody said, and then the talk turned to the peacocks and the hedgehogs and the geese and the turkey and all the other creatures that had inhabited the Willyards' world on the city's near North Side. None of them live there anymore.

"Daddy was going to get a kangaroo," Sheila said. "He had always wanted one, and he was going to get a baby kangaroo at the animal auction in Fruitland, but he was killed the night before."

———

VOLUNTEER HAS FOUND A HOME AT OLD COURTHOUSE

FEBRUARY 19, 2003

While a group of schoolchildren toured the Old Courthouse Tuesday morning – in other words, it seemed like an ordinary day – most of the courthouse employees gathered in a conference room to honor Chester Bold on his 25th anniversary as a volunteer at the site.

Rick Ziino, who runs the volunteer services for the Jefferson National Expansion Memorial, told the assembled crowd that he had been in contact with his bosses in Washington. He said they had told him that there were only one or two volunteers in the entire country who could match Chester's record of service. The crowd applauded. Chester, who was decked out in a yellow shirt adorned with a National Park Service patch, raised his arms over his head in triumph. The crowd responded with more applause. Chester smiled. It appeared, though, less a smile than a wince. That's part of his condition. His smile looks like a wince. On this particular day, he seemed to be wincing a lot.

He was born 53 years ago. His father was a firefighter in Lemay. Chester was the second child. When he was 2 years old, he got hold of some fuel oil. He drank it. He survived, but suffered brain damage. He says now that the antidote is what caused the problem. "It doped up my brain," he told me.

His mother – Ruby was her name – blamed herself for Chester's condition. She was very protective of him. There were other kids – an older brother, a younger sister, and then, when Chester was 12, his mother died while giving birth to another boy. The father took his three kids and his infant and moved in with his mother. They lived in a small house in south St. Louis.

With Chester's mother gone, the world was a darker place. School was difficult. It is not that he wasn't smart, he was just easily overwhelmed. "They put stuff on the blackboard, and you were supposed to read it, and learn it, but it was just all too fast," he said.

He went from school to school, and finally, at the age of 16, he graduated from eighth grade. It was a special program, he told me. That same year, his father remarried. Chester remained with his grandmother.

When he was 18, he was sent to the State School and Hospital in Bellefontaine Neighbors. Three years later, he was moved to the State Hospital on Arsenal. He considered that an improvement, except for the medication. "Too much medicine," he said.

After a couple of years, he moved to a boarding home. He also was a client of Places for People, and in 1977, a social worker from that agency took him to the Gateway Arch and the Old Courthouse. He saw the volunteers, and in February 1978, he began working as a volunteer for the Jefferson National Expansion Memorial at the Old Courthouse. Mostly, he was assigned clerical work – stuffing envelopes, folding things and shredding old documents.

In 1981, the boarding house was shut down, and Places for People helped Chester find an apartment.

Life took on a comfortable routine. Three days a week, he would take the bus downtown and go to the Old Courthouse. Other days, he would go to Places for People. His Social Security check was sent there, and caseworkers made sure his bills were paid. Three times a week, he was given cash. In the evenings, he would stay home and work on model railroad cars. There was no track on which to run them, but building them gave him pleasure. Still does.

And then Tuesday, a celebration of 25 years. Chester got a framed certificate of achievement, and a plaque. Friends spoke of his devotion to Miss Piggy and his love of model railroads. A caseworker spoke about Chester's knowledge of St. Louis history. Even his landlord was there and asked to speak. "I'm not his landlord. I'm his friend." And, of course, there was a cake. Finally, the assistant superintendent gave Chester a large glass Arch.

Chester raised it over his head. The crowd applauded, and Chester seemed to wince so hard that I thought he might cry.

—

PARISHIONERS MAKE SURE FAMILY IN NEED CAN SEE THE LIGHT

FEBRUARY 4, 2001

Christy Berg loved Christmas lights.

He was born 57 years ago and he grew up in a fine house on Forsyth Boulevard, a little west of Big Bend, not far from Our Lady of Lourdes church. His father died while Christy was in high school, and as the oldest son, Christy became the man of the house. Before long, the house was known for its Christmas decorations. Some thought the display was overdone – as if you can have too many lights – but most of the neighbors thought it was spectacular. Christy also took over the family business – the Berg Vault Company. The vaults were burial vaults. High-end vaults, expensive vaults. The business kept him very busy, and he was almost 40 when he married Emma 20 years ago. She was nearly a decade younger than her husband, and she was, in those days, smallish and petite, while Christy was a bear of a man. He was well over 6 feet, and he was heavy. They had their wedding reception on the lawn at the house on Forsyth. It was all very upper middle class, but truth is, the family business was sliding. Consumers, and consequently, the funeral homes, were becoming ever more cost-conscious.

In 1985, the business was closed, and Christy went to work for the Catholic Cemeteries of the Archdiocese. He was a salesman, a counselor. He was good with people, kind and not pushy, and he was particularly adept at dealing with people who had lost a child.

That's because he and Emma had lost a child. Their first daughter was stillborn. They put a painting of her above their fireplace. They were then blessed with a second daughter, and then, as the years went on, two more. The three sisters – Sarah, Hannah and Mary – are now 12, 9 and 6.

Several years ago, between the births of Hannah and Mary, Emma began feeling weakness in her arms and legs. Well, of course. Small kids. Who wouldn't be fatigued? But it seemed like more than that. At about the same time, Christy's vision began to deteriorate. He had surgery to try to correct his failing vision. The surgery was unsuccessful. Emma's condition continued to worsen, too. Finally, she was given a diagnosis – multiple sclerosis. By then, she was unable to climb stairs, and the family left the house on Forsyth and moved to a small, one-bedroom apartment.

Three days before Christmas of 1994, Mary was born. She was healthy. The Christmas lights blazed brightly in the small apartment.

Christy continued to work even after he was legally blind. Finally, though, in 1996, he retired. Emma was very ill, almost helpless. Christy took care of her. Apparently, the landlord felt that five people were too many for the small apartment. He forbade Christmas decorations in the windows. No problem. Christy decorated the van that he could no longer drive. Ribbons and pine branches. The next best thing to lights.

Finally, an apartment opened up on Forsyth. A larger place, too. The girls could walk to the school at Lourdes. The family became a part of the parish, but the parishioners had to be careful. Christy was a fiercely proud man. He wanted no one to pity his girls. People didn't. What's more, people admired Christy. He was raising three girls and taking care of his wife. Still, he sometimes needed help. The parishioners of Lourdes learned to walk the fine line between friendship and charity.

It seemed to work out for everybody.

It makes a community better, somehow, when you're looking out for someone, a parishioner told me. And, of course, as proud as he was, even Christy would admit that it was good to be part of a community that cared.

There were plenty of highs. Two years ago, Sarah's teachers at Lourdes nominated her for a "Do The Right Thing" award from Channel 4 for all the help she provided at home for her parents. She won and the family went downtown - a huge adventure - for the ceremony. Christy pushed Emma in her wheelchair. The blind leading the disabled, but no self-pity. Just pride and love.

There were plenty of laughs, too. Not long ago, Christy dyed Emma's hair. The color was a little off, but who could tell? Christy couldn't see, and the only mirror in the apartment was too high for Emma to use from her wheelchair.

Two years ago at Christmas, a parishioner offered Christy "anything he wanted" for his family. Christy did not have to think very long. He said he wanted the family to see Christmas lights. The benefactor rented a special van to accommodate a wheelchair, and the family was driven through the Christmas display at Tilles Park, and then on a tour of the area to look at the lights. The girls described them to their father.

This past Christmas, the benefactor offered another tour, but Emma's health had slipped too badly. Still, there were decorations. Christy heard an ad on the radio for Suburban Lawn Center, and he called to see if they would deliver an artificial tree. "Don't you want to see it first?" the salesman asked. "I'm blind, and I can't leave the house, anyway," Christy said. Within an hour, a truck arrived with a fully decorated tree. A big tree, too. The lights and the ornaments were free.

Christy died Monday morning of heart failure. He was 57. His funeral was Thursday. Emma is in the hospital. The girls have stayed with friends from the parish and with relatives. The future is uncertain, but there is no shortage of people willing to help.

By the way, the Christmas tree is still up. The girls figure it's what their father would have wanted.

—

FLOWER SHOP OWNER BLOOMS THROUGHOUT A LIFETIME OF CHANGE
AUGUST 13, 2000

Henrietta Rohlfing had a birthday Friday, but she went to work, anyway. She runs a small nursery and florist shop in Morrison, which is a town of about 160 and lies 15 miles west of Hermann on Highway 100. The flower business is mostly about holidays and anniversaries and weddings and funerals, but still, summer tends to be a slow time. Things pick up once the teen-agers go back to high school in nearby Chamois.

"We sell a lot of roses when school is in," Henrietta said. "Kids are always in love." Is it the boys giving roses to the girls, or do girls give roses to boys?

"It's both ways," Henrietta said. "That's the modern way."

And she's fine with that. She really is. One of the secrets of serenity is keeping an open mind about change. Henrietta has seen a lot of it.

She was born in 1905 on a farm just across the river from Hermann. She was the fifth of the seven children of Henry and Henrietta Stutenkemper, and she can still, at a moment's notice, spell her maiden name backwards. "We used to do things like that," she told me, as she recalled a childhood before television and radio. She had a stubborn streak, too, and she insisted on finishing the eighth grade. She was the first of her family to do so.

High school, though, was out of the question. For one thing, there was no high school nearby. She would had to have been a boarder somewhere. Also, why would anybody, especially a girl, need that much education? The bottom line, though, had to do with all the work that needed to be done on a farm in the early part of the century.

Her father had come here from Germany in 1882. He was 21 years old. Perhaps he had left Germany to avoid military service. But that's conjecture. He was a man of few words. He homesteaded 160 acres near the Missouri River, and with a farm that large, there was almost always a hired hand or two. That meant there would be 10 or 12 at the table and at three meals a day, there was a lot of cooking and cleaning. Once she finished grade school, Henrietta's life revolved around that kind of work.

She was 14 when she met Albert Rohlfing. He was 20. He came with his uncle to the Stutenkemper farm to help build a barn. After the barn was built, Albert went to Kansas and worked a harvest season. When he returned to Missouri the next year, he visited the Stutenkemper farm. He was soon a regular visitor. In the spring of 1923, when Henrietta was 17, she and Albert were married.

They bought a farm near Morrison. They worked the land, and they had four children. In 1940, after years of drought and years of flooding, Albert gave up the farming life and became a carpenter. He worked at that as tirelessly as he had worked the land. When Henrietta decided to go into the florist business in 1949, he pretty much rebuilt the building she used as her shop. When a tornado destroyed the building, he rebuilt it. "I'm going to work until I'm 80, and then I'm not going to do a damn thing but fish," he told his wife, and that is almost exactly what he did. He died in 1993 at the age of 95. He was buried in the Good Hope Cemetery, which is next door to the florist shop.

Henrietta's home is on the other side of the florist shop, and she kept working. She has had three heart attacks, and she once broke her back, but she is in her shop six days a week, and she spends most of her time on her feet. Her mind is still sharp, and she likes the flower business, she told me, because flowers make people happy. One of her daughters, Darlene Haeffner, works with her. Darlene is 75 and also a widow.

Because the little shop is more than 50 years old, it is not unusual for the two women to do second-generation weddings. In those instances, a young woman will inform them that the shop provided flowers for her mother's wedding.

In 1993, the two women sold the shop, but they got it back less than a year later. They no longer have any plans to sell. One day it will close and that will be it, said Darlene.

That day is probably far in the future.

"I'm too old to retire," Henrietta told me on the day she turned 95.

—

FOR THE RICH, NEW BUSCH IS A CHANGE FOR THE BETTER

MAY 12, 2006

Is evolution really good science? If you believe that it is, you believe that things are constantly evolving, and as things evolve, they generally get better. Opposable thumbs are better than non-opposable thumbs. Big brains are better than little brains. Evolution suggests improvement.

In an effort to test this theory, I went to a game at the new Busch Stadium.

Let me say right now that I do not intend to discuss the architectural merits of the new stadium. It is what it isn't. In other words, it's a faux old stadium. This retro look is all the rage these days, and while it might seem silly to tear down an old stadium to build a new stadium that looks like an old stadium, it actually makes some sense. That's because baseball is a retro sport, slow-paced and leisurely. It is no coincidence that the golden age of baseball and the golden age of radio were one and the same. If baseball had not already been ingrained into the American fabric, it might not have survived television.

When I began going to baseball games at Wrigley Field, a grandstand seat for a child under 14 was 60 cents. Bleacher seats were 75 cents. My ticket for Wednesday's game was $170. It was a gift from a friend.

That is not a misprint. I had one of the most expensive seats in the house. I was in the fourth row between home plate and the visitors' dugout. I was close enough to the man in the on-deck circle that I could have said, "How much do you make?"

That would have been a good question for our discussion about evolution. Next to the designated hitter rule and the expanded playoffs, the biggest changes in baseball have to do with money. When I was a kid, baseball players had winter jobs. They needed them. I did not know much about salaries, but I had the impression that an average player made about as much as my father, who was a union electrician. Maybe electricians had ballplayers beat. As late as 1970, the average salary for a major league player was $29,303.

Part of the reason for low salaries, of course, was that there was no free agency. Ernie Banks was a Cub. Stan Musial was a Cardinal. Hank Aaron was a Brave. Except for the occasional trade or the emergence of some rookie phenom, teams stayed the same year after year.

So does all of this change represent evolution?

To the folks in the $170 seats, it does. Rich people used to be an afterthought at the old stadiums. They had essentially the same experience as the rest of us. Not so at the new Busch. The $170 ticket does more than get you into the game. At the $170 level, it's like you're watching the game while spending the day on a cruise ship.

First, I had lunch at a restaurant in the ballpark. Did I want the sea bass with sun-dried tomatoes, the cheese ravioli or the open-faced pork sandwich? All three, please. And an Old Fashioned with which to wash them all down.

It's difficult to not overeat when the food is tasty and free, but doing so, it turned out, was a mistake. Why? Because in the $170 seats, even the standard ballpark food is free. You want a hot dog and a beer? Just tell your server and she brings it to you. If beer isn't your thing, you can have a glass of wine. There were limits, though. A fellow in the row in front of me asked for a bottle of merlot. No bottles, he was told.

He was a gentleman about it. He didn't complain. For that matter, the folks around me seemed uniformly upbeat. And why not? The Cardinals were winning, Congress was extending the tax cuts on capital gains and dividends, the cell phone reception was good and it was comforting to know that the new stadium does not ignore the wants of the affluent. The rich are no longer an afterthought at the ballpark.

That is clearly evidence of evolution, at least if you happen to be sitting in a $170 seat.

—

THIS VIETNAM VET HAS WAITED YEARS TO BE A U.S. CITIZEN

OCTOBER 26, 2001

Hinh Van Vu went into the emergency room at St. Mary's Health Center in Richmond Heights on Thursday night last week. Such bad timing. Last Friday was supposed to be one of the greatest days of his life. He was going to become a U.S. citizen.

His journey to citizenship had been a long one. He was born in October 1949 in the northern part of Vietnam. When the French lost their war in 1954 and the country was partitioned, Vu's parents moved south. They did not want to live under communism.

Vu grew up in Saigon. His father was a laborer. His mother was a street merchant. When the Americans came, the Vu family was very pro-American.

Vu joined the Army when he was 17. He was in an elite unit connected with the American Special Forces, a unit called a "Studies and Observation Group."

The all-Vietnamese 11-man reconnaissance team was airlifted into very dangerous places. In January 1967, Vu's team was sent into North Vietnam to observe traffic along Highway 8. They were dropped almost on top of a large North Vietnamese Army unit. For two days and nights, Vu eluded capture.

Then he was caught.

The North Vietnamese were not kind to these men whom they considered lackeys of the Americans. For more than a year, Vu was kept chained in an underground cell. He lived in darkness.

Even after South Vietnam fell in 1975, Vu was denied the relative freedom of a "re-education camp." He was finally released in 1982.

He moved back to Saigon, which had been renamed Ho Chi Minh city. Life was not easy for a man with his history. But he survived. He got married. And always he harbored the dream of immigrating to the United States.

Because of his military record, the United States agreed to accept him, and he came to this country on January 12, 1992. He originally settled in Chicago, but a childhood friend lived in St. Louis and urged Vu to move here. He moved in October 1992.

Freedom does not guarantee that all of one's luck will be good, and Vu's life here has not been without heartache. His oldest son drowned in the Meramec River on an outing this summer. The young man was 17. Vu's other son has cerebral palsy and is severely disabled. Vu's wife devotes herself to his care while Vu supports the family. Most recently, he has been working as a manicurist.

In his spare time, Vu studied for his citizenship exam. He passed that exam on the first day of August. He was one day away from taking the oath when he went to the emergency room with an unknown ailment.

Dr. Nancy Marshall heard of Vu's plight last Friday morning from a resident. He was not yet ready for release, and diagnostic tests were planned. Marshall called Ken Lukhard, the hospital president, and he called Steve Hoven, the vice president of public affairs for SSM Health Care. He said he would talk to Sen. Christopher "Kit" Bond.

Bond's office could do nothing without the requisite paperwork, and

Katie Cusick, a hospital social worker, began working on that. Nurse case managers Robin Warchol and Joanne Dunstan also worked on the case, coordinating things between Vu's family, the senator's office and INS officials.

Vu is still in the hospital – the test results are still pending – but this afternoon, a federal judge and an INS official will go to St. Mary's and administer the oath of citizenship to Hinh Van Vu.

I visited him Thursday. An American flag was on his dresser, sitting next to a framed copy of a presidential unit citation for the work done so long ago by the "Studies and Observation Group."

Congratulations, I said. Thank you, he replied, but I thought to myself that it is really we who should be grateful that people like Vu want to join us.

—

SURPRISE WITNESS REVIVED PROSECUTION IN KILLING OF BOXER

FEBRUARY 10, 2002

"In the clearing stands a boxer, and a fighter by his trade ..."

On an early December evening 14 months ago, Robert Kibby drove to the front of the city's recreation center at 12th and Park. Kibby, who was then 20, worked at the center, and on this night, he was dropping off some uniforms and equipment from a youth football team. Carrying a bundle of uniforms, he approached the door. A man standing in the foyer saw him approach and opened the door. The man was wearing tan coveralls and a dark skull cap. Kibby carried that first load of uniforms into the center and returned to his car for a second load. Again, the man in the coveralls opened the door. After a third trip, Kibby went to move his car into the parking lot. While he was gone, somebody shot and killed Ray Lathon, a boxer who had just finished a workout. The assassin shot Lathon four times in the head and then fled into the night.

The cops talked to everybody who had been at the center at the time of the shooting. There were people who had seen the killer, but these witnesses weren't much help. They said the killer had been wearing tan overalls and a ski mask.

Somehow, Kibby was overlooked. Perhaps that's because he had been looking for a parking space at the time of the shooting.

Approximately two hours after the shooting, the cops got a call from Michael Stuart. He told them he had gone to the recreation center with a friend, Ahmad Adisa. While Stuart stayed outside in Adisa's truck, Adisa went inside. He took a gun with him. About 20 minutes later, he came running out. He said he had shot a guy in the head. That was Stuart's story.

The cops asked what Adisa was wearing when he went into the center. Tan coveralls, Stuart said. Based on that information, Adisa was arrested.

But there were problems with the state's case. First, no gun was recovered. Stuart said Adisa had thrown it out of the truck as they drove from the center. Cops searched for the gun that night but couldn't find it. Nor were any tan coveralls recovered. No ski mask. So the entire case would depend on Stuart's testimony, and his credibility was sure to be an issue. He had just gotten out of prison three months earlier. He had a history of stealing and fraud. On the day of the shooting, he had left his girlfriend's apartment after she called police and told them he had threatened to kill her.

Even the prosecutor, Dwight Warren, figured he had a loser. Adisa's family had hired a top-notch defense attorney, Scott Rosenblum, and Rosenblum would likely make mincemeat out of Stuart.

The trial was supposed to start Tuesday. But on that morning, one of the state's witnesses, a woman who had been working at the center the night of the shooting, wondered aloud to Warren why the cops had never talked to Kibby. "Who's Kibby?" the prosecutor asked. He's the young man who saw the killer before he put on his mask, said the woman.

The cops were dispatched to find Kibby. They did, and he said, yes, he had seen the shooter. Would you recognize him now, 14 months later? I think so, he said. He was brought to the police station and shown five photographs, a mug-shot lineup. He pointed to Adisa's photo. He said he was certain. The trial was postponed for a day, and the state had a new star witness.

"I feel like the Rams," Rosenblum told me. "I was a heavy favorite going in, but now I think I'm down. But you know something? Do you really think you could see somebody for just a few seconds in a dimly lit place and then remember them 14 months later? We might not be out of this yet."

The state is not required to provide a motive, but Warren was prepared to argue that this had been a contract killing. Lathon was arrested in October of 1999 on an assault and kidnapping charge. The victim was a drug dealer, and the dispute concerned a turf war. The charges were dropped when the drug dealer refused to cooperate with the cops. Instead, he had put out a contract on Lathon.

That was the state's theory, and it seemed terribly sad: Lathon, a leg-breaker; Adisa, a hit man. Go back a few years, and both of these fellows were young men of great promise.

In 1989, Lathon was the U.S. Amateur champ at 165 pounds. He won the national Golden Gloves title that year, too, and also a gold medal at the U.S. Olympic Festival. He turned pro in 1990 and won his first professional fight with a first-round knockout. Old-timers compared him favorably with St. Louis boxing legends like Archie Moore, Sonny Liston and the Spinks brothers. Although he never lived up to his potential, he was 22-1 as a pro and was training for a North American Boxing Federation title match when he was killed. He was 34 years old.

Adisa, who is 28, was once on a college-bound track at Metro Christian School in St. Louis County. He was a guard on the basketball team. Then, shockingly, the young man everybody knew as "Pumpkin" was arrested in a killing. He was 16. He was charged with shooting a man during a street robbery. He eventually pleaded guilty to voluntary manslaughter and did seven years in prison.

Members of Lathon's and Adisa's families showed up for the trial, and both families behaved with remarkable grace. Lathon's mother, Jessie Smith, told me she used to go to her son's boxing matches. She talked about the one professional fight he had lost. That was in California, she said, and she had been there.

What went wrong? I asked. Why had Ray never been able to shake the influences of the street?

She shook her head. Friends, she said. The wrong kind of friends.

Adisa also had an extended family at the courthouse – his mom, his dad, his stepmother, two brothers and an uncle. Jeanette Walker, Adisa's mother, told me that Ahmad was the only one who had ever been in serious trouble. She said she couldn't explain how any of it had happened, but she was convinced her son was innocent. He had pleaded guilty in that first killing because he was tricked, she said, and this charge had just flowed from that first one.

"Once you get in the system," she said, and then her voice trailed off.

Well, who knows? It's hard to argue anything when the state's case gets a last-minute boost because a hit man allegedly opened the door for a stranger. A random act of courtesy from an unexpected source.

—

WRECKING AND SALVAGE FIRM STRESSES LATTER WITH EMPLOYEES
October 14, 2005

Noah Young was in court 2 1/2 years ago for a probation revocation hearing. He was out of the ordinary. At 56, he was a good deal older than most of the other defendants. And while all the other fellows on the docket wanted a second chance – or, more accurately, a third chance – Young seemed intent on going to prison. Actually, he didn't seem intent about anything. The word I used at the time was "relaxed."

He had been arrested with another man for stealing radiators at a junkyard. He had been charged with felony stealing and tampering. Tampering translates to car theft. The men had been using a stolen truck. Young pleaded guilty and was put on probation.

He was ordered to pay $500 restitution to the owner of the truck. He decided he shouldn't have to pay restitution because he had not known the truck was stolen. And if the truck was damaged, it had been dam aged before Young got in it. Because he refused to pay restitution, he was brought to court for a revocation hearing.

Judge Mark Neill looked at Young's record and saw that it wasn't too bad. A number of scrapes over the years, but nothing serious. In fact, Young had never been to prison. Why waste a cell on somebody like this?

Neill explained that the restitution could be paid over time. I'm not paying it, Young said. Then I'll have to send you to prison for two years, Neill replied. Fine, Young said. I'm going to continue this hearing for three weeks and I'll let you sit in jail and think about this, Neill said. I'll consider those three weeks as a down payment on my two years, Young said. He wasn't angry or anything. Just unconcerned. Relaxed.

So Young was led away and I wrote a column that concluded, "It's always odd to see a fellow turn down a second chance."

A couple of days after the hearing, Neill ran into a friend, Don Bellon, who owns Bellon Wrecking & Salvage Co. Neill told Bellon about Young. This guy does not belong in prison, Neill said. Bellon had an idea. "Why don't I hire him and then pay the restitution out of his salary?"

Which is what happened.

You have to understand that Bellon Wrecking & Salvage is slightly misnamed. The company's emphasis is more on salvaging than wrecking. And when Bellon does demolish a building, he tries to recycle and reuse as much as possible from the demolished building. Earlier this year, the company received the Mayor's Spirit of St. Louis Award for its work at the corner of Vandeventer and Chouteau avenues, where the company is headquartered. That is also the site of Bellon's Deli and Pizzeria.

I had lunch there earlier this week with Bellon and Young, who has been a full-time employee since he was hired shortly after the probation revocation hearing. The building is an example of Bellon's zeal for recycling. Some of the booths in the deli are old church pews. What seem to be decorative railings in the restaurant are actually old elevator doors turned on their sides. The terra cotta on the outside comes from the old annex to the Sheldon concert hall.

"I guess you could say Noah was our human recycling project," Bellon said. Young laughed. He still seems relaxed. He and Bellon seem to have an easy manner with each other.

Actually, though, it was Mary Bellon who had the most daily contact with Young. She pretty much ran things at headquarters while her husband was out on various jobs. Mary died in December. She was playfully swinging on the pole of the family's basketball hoop when the contraption fell on her. She was a longtime volunteer for Habitat for Humanity, and she was active in her church, Our Lady of Lourdes.

And, of course, she helped her husband run the wrecking and salvage company, with the emphasis on salvage.

—

VIETNAM VETERAN HAS NEVER FORGOTTEN THE ULTIMATE GIFT

MAY 26, 2002

Lenny Miller celebrated his 20th birthday on a hill southwest of Da Nang in the Republic of South Vietnam. He was a member of a 12-man U.S. Marine reconnaissance team. On this particular mission, the team was supposed to sit on the hill for a few days and watch the valley floor. Miller's birthday – Sept. 4, 1967 – had been quiet. The team had dug a hole a little bit down the hill to serve as a listening post during the long, dark night. Miller's best friend, Melvin Riley, who was, like Miller, from the St. Louis area, offered Miller a birthday present.

"Sleep in tonight. I'll take your watch." "No need to do that, man."

"Happy birthday."

So it was that Riley, and not Miller, was in the forward hole when the Viet Cong came up the hill.

I visited Master Gunnery Sgt. Lenny Miller earlier this week. For a good part of the last 20 years, he has been in St. Louis on recruiting duty. He will retire in June, and with some fanfare. He is the last enlisted Marine who was on active duty during the Tet offensive of 1968.

For all practical purposes, he's retired now. He had an operation on his back earlier this month, and he doesn't figure to make it back to the office. He's recuperating from that operation now. On the day I visited, he was wearing a T-shirt that said, "Pain is weakness leaving the body."

Miller joined the Marines in June 1966. He went in with a pal, and they went through boot camp together. They were in infantry training together when a staff sergeant from Reconnaissance came to talk to the infantry training company.

"We're the eyes and ears of the infantry. We go out in small teams. We're looking for volunteers," he said.

Miller's pal nudged him. This sounds neat, he said. Small teams doesn't sound so neat to me, Miller said, but finally, he relented and stepped forward. Just then one of the other fellows asked about life expectancy for recon Marines. "Two minutes and 36 seconds in a hot LZ," said the staff sergeant. Miller's pal stayed in the formation, and went to Vietnam as an infantryman.

"He was shot and wounded three months after arriving in country," Miller said. "So who knows?"

Miller arrived in Vietnam in March 1967. The recon fellows were a breed apart. Peepers and creepers, they were called. They'd go out for seven to 10 days, and then they'd spend several days at division rear before going out again. They had two kinds of missions. The first was an area reconnaissance. They would spend the mission on the move. The second was stationary observation. They'd set up on a hill and stay there. An ideal patrol meant no contact. See and not be seen. But because the recon teams were sent into areas thick with enemy troops, it was hard to avoid contact. During Miller's 21 months in Vietnam, he went out on 37 long-range patrols. Twenty-three of them involved contact with the enemy.

The weeks leading up to Tet were rough for the recon teams. "The teams were having contact almost all the time. We were losing a lot of people. Still, we didn't realize anything big was coming," Miller said.

Oddly enough, Tet itself was almost peaceful for the Marines who had the most dangerous job in the war zone. January 31, 1968, found

Miller's team on another hill. "I was the assistant patrol leader, and somewhere around midnight, I guess, one of the guys woke me up. 'You gotta see this,' he said. Out there in the dark, all around us, but miles away, you could see flashes. Mortars, artillery, gunships, everything. It was like the Fourth of July." The team radioed headquarters – Grim Reaper – and headquarters told them to sit tight. They did.

Six months later, Miller's team was on yet another hill. They'd been there four days, and they'd seen a lot of activity below them. They'd rained artillery on the enemy. Early on the evening of that fourth day, they began to take sniper fire from another hill.

They'd been spotted. The assault came around midnight. The team radioed for fire support. They couldn't get any. Some rifle companies were taking a beating, and all available fire support was going for them. The recon team would have to hold on.

The team's machine-gunner was hit and killed by a rocket propelled grenade. Miller knew they needed the firepower from the M-60, so he made a dash for the gun. A grenade landed a few feet away from him. Shrapnel tore into his right leg and left foot. For a moment, he thought his legs had been blown off. He recovered and made it to the M-60. Somehow, the recon team held until helicopter gunships were available. They came in firing 15 feet from the team's position.

"For a while, I didn't think we'd get off that hill," Miller said. He was awarded the Bronze Star for his heroism that night.

Miller left Vietnam in November 1968. His hitch was up in January 1970, and he joined the Marine Corps Reserves. He missed active duty, though, and as time went on, he missed it more and more. Eleven years after getting out, he went back in, and became a recruiter.

He has had recruiting duty in Kansas City and Minneapolis, but every year, he has made it back to St. Louis for Memorial Day. Every year, he does the same thing. He visits the grave of Melvin Riley.

On Sept. 8, 1967, this newspaper published a short notice of Riley's death. The story was on page nine. As for what happened, it said only that he was shot while on patrol.

Bill McClellan

CHAPTER FIVE

LIFE'S UNEVEN MOMENTS

WITH THE PROPER SPIRIT, CHRISTMAS CAN PUSH FAMILY RIGHT UP A TREE

DECEMBER 23, 2002

The Bickersons were sitting at the breakfast table, talking about putting up their Christmas lights. Actually, re-putting up their Christmas lights. And bickering about it, of course.

"Why does Mom have to be such a perfectionist?" asked the teenage son. He asked the question of his father, but Dad Bickerson just shrugged his shoulders.

"It's stupid," said the son. "The lights are fine. Be honest, Dad. Don't you think the lights are fine?"

Dad shrugged his shoulders again and took another sip of his egg nog. He was not going to be drawn into this argument, but truth is, he agreed with his son. The lights looked fine to him. Lights are lights. Who cares if they're perfectly arranged?

Mom Bickerson does. That's who. The previous night, she had noticed a certain unevenness in the lights on the spruce in the front yard. It would only take a few minutes to fix, she decided.

"They're fine," the son repeated. "Honestly, Mom, why don't we just leave them as they are? We'll never be able to get them completely perfect."

"You'll spend more time complaining about it than it would take you to do it," said Mom.

"Mom's right," said the Bickersons' daughter. She had just come home from college, and this was her first opportunity to get in the Bickerson spirit.

"Why don't I help Mom fix the lights?" said Dad. Actually, he figured the exercise would do him good. He was – is – facing an embarrassing Christmas morning. He's getting pants this year. Pants for his birthday would make some sense. His birthday is in the summer. But Christmas comes in the heart of egg nog season, and Dad Bickerson is something of a nogaholic. In other words, the pants weren't – aren't – going to fit. At least not for a few weeks.

"I'm going to do it," said the son.

"No, I'll do it," said the father.

"Why don't you two just stay here and fight about it, and I'll help Mom," said the daughter.

"I'll do it alone," said the mother.

The Bickersons, all four of them, went out to re-string the lights on the spruce.

The spruce is about 12 feet tall, and the son went to the back yard to get a ladder. While he was gone, the father gazed at the tree. Years ago, it was a Mother's Day gift. A symbolic kind of a gift, he had thought when he planted it. A young tree is like a child. You'll nurture it, and watch it grow, and you don't even know the people who will someday enjoy it.

The son came back with the ladder. The Bickersons argued briefly about who would do what. The mother had the best feel for the job. She should be the one to climb the ladder and rearrange the lights. After all, she was the one who had spotted the uneven spots on the tree. Then again, that made her the perfect choice to stand on the sidewalk and supervise the rearrangement of the lights.

Why couldn't she do both?

So she did. She went up the ladder and rearranged the lights. The rest of the family stood below. Then she went to the sidewalk and examined what she had just done. It still wasn't quite right, she decided. "It's perfect," said the exasperated son. "I think Mom's right," said the daughter. "Well, Mom's right, but there's something nice about imperfection," said the father. That comment drew a glance from his wife. She tolerates imperfection but doesn't applaud it.

She went back up the ladder. She made some very slight adjustments to the strands of lights and went back to the sidewalk to review her handiwork.

"It's perfect," said the son. "You're just saying that," said the daughter.

"Life itself has an uneven quality," said the father.

His wife continued to study the tree. "I think that's as good as we're going to get it," she finally said.

It's more than just good, thought the father. And he wasn't thinking about the lights.

—

WITH NO WEAPONS AND NO NAME, CASE MAY GO NOWHERE

MAY 9, 2004

One day last month, a ragged-looking man waved over a city cop on Broadway just east of Chouteau. I witnessed a murder, he said.

The officer took him to headquarters and turned him over to detectives from the homicide squad. The man told the detective he had been staying in a shanty by the river. He said that several nights earlier, he had seen two men stab a third and then push him into the river. The man seemed a little shaky, but the detectives asked him if could take them to the shanty. Sure, he said. As they approached the river, he pointed to two men walking toward downtown from the river. That's them, he said. The detectives called for a patrol car and had the two men taken to headquarters. They then continued to the shanty with their witness. Several people were there. Some confirmed the witness's story. A man named Slick attacked a woman, and two other men then attacked Slick. He had been stabbed and then pushed into the river. The detectives returned to headquarters to talk to the two suspects. Each confessed. The detectives went to the circuit attorney's office and applied for warrants.

But witnesses and confessions aside, there was no body. And who was Slick? It's tough enough to prosecute a case when you have no body, but when the body you don't have has no name, the case gets even more complicated. There were no weapons, either. The men said they had thrown their knives into the river. Cars go into the river and disappear. Forget about finding knives. Finally, everybody involved was homeless. Some of these people seemed vaguely confused. Would they even show up for a trial?

The warrants were taken under advisement. One of the suspects was wanted in North Carolina. We'll take him, said the officials from that state. The other was wanted on a drug possession case in Oregon, but officials from that state didn't want to extradite him. He was released.

On Thursday, a body surfaced a couple of hundred yards south of the shanty. The best guess is it had been stuck under a barge, and when the barge moved, the body popped to the surface. As of Friday afternoon, the body had not been identified. But speculation centered on Slick.

Bill McClellan

The shanty is a couple of blocks south of Chouteau. It looks like a boxcar on stilts, but less substantial. There is no electricity or running water. Five people were there when I dropped by Friday.

Christine is 21. She said she was the woman Slick attacked. John is 23. He said he is Christine's fiance. They moved into the shanty together in January.

They said they met Slick, who police say was in his mid-40s, a couple of days before his death. He had been at a gas station nearby trying to sell some stolen clothes. He was befriended by one of the men who later allegedly murdered him. This man and the other suspect were living at the shanty. Slick came back with his new friend. He stayed.

On the night of the murder, a church group came by with sandwiches. This is a fairly common occurrence, the people at the shanty told me, and one of their main sources for food. Also, some of the men get day-labor jobs. All of them are looking for work, they said.

At any rate, Slick had been in a nearby abandoned tractor-trailer with a woman for a while. He may have been high. (The group at the shanty told me they don't allow drugs at the shanty.) According to Christine, she was in bed sometime after midnight when Slick attacked her. He ripped at her blouse, she said. She screamed.

One of the men then attacked Slick. He may have stabbed him – police found blood in the shanty – but Christine didn't see a knife. Slick went outside, and the other man stabbed him, Christine and John said. Slick took several steps and collapsed.

The two men pulled him to his feet and guided him toward the end of the little platform on which the shanty sits. There is a drop of about 35 feet from the platform to the river. They gave him a push.

Police hope to have the body identified sometime this week.

—

COUPLE THAT WAS FLORISSANT FIXTURE THRIVES IN FLORIDA

JUNE 11, 1999

They met at the Casa Loma Ballroom in the fall of 1954. Marie was 20 years old, and lived in north St. Louis. She took care of her father and two brothers. Bud was an electrical maintenance worker who lived on the city's South Side.

One night the manager of the ballroom asked Bud if he had a dancing partner. Bud said he didn't. The manager looked around and saw Marie. He introduced the two. They never stopped dancing.

There was no need to actually date. They'd just meet at the Casa Loma three or four times a week. Mostly, they were ballroom dancers, but they were quite the jitterbuggers, too. In fact, they did jitterbug exhibitions on the Admiral. They weren't paid for these exhibitions. They just did them.

A couple of months after they met, they began to formally date. Of course, it was dancing dates, and generally at the Casa Loma. Instead of meeting at the Casa Loma, Bud would go to Marie's father's house and pick her up and later take her home. It was as if they formalized something that had been understood.

They were married in July 1955. They spent a couple of days at Pere Marquette for their honeymoon. Then it was on to life.

In those early days of marriage, they lived with Marie's father in his home on Montgomery Street. The dutiful daughter needed to watch her dad. He died in 1960, and Marie and Bud moved to Florissant. By this time, they had two children.

Bud worked as a dispatcher for a trucking firm.

On April 19, 1976, Marie had a bad headache. She didn't think anything about it. Maybe it had to do with stress. Bud's mother had died three days earlier. In fact, Marie first noticed the headache at the funeral home.

It turned out to be an aneurysm that had burst in her brain. Marie was in a coma for three weeks. When she woke up, she was paralyzed on her

Bill McClellan

left side. That would be a permanent condition, the doctors said.

The doctors also said she should try to walk.

So she did. They did, actually. There was no way Marie could walk alone. She had no balance.

They walked up and down the sidewalks in the Thunderbird Hills subdivision. But despite the name, there weren't much in the way of hills and so they soon changed their route for more of a challenge. Up and down Waterford Drive they began to walk.

They did so for years.

Their hours varied depending on Bud's shift. When he worked the night shift, they walked in the afternoons. When he worked the day shift, they walked in the mornings.

They became a part of the landscape. And then one day, they vanished.

A retired English teacher, Mary Louise Hawkins, wrote me a letter. She said she had seen the couple every day, in all kinds of weather, when she worked at McCluer North High School.

She said the walking couple had touched so many people's lives. Their story seemed to be one of devotion and love. But what had happened to them?

I printed Hawkins' letter. I then got a call from Debbie Kasterup. The people you wrote about are my parents, she said. Their names are Bud and Marie Frederich, and they have retired to Florida.

I called them. I told them that a number of people had called to say that they, too, remembered the walking couple. You two were famous, I told them. I asked if they had known that.

"People used to honk. We didn't pay much attention," said Bud.

I said that people were inspired by them.

"My husband is an angel," said Marie. "I once had a doctor tell me that a lot of women would take my disability if my husband came with it. I told the doctor I'd keep them both."

They now live in Lakeland, Fla., and yes, they spend much of their time walking. In their new place, they have a picture of the Casa Loma Ballroom, a reminder of the time when they were dancers, before they were walkers.

—

A JUDGE RIGHT HERE COULD HAVE MADE FLORIDA IRRELEVANT

NOVEMBER 12, 2000

Early Tuesday evening, I was in the car headed from Bill Federer's party in South County to the Democrats' shindig at the Chase Park Plaza. I was listening to election news on the radio when the announcer said that a Circuit Court judge had ordered that the city's polling places be kept open until 10 p.m.

Judge Evelyn Baker had issued the order, the announcer said. I couldn't believe it. A local judge – somebody I know personally! – might help the Democrats steal the first election of the new millennium.

You see, I already knew that the election was going to be close. (In fact, it was so close that had Al Gore won Missouri, he would not have needed Florida.) If the judge could keep the polls open long enough for the Democrats to get enough people to the polls to give Gore the state, they might well steal the election.

Let me tell you right away that I am not a prude when it comes to stealing elections. I was raised in Mayor Richard J. Daley's Chicago, and we used to have wet ballots.

Our clumsy election officials were always spilling things on bunches of our ballots, and they could not be counted until they dried, and they were never dry until all the votes had been counted from the Republican strongholds downstate.

Bill McClellan

Incredible as it may seem, we always ended up with just enough Democratic votes to prevail. As long as Mayor Daley liked the candidate, that is. If the mayor didn't like the guy, then we wouldn't have enough, and the Republicans would win.

History will tell you that the mayor liked John F. Kennedy, and when our ballots finally dried out in that 1960 election, we had just enough to put Kennedy over the top.

By the way, the fellow Gore sent down to Florida to oversee the recount is the mayor's son, Bill Daley. I watched him on television talking about "the integrity of the electoral process" and I have to give him credit for keeping a straight face. Considering his bloodlines, that was no mean accomplishment.

At any rate, Bill Daley's dad was a very powerful man, and I grew up thinking that only powerful men – powerful white men – could steal elections, and it seemed kind of nice that as we hit a new millennium, an African-American woman like Judge Baker might be at the forefront of swiping one.

In addition, Judge Baker is not really considered a powerful person. For instance, when people speculate about which judges might get bumped up to a higher court, you never hear Baker's name.

Maybe that's because she is known to enjoy an occasional drink at lunch. I'm known for the same thing, so naturally I don't hold daylight drinking against the judge, but these days it is often counted against us.

She was appointed to the bench in 1983 by then-Gov. Kit Bond – another guy who's not averse to a nip at noon! – and her career has been steady but not spectacular. She does, however, have a fine sense of humor.

Her husband died in 1994. His name was John Joseph Hughes, and he was Irish. He used to spend many an afternoon in a little saloon near the courthouse.

After he was diagnosed with terminal cancer, he told his wife that he wanted an Irish wake at the place where he and she had shared so many good times. The judge honored her husband's request.

I was sitting next to the judge when the pallbearers carried the casket in and set it on the bar itself. I raised my glass in toast, and the judge said, "You know, this is the first time John has been carried into a saloon."

You can see, I hope, why I think so highly of Judge Baker, and why I was thrilled at the notion that she might be able to help steal a presidential election. What a feat it would be. How far the country has come since my youth.

I don't mean to suggest that she did not have reasons for keeping the polls open.

Personally, I thought it was the wrong thing to do, and when the Democrats had, at the ready, a tape-recorded message from Jesse Jackson urging people to take advantage of the new hours, well, it did seem peculiar.

But still, it would be impossible to argue that things were going smoothly with the city's voting process. Things were a mess. Voters who thought they were registered weren't, and the situation at the Election Board downtown was chaotic.

You know who I blame for that?

The late Mel Carnahan. I liked him very much when he was alive, and I voted for him after he died, but he is the one who appointed the members of the Election Board.

Frankly, these kind of appointments often have more to do with politics than with competence, and it was certainly that way when Carnahan moved into the statehouse.

I remember when he named political cronies to the Election Board, and then had to watch in embarrassment as the entire board was forced to resign because they all had forged alliances with riverboat casino companies.

Shortly before the mass resignation, the new chairman fired two long-time employees and replaced them with politically connected people. A federal judge rescinded the firings, so new jobs were created to keep the politically connected people on the payroll.

You can't expect an election board like that to be very efficient. Not surprisingly then, things got out of control on Tuesday, and that gave Judge Baker the chance to step forward.

Now as I watch the news from Florida, I have a hard time forgiving the state appellate court judges who overruled her. Had her order stayed in place, Florida wouldn't matter. Judge Evelyn Baker and the Democrats here might have stolen the election.

It didn't happen, but next time I run into the judge at lunch, I'm proposing a toast: To what might have been.

—

AN IMPERFECT WORLD FORCES ANGIE TO MISS HER CALLING

JANUARY 7, 2001

I'm a voice guy. A well-turned ankle is nice but there's something about an attractive voice. Whatever it is – an inflection, a certain lilt – some women just have it. Angie does. She called me at home early Wednesday night. Just about dinnertime, actually.

"William?" she asked.

"Yes," I said, instantly smitten. Nothing sultry, nothing flirty. Very professional. Very cool. I tried to answer in the same vein. "This is he. Or him. I'm William."

"I'm Angie," she said.

I don't know any Angies. And that's fine. I'm happily married to a woman with a wonderful voice.

But still, Angie's voice had me mesmerized. Scared, too, the way a wild animal is scared when it hears an unnatural sound in the forest.

A twig snapping, brush moving on a windless day. Teachers used to call me William when they were angry with me. Nothing good has ever come from a conversation in which I've been called William.

"I'm with a collection agency," Angie said.

She informed me that I owed $64 to a doctor from the Washington University School of Medicine. He had provided some kind of service to my son, Jack, and I had not paid. He had turned me over to the Midwest Collection Service, the agency for which Angie works.

Even aside from her voice, I liked her. That is, I admired her. What a difficult job she has. For all she knew, I was buried under medical bills. Children's medical bills. Now with utility bills going sky high, I could be buried under heating bills, too. In her mind, I was probably broke and desperate, a character out of a Victor Hugo novel, trying to decide whether to spend his last dollar on heat, food or medicine.

I tried to ease Angie's mind. I told her that the whole situation was a misunderstanding. I've got health insurance that pays for everything. Sometimes doctors or hospitals send incomprehensible paperwork to the house. If I look hard enough, I find a small notation, "This is not a bill." Well, why send it to me then? Even if I don't find that notation, I don't worry. Eventually, somebody at the doctor's office will figure out that the insurance company should be billed.

"Why don't you send me a copy of the bill? I'll take it to the benefits department, and I'll make sure this thing gets paid," I said.

"This is not about your benefits department," Angie said, and although her voice was still cool and professional, I had the impression she didn't believe I had a benefits department. "This is about you."

She was absolutely right. I had a vague recollection of getting a bill from some doctor, and ignoring it, figuring it had been sent to me in error. I should have taken it to the benefits department immediately. Or at least turned it over to my wife.

On the other hand, maybe this isn't just about me. What does this say about our faceless society? Washington University School of Medicine is part of the BJC apparatus. Both my kids were born at Jewish. Between emergency room visits and operations of various sorts, I've given BJC thousands of dollars worth of business. You'd think somebody over there would see that unpaid $64 bill, and say, "This must be a mistake. This guy's insurance always pays."

But that's not the way it works these days. Everything is impersonal. You call a business or a government office, and you get an automated menu. Heck, I get calls from solicitors who ask if I want to subscribe to the Post-Dispatch. Why should I expect BJC to remember me?

I pleaded with Angie. Just send me a bill. I'll get it paid. She was firm. The bill was already eight months old. The doctor had waited long enough for his money.

"You're in collection," she said, and there was no point asking exactly what that meant. I thought of a friend who was stopped by a cop in Texas. The cop told him to get out of the car and then very casually said, "The Position." When my friend looked puzzled, the cop sighed and said, "Don't act like you don't know what I'm talking about." My friend then figured it out, and turned around and put his hands on the car in preparation of being frisked. The worst part of the experience was feeling naive, he said.

So while I wondered if my credit was already ruined or just on the verge of ruination, I didn't let on. No guy likes to act naive in front of a woman he admires.

I asked to speak to Angie's supervisor. His name is Dan. Like Angie, he was very professional. Dan suggested I pay the $64 and then go to my benefits department.

That's probably what I'll do, but I still say that in a perfect world, the gang over at BJC would have checked my history before turning me over to a collection agency. Then again, in a perfect world, there'd be no medical bills, no collection agencies and Angie would have a job in radio.

———

MEETING JACK KEROUAC'S GHOST IN A CUP OF COFFEE

The Swine Flu swept through town the other day and I caught it. I should have seen it coming. When I was pouring myself a cup of coffee that morning, I felt an urge to put Kahlua in it. I resisted, of course, but the very thought of alcohol in the morning should have filled me with foreboding. What in the world was I thinking? Instead, the moment passed like a shadow on a mostly sunny day.

Later, I went to a dinner party. I had a couple glasses of wine and was telling a few stories when my wife said to a lawyer sitting across from her, "Richard, I bet you have some good stories."

He smiled. "They're only stories if you tell them," he said.

"I admire restraint," I said, "the same way I admire moderation. Secondhand and at a distance." I reached for a wine bottle.

In my defense, one expects restraint from an attorney, but not from a newspaper person. Oh, sure, we know a few secrets, but most of the stuff we learn we pass on to the readers. We're in the storytelling business, and it's like the lawyer said, They're only stories if you tell them.

Somebody then announced that it was the 50th anniversary of the first reading of "Howl."

Perhaps that's what had gotten into me with that impulse about Kahlua. It was a beatnik thing. Allen Ginsberg and Jack Kerouac and the rest of them were trying to make a psychic connection through the years. "Put some Kahlua in that coffee. This is an important anniversary."

I was once a kindred soul. Like a lot of young people, I read "On the Road" and was hooked. I don't care that Truman Capote said of Kerouac's work: "That's not writing. That's typewriting." I wanted to be a beatnik, and listen to jazz and talk excitedly into the long night. Fortunately, or unfortunately, the timing was off and I was too late for the Beats. If I wanted to be slovenly and avoid working, I had to be a hippie. So I became one. I enjoyed the lifestyle.

But who were the great hippie writers? Richard Brautigan? Ken

Kesey? They appealed to hippies, but were they hippies themselves? I think not. Perhaps the great hippie writers only thought about writing.

At any rate, the host of the dinner party decided he should read "Howl." If you know your beatnik history, you know that Ginsberg read "Howl" at the City Lights bookstore in San Francisco. Kerouac sat in the audience, drinking wine from the bottle, and hollering, "Go! Go! Go!"

The host began, "I saw the best minds of my generation destroyed by madness, starving hysterical naked . . ."

I grabbed a bottle.

". . . angelheaded hipsters burning for the ancient heavenly connection to the starry dynamo in the machinery of night . . ."

"Go! Go! Go!" somebody shouted. It might have been me.

Well, I overdid things terribly. Had the Swine Flu the next morning. A day of my life wasted. A precious day. They're finite, you know.

I resolved to begin treating my body like the temple it is. From now on, it gets only quality stuff, I promised myself. I drove to the Hill and got an Amighetti's special and a bottle of Fitz Cream Soda. I took my lunch over to Berra Park.

Berra Park on the Hill. For whom is that named? Nope. Yogi Berra might be the most famous person to come from the Hill, but he was never an alderman. The park is named after the late Louis "Midge" Berra.

I found a picnic table under a tree. The lunch was everything I expected. An Amighetti's special is the best sandwich in town, and Fitz Cream Soda is the true nectar of the gods. It is ever so much better than wine. Why had I not realized that before? Why did I have to lose a day to see the truth? I sat there, muttering insults to myself when suddenly, from the branches above me, a bird made his presence known. Right on my head. A beatnik or a hippie would have ignored it. I went home and showered.

GIVING BASEBALLS BACK TO MCGWIRE IS NOT A CAPITAL IDEA

SEPTEMBER 9, 1998

Thank goodness that 62nd home run didn't make it into the stands.

Chances are, some goofy fan would have given it to Mark McGwire. What would people have thought of us then? I mean, this used to be considered a tough town, a blue-collar town, a union town. A beer and a shot town. A place you wouldn't want to have a flat tire at night town.

This was a town where people looked out for themselves and were darned proud of it, because if you don't look out for you, nobody else will.

So why are people giving historic baseballs back to McGwire?

Consider Mike Davidson, for instance. He ended up with home run No. 61 on Monday afternoon. It literally rolled under his seat.

That ball could be worth thousands and thousands of dollars.

"I'm going to give it to McGwire," Davidson told reporters. "Because it would mean more to him and to baseball than it would to me, more than a million dollars."

So Davidson gave it back to McGwire. The millionaire slugger gave him two autographed bats and two autographed jerseys.

Two days earlier, Deni Allen got Home Run 60. That, too, had some potential value.

"I knew no matter what, I was giving it to him," Allen told reporters. "I believe it's his ball and he deserves it."

Allen walked away with some trinkets, too.

Something is wrong here.

If a ball goes into the stands, it does not belong to the player who hit it. It belongs to the fan who ends up with it. If that ball happens to be worth some money, well, that's good news for the lucky fan.

Bill McClellan

It's true, of course, that as baseball players go, McGwire does not seem like a particularly greedy fellow. He signed a contract to play here for less money than he could have gotten elsewhere. Then he turned around and pledged a million bucks to charity.

But still, he is getting more than $9 million a year. Plus, of course, he gets a buck for every ticket sold over 2.8 million – and the Cardinals are headed toward 3.2 million this year.

So even without any endorsements, he's up there in the $10 million-a-year range.

If he really wanted those historic baseballs, he could pay for them.

In fact, if the fan happens to really like McGwire – and who doesn't? – he or she could do what McGwire did for the Cardinals. Accept a little bit less than what could be obtained on the free market.

After all, McGwire didn't say, "I'll play for nothing." He said, "I'll play for a little less, but I still want a lot."

That's very reasonable. Maybe even soft-hearted.

There is nothing reasonable about giving things of value to a millionaire. Even if he's the nicest, most popular millionaire in town, he's still a millionaire, and it is not reasonable for working people to give millionaires money.

It wouldn't normally happen in this town.

Right now, of course, St. Louisans are intoxicated with this home run thing. I understand – better than most, unfortunately – that when a guy gets tipsy, he'll do silly things.

Eventually, though, you wake up.

In just a couple of weeks, this particular party is going to be over. Life will resume. Bills will have to be paid.

And how are our generous fans going to be feeling on that Morning After?

If I went to the game and happened to catch a baseball worth thousands and thousands of dollars and I came home and told my wife that I had given my windfall to a millionaire and he had given me a bat, well, I suspect that my wife would know what to do with that bat.

We're going to have more chances. He's going to hit more home runs during the next home stand. Each of those balls is going to be valuable.

If you get one, do the right thing.

—

MURDERER'S SENTENCING IS LATEST CHAPTER IN FAMILY'S SAD HISTORY
DECEMBER 3, 2000

Charles Reisinger Jr. came into court Thursday for his sentencing. He was wearing a gray-and-white striped uniform of the sort seen in James Cagney prison movies. The booking card at the Montgomery County, Ill., jail lists Reisinger as 5 feet 5 inches and 250 pounds, and he looked almost comical in the old-fashioned jailhouse garb. He seemed cheerful, upbeat and courteous when questioned by the judge. Had he read the pre-sentence report? Yes, sir. Any questions or corrections? No, sir. Was he on any medication? None whatsoever, sir. Satisfied with his lawyer? Yes, sir.

Two friends testified on Reisinger's behalf before the judge passed sentence. A young man told the judge that Reisinger had always been a good father and a loving husband. A young woman said that Reisinger and his wife used to baby-sit her kids. She described Reisinger as a "big teddy bear," and she added that he couldn't bring himself to discipline his own children. Reisinger's mother was the final witness. She said her son was not the violent type. He previously pleaded guilty to first-degree murder for killing his wife, Jennifer. In Illinois, first-degree murder carries a range of 20 to 60 years. Current law requires that a person serve the entire sentence. The assistant state's attorney, Chris Matoush, recommended a sentence of 40 years. Public defender David Grisby pointed out that Reisinger, who is 35, had never been in trouble before. Grisby asked for a 20-year sentence. Judge Mark Joy looked at Reisinger. "You don't seem to be the type," he mused. Then the judge talked about the seriousness of the crime, and finally, pronounced sentence. Thirty-five years.

No one had come to court on behalf of Jennifer. Unless you count Mata Weber. She sat in the back of the courtroom and wore a button that said, "We Remember Karen." Karen was Weber's daughter. She used to work in a roadside tavern. Charles Reisinger Sr. abducted and murdered her almost 20 years ago. He was convicted of first-degree murder. That conviction was overturned. He then pleaded guilty to second-degree murder and got 25 years but was released several years ago after serving half that sentence.

Now that Karen's murderer's son was being sentenced, Weber felt she should be there.

As I left the courtroom, Reisinger's mother spoke to me. "I hope you get it right," she said. "This is not, 'Like father, like son.'"

Admittedly, it was that notion that first attracted me to the case. Jennifer Reisinger was killed in December 1999. One year ago Monday, actually. A fellow riding an ATV found her body in a remote area near Raymond, Ill. She had been strangled, and then someone had stuffed a 30-gallon plastic bag into her mouth. She was 30 years old.

The cops brought Charles Reisinger Jr. in for questioning, and he confessed. The next month, he went to court to get his confession thrown out. He claimed that the confession had been coerced. That hearing was in January.

Shortly before the hearing, I talked to a detective with the Illinois State Police. He is one of the fellows who arrested Reisinger's father. The father was mean, the detective told me. Tough, too. A dope dealer, a brawler. Nobody was surprised when he was picked up for murder. I asked if he had confessed. The detective shook his head. Confess? Not this guy. He'd just look at you and tell you you'd have to prove it, said the detective.

I then went to the hearing. Deputies brought the son into the courtroom. Short and very heavy, he looked silly rather than sinister. He reminded me of the computer guy in "Jurassic Park" who stole some dinosaur embryos. Two detectives from the state police testified at the hearing. Not only had there been no coercion, there had been no need for any, they said. Reisinger had been very cooperative, they said. "It was the most co ngenial atmosphere of an interview like this I've ever seen," said one.

Reisinger was theatrical when he testified. He said he had confessed only because he had been stressed out. That was largely due to coffee, he said. He had been thirsty and all they had at the police station was coffee. Coffee, he said, and then he sighed heavily. His motion to suppress the confession was denied.

Jennifer's life was something of a mystery. I was told she had been taken from her biological parents as a small child. Then there were a series of foster homes. In one such home, her foster parents allegedly kept her in a cage. She was eventually adopted by Roger and Sheri Dolash, but they were killed in a car crash. Roger's brother lives in Ohio, and he confirmed that Jennifer had had a horrific childhood.

A stepsister said she couldn't really add much to what I'd been told, but she did say she met Reisinger shortly after Jennifer married him in 1997. What was he like? He was a teddy bear, the stepsister said.

Jennifer was a plain young woman. She was 5 feet 1 inch and weighed 146. Still, there had been plenty of men before Reisinger. At least one husband. Maybe even a couple of children who had been taken away. At the time she met Reisinger in late 1996, she had a toddler, a little girl. She became pregnant, and she and Reisinger were married in June of 1997, three months before their daughter was born.

Reisinger was the oldest of four children. He was 6 when his mother divorced his father. The divorce petition cites mental cruelty and abandonment. While his siblings were thin, Reisinger was always heavy. His mother blames herself. She says she kept him on baby food for too long. He was a loner in school. He was very quiet. He was put in remedial English. He may have had dyslexia. He went into the Army after high school, but that didn't work out. He was given an honorable discharge and released early.

He got a job as a truck driver. He met a woman. He thought it might get serious, but then she had somebody else's baby. Then he rented half of a duplex. Jennifer and her then-husband were living in the other half. Jennifer and her husband got a divorce, and the ex-husband moved to Michigan. Jennifer and Reisinger became a couple.

If any marriage should have succeeded, it was this union of two people with such unhappy pasts. But the marriage lasted only a little more than two years. Jennifer and the two children moved out in September 1999. She got a job at a nursing home in Carlinville, Ill. She and the kids lived in a nearby housing project. Records show a man lived with them. He was 21.

In his written confession, Reisinger said he went to the nursing home where Jennifer worked. He said they went for a ride to talk things over, and she told him she was going to take the girls and move to Alabama. He said what started out as an argument progressed into a fight.

"I was getting mad and I saw red," he wrote.

After the sentencing, I asked Mata Weber if Charles Reisinger Jr. reminded her of his father. She shook her head. I felt the same way. Two very different men.

Meanwhile, there was a trial going on in the other courtroom in the Montgomery County Courthouse. A young man was charged with murder. Oddly enough, his father had been convicted of murder.

—

THE POWER OF PAINT TURNED HOUSE INTO CONVERSATION PIECE
FEBRUARY 7, 1999

Harold Schoessel was born in September of 1914. His father was the village blacksmith in Imperial. His mother was a housewife who loved to sing. They lived in a small frame house. It was painted white.

The family moved to St. Louis when Harold was a child. They lived in another frame house. It, too, was painted white. Harold graduated from grade school just as the Great Depression was beginning. High school was considered an impossible luxury. Harold went to work. He did whatever he could. He shoveled coal. He sorted through a city dump looking for things of value.

Years passed.

Harold was 41 years old. He had a steady job. Like his mother, he loved to sing. One day, he went to a friend's house with his guitar. He was singing a country song when one of the kids in the house - his friend's daughter - came running up to Harold with a woman's shoe.

It belongs to a princess, the little girl said. If you find the princess whose foot fits the shoe, you can marry her, the little girl said.

There was only one woman in the room who didn't have a shoe. She was embarrassed. This had not been her idea. Her name was Lora, and she was a cousin of Harold's friend. She was 40 years old.

Like Harold, she had never been married.

She was a country girl, and even at 40, a wisp of a thing. Her father had died when she was 2. She had been brought up by her grandmother. Lora was very quiet, and Harold liked that.

They were married in May of 1956. They bought a home in Manchester on Route 141 just south of Manchester Road, and moved in on the day of their wedding. It was a small frame house, and Harold and Lora were its first occupants. It was painted white.

To say that Harold and Lora were reclusive would, perhaps, be overstating things, but not by much. They had no children. They seldom went out. Rarely did they have visitors.

Harold retired in 1979. He spent most of his time fiddling with plants. He was forever trying to grow things. Special tomatoes, unusual flowers. He maintained books of notes on his various efforts.

He had a fine garden, but not much came of his experiments. It seemed that Harold and Lora Schoessel were destined to live out their lives in anonymity.

Then in 1984, Harold decided to paint his house. Not white, though. He had lived in white houses all his life.

He decided to paint his house the color of one of his favorite flowers. The name of the flower was the Iris Lorelei. A pretty flower with a name close to the name of his wife. Perfect.

He went to a decorating store in Manchester. He found a color of paint that seemed to match the flower. The color was called Mardi Gras. The salesman said that he didn't know anyone who had painted a house

Mardi Gras, and he explained that it might not come out exactly the way Harold was envisioning it. It might turn out, well, strange.

Harold didn't care. He began painting his house in July. From the very beginning, Harold could tell that it wasn't exactly the way he had envisioned it. It was darker than he had thought it would be.

Actually, it was purple.

Harold finished his painting job at Thanksgiving. It was an immediate sensation.

My colleague, Harry Levins, wrote about the house in December of 1984. He explained that the color was supposed to be rose orchid.

"Ok, it's rose orchid. Still, it looks purple. Bright purple. Day-Glo purple. The shade of purple that Frederick's of Hollywood reserves for its naughtiest underthings."

It became a landmark. Strangers came into the yard and took pictures of it. People gave directions by it. A nursery advertised itself as being six-tenths of a mile south of the purple house.

Harold repainted it in 1996. Same color.

In 1997, Harold and Lora learned that a long-rumored widening of 141 was going to happen, and it was going to swallow their house. Harold began making plans to build a new one. It would be the same dimensions. He would recreate the house in which he and Lora had spent their entire married life.

The color didn't matter. In the end, the color doesn't matter.

Looking back on it now, Harold figures he worked himself into too much of a frazzle trying to make plans to recreate the house. At any rate, he wore himself out and ended up going into the hospital. That was in February.

In April, he and Lora moved into a senior citizens' residence.

The state is going to knock their house down sometime this week. Probably Monday.

I visited Harold and Lora Friday morning, and asked Harold if he were interested in taking one last look at the purple house.

"No, it would make me cry," he said. "You spend 42 years in a place, it grows on you."

Later, I drove out to the purple house. A young man who works for the highway department came by.

His name is Todd Strong, and he's a construction inspector. He'll be in charge of tearing down the purple house.

"I grew up on 141," he told me. "This place has sure been a landmark."

—

IT'S GAME, SET, MATCH FOR ME AS A PARENT SPECTATOR

MAY 29, 2006

I remember going to a high school softball game at Shaw Park several years ago. It was an afternoon game, which meant that most parents were unable to attend. There were only four or five of us in the bleachers. I was the only man.

"I wonder who we play next," said one of the mothers. "St. Elizabeth," I said.

"I wonder if they've got a good team," said one of the other mothers.

"We beat them 2-1 last year, and the game ended with one of their players being thrown out at the plate," I said.

One of the mothers looked at me and shook her head. "You need a life," she said.

"This is my life," I said.

Bill McClellan

And so it has been for eight years. I have the sort of make-believe job that allows me to juggle my schedule, and I haven't had to miss many games. But you can't juggle away time, and mine ran out last Thursday at the Missouri high school tennis championships in Springfield.

The semifinal matches are played in the morning, and the winners meet for the championship in the afternoon. Each team has six players. The six players each play singles and then form into three doubles teams. So there is a potential of nine points in a match. I say a potential of nine points because as soon as one team wins five points, the match ends.

Team tennis is an odd sport to watch. It begins, as I said, with six games going on at once. It's hard enough keeping track of the match you're watching – Was that ball in or out? Whose point was that? – and it's impossible to know what's going on in the other matches. You can glance at another court and see a ball hitting the net or flying out of bounds, but you don't know if you're getting an accurate sense of what's going on.

Another thing that's odd about team tennis is the best player counts no more than the sixth man. If your No. 1 guy beat the other team's No. 1 guy, you get a point. If your sixth man wins, you get a point.

My son, Jack, was the No. 4 player on the Clayton team. That's remarkable. First of all, he's not a year-round tennis player. He is, or was, also a soccer player. Second, his athletic abilities are a powerful argument against genetics, which, like evolution, is no more than a theory.

Thursday morning, Clayton played Westminster. I watched Jack's match against Joe Hunsicker. Two out of three sets. Joe played well and won the first one. From a nearby court, I heard loud cheering. I glanced over. The wrong people were cheering! All told, four of the Clayton six lost their first sets. But Jack and Bohan Li, the No. 6 player, came back to win their matches, and along with wins from the always reliable No. 1 Joey Nicolazzi and No. 3 Jonathan Pang, the team went into the doubles with a 4-2 lead. Pang and No. 2 Max Shapiro quickly won their doubles match, and Clayton moved on.

In the championship match against Pembroke Hill, Nicolazzi and Li were the only winners in singles for Clayton, and Li's match was a long one. If he didn't win, there would be no doubles, but he hung on, and so the No. 6 player carried the team into doubles. That's pretty cool.

In a match a week earlier against Country Day, the hero had been Steve Golembieski, the No. 5 player, who had prevailed in a third-set tiebreaker that had set up a dramatic match-clinching victory in doubles by Nicolazzi and Jack.

Clayton needed all three doubles to win the championship. Li and Golembieski won in straight sets. Nicolazzi and Jack lost the first set and won the second, but the match ended when the other doubles team lost a tough, close match. Coach Susie Luten and assistant coach Greg Fitzgerald congratulated the boys on a fine season. The boys then lined up to shake hands with the champs from Pembroke Hill, and I began looking for a new life.

—

DEATH HAS DOWNTOWN NEW HAVEN FEELING EMPTIER THAN EXPECTED

NOVEMBER 16, 2003

Louis LaBelle arrived in the small Missouri town of New Haven several years ago. He quickly became a recognizable part of the downtown scene. Then again, downtown New Haven is small – one square block along the Missouri River. It's an old downtown, and it looks like a movie set.

LaBelle could have come from a movie, too. He was unorthodox, to say the least. He did odd jobs. (He was very handy.) He was friendly. He was kind. He was intelligent. He was usually smiling. He often carried flowers to give to the ladies who worked downtown – in the City Hall and in the restaurant – and they much appreciated this kindness, even though they understood that LaBelle had filched the flowers from somebody. "I have gardens all over town," he used to say. He slept wherever he could. For a while, he lived in a horse trailer. Then he lived in the basement of an abandoned building in a newer section of town, and finally, he found an open door in an empty building downtown, and he moved in. He drank a great deal, and he sometimes introduced himself as T.D. As in, town drunk.

And maybe he was, but the people of New Haven are a tolerant lot. LaBelle stayed busy with odd jobs – as busy as he wanted, at any rate. As a downtown resident, he patronized the Riverfront Mercantile store. His standard purchase was a 40-ounce can of Miller High Life. That was $1.19 plus tax. Ralph Haynes, the owner of the store, displayed on the counter a plastic cup on which he had written in magic marker: "Louie's Change." So LaBelle would give Haynes two bucks, and Haynes would put the change in th e cup. Other folks, especially the downtown crowd who knew LaBelle, would sometimes put their change in the cup, and it was seldom empty.

LaBelle died last month. He was about to cut somebody's lawn, and he was trying to start the mower, and boom. He had a heart attack. He was 59 years old. LaBelle has a daughter, Peggy Sue Fairow, who lives near Dutzow. She agreed to donate her father's eyes for transplant. His body was cremated.

An odd thing happened after LaBelle died. People missed him more than they would have suspected. Some were surprised to discover they missed him at all. He had become, it seems, a bigger part of New Haven than people would have guessed. So his friends held a memorial service for him Monday night at Aldo's restaurant, which is the restaurant in downtown New Haven. About 45 people were there.

Tab Armstrong and Kathy Trentmann work at City Hall. They told me there were times when they would go to work, and awaiting them would be a couple of flowers stuck in a beer bottle. "Louie had been there," Trentmann said.

Sometimes those flowers had belonged – in a technical sense – to Ellen Zobrist, but she was at the memorial, too, and she said she never begrudged LaBelle any of her flowers. He knew their names, she said. He knew about botany.

Louie knew about metal, too, said Ben Armstrong, a bartender and a carver. He brought me a knife once, and he talked about iron and the quality of the metal, and he was right about it all, said Armstrong.

Mostly, though, people talked about what a good fellow LaBelle was. Randy Barks is a bricklayer who spends a lot of time fishing. LaBelle loved the river, too, and the men became friends. "He was just happy-go-lucky," said Barks, who added that LaBelle was also a world-class scavenger. Barks once needed a bell for some project he was working on, and sure enough, LaBelle came up with a bell. He wouldn't accept any money for it, either, but he did take a 12-pack.

Steve Roth, the editor and one-man staff of The New Haven Leader, stopped by the memorial, and that showed a bit of backbone. He had written a column about LaBelle's death in which he had referred to La-Belle as the town drunk. That was, as I have mentioned, the very name that LaBelle had applied to himself, but still, the column upset some people, and Roth later published an apology.

Incidentally, that column did not bother LaBelle's daughter. "It's the way I'd introduce him to people. 'This is my father, the town drunk of New Haven. Watch out. Your town might be next,'" she said. She explained that she had long ago accepted her dad's unorthodox lifestyle. She also said she wasn't surprised that so many people had turned out to remember him. "He was kind. He helped everybody," she said.

Cindy Bumgarner, who used to work as a waitress at the Front Street Grille, which later became Aldo's, began the formal part of the memorial by reading a speech directed to LaBelle. "I will miss your smile and great heart. A lot of us learned a lot from you," she said. Dennis Connolly, who owned the Front Street Grille, opted for humor. "I sometimes had to ask him to leave, but I never had to ban him," Connolly said. "He was a character."

Blanche Rowold, who is 84 and seems to be a character herself, stood up and declared that LaBelle was one of the greatest people she had ever met. She said she used to drink with him.

Haynes from Riverfront Mercantile announced that LaBelle may have had a premonition about his death. In the final week of his life, he had drawn down the money in his change cup to less than a buck. Haynes also announced that he would be keeping that change cup on his counter as a memorial to his late friend.

Another memorial was on display. Aldo Alu's wife, Susie, had kept some roses that LaBelle had given her the day before he died. They were on a table next to some photographs.

The service concluded with a prayer from Bob Mueller, who owns the local Robller Vineyard. "Lord be with us as we remember a friend who touched us in many different ways," he said.

Bill McClellan

That concluded the program, but Ben Armstrong, who was drinking Jim Beam whiskey, raised his glass to the crowd. "In the spirit of Louie, we should make Aldo push us all out of here," he said. The memorial was still going strong a while later when I stepped out into the downtown street that seems, somehow, to be missing a certain spirit since Louie LaBelle passed away.

—

A POLICE DETECTIVE WHO REMEMBERS AND IS REMEMBERED

JANUARY 16, 2004

Pantazo's Market is long gone. The building at 3201 Arsenal was most recently the headquarters of a construction company, but when I stopped by Wednesday morning, the building was unoccupied, and a sign on the door said the company had moved. I stood outside for a moment and tried to imagine what it was like on an evening in February 1971.

Katherine Pantazo was behind the counter. She was 24 years old. She was a schoolteacher. She taught fourth grade at Bryan Hill on Gano Avenue. Her class had the best achievement and attendance record at the school. She still lived at home with her folks, and she sometimes filled in at the grocery store. That's what she was doing on a Friday night almost 33 years ago. Cloyd Richardson was just out of prison. He went into the store to rob it.

Charles Baker lived in an apartment next to the store. He was a security guard. His wife wanted a pack of cigarettes, and Baker volunteered to go to the market. He was wearing his uniform. He walked into the store, and Richardson shot him. In the face and then in the back. Richardson then shot Katherine in the head. He left without taking any money.

Baker died. Katherine was very near death that first night. "She's not going to make it," the doctor told her mother, Eugania. "She will live," said Eugania. Katherine was in a coma for weeks, but she did live. She did not remember the shooting, but fortunately, her testimony was not needed. Richardson was convicted, largely on the basis of his video-taped confession. It was the first time such a confession was used in a St. Louis courtroom.

Katherine never returned to teaching. Her mind is fine, but her body never really recovered. On her best days, she can move around with a walker. For the most part, she stays at home. For the past 33 years, her mother has been her caregiver.

After a brief flurry of interest – the case was big news – the spotlight turned elsewhere, and the Pantazo family was forgotten. But not by Joe Burgoon. He was one of the detectives who worked that case, and over the years, he has stayed in touch. He dropped by recently with some fudge.

"He is the best policeman in the world," Katherine told me later. "I love him."

Best ex-policeman. Burgoon has just retired. He turned 65 this week. He spent 43 years on the Police Department, 27 of them in homicide. In a list of most memorable cases, the shootings at the Pantazo Market would not rate high. That is, there was not a lot of detective work involved. Richardson's stepson called the police and told them what his stepfather had done.

When a legendary detective retires – and Burgoon qualifies – you'd expect his colleagues to talk about the tough cases, and to recall the way he could sort through facts, and figure out what was important and what just seemed important. With Burgoon, though, everybody feels obligated to mention how nice he is. In a feature about Burgoon that appeared in this paper last week, retired detective Mike Guzy said: "He's the best homicide investigator I've met in my life, bar none. Oh, yes, and he's embarrass ingly nice."

I read that quote, and I thought about Katherine Pantazo. I thought, too, about a young woman who called me a couple of months ago. She was 8 years old when her mother was murdered in 1983. She had wit-nessed the murder and had testified against the killer. Now she had heard that he might get out of prison. I asked her if she remembered any of the homicide detectives who had worked the case. Joe Burgoon, she said.

I went to the station on Sublette where Burgoon was working. I asked, foolishly, if he remembered the young woman. He reached into his wallet and pulled out her photo. We stay in touch, he said.

Bill McClellan

The killer, by the way, is not getting out.

—

FAMILY BEHIND THE SCENES HELPED WRITE HISTORY OF KEMOLL'S

NOVEMBER 9, 2003

Kemoll's is an exclusive Italian restaurant in downtown St. Louis, and a short history of the establishment is included in the leather binder that contains the wine list. The reader learns that the restaurant was founded in 1927 by Joe Kemoll –he had come to this country as Vincenzo Camuglia, but the immigration officials decided to Americanize his name – and the restaurant is now run by grandson Mark Cusumano. Because the recipes came from Kemoll's mother-in-law, Grace Danna, Cusumano is called the fourth generation. The official history ends with this note: The fifth generation is already chipping in.

As is often the case with restaurants, there is a parallel universe. Katie Bell worked for Joe and Gaetana Kemoll even before they opened their restaurant. You could call her a maid, I suppose, or maybe a nanny. She probably did some cooking, too, and that must have been a high-pressure task, cooking for people who so loved food that they would eventually open their own place. And when they did open their restaurant, Bell was one of the first employees. It was an Italian restaurant, and the recipes came from Sicily, but Bell, an African-American woman, was one of the first cooks.

Her daughters, Beatrice Johnson and Louise Jackson, followed her to the restaurant. They both spent their entire working careers at Kemoll's. Like their mother, they were cooks. As Kemoll's evolved into a fancy place, a cook became what laypeople might call a helper. A chef prepared the actual meals. The cooks helped the chef.

Johnson worked for 45 years before she retired, and by then, her daughter Marguerite McNeal was working as a cook. She had started as a salad maker in 1975. Perhaps because she was the third generation of her family to work at the restaurant, and Gaetana Kemoll was a person who took family seriously, McNeal was soon selected for a special task. She was put in charge of making the appetizer Calzone Romano. It's a turnover pastry filled with Italian meats and cheese. It is a house specialty.

"Mrs. Kemoll used to tell me, 'You were made to make calzone.' Maybe so," McNeal said with a shrug. We were talking in the restaurant after lunch on Thursday.

I asked if she ever made calzone for her family. She has raised six kids, and I figured those kids would have had an occasional party, and it was a probably a kick to serve such a delicacy. Or maybe make a batch for yourself some night when you're going to watch television. McNeal gave me a strange look.

"I make enough calzone. I don't want to see a calzone," she said. "I don't eat them. It's the truth."

Well, what does she do for parties? She's the third generation to be employed as a cook at one of the city's finest restaurants.

"I go to Schnucks and buy something already prepared," she said.

She usually works an early shift. She catches the Lee bus at Kossuth and Grand in the morning, and arrives at the restaurant about 9 a.m. She helps get the kitchen organized for the day, and then she works the lunch hour that ends at 2 p.m. And, of course, she makes the Calzone Romano.

"That doesn't take much time," she said. "I make the dough from scratch, of course, with yeast, and flour, and water, and oil. Then I cut the cheese and the meats. It's not hard."

By the way, she's the third generation to be employed as a cook at Kemoll's, but not the last. Her daughter Nitra McNeal is also a cook, and Nitra's daughter Reenisha Hughes is a busperson.

So it really is like it says in the history that comes with the wine list: The fifth generation is already chipping in.

It's just that there are two fifth generations, and two families, coexisting quite nicely, in one of the city's most exclusive restaurants.

———

Bill McClellan

Bill McClellan